AF228443

Enchanted Forests

ENCHANTED FORESTS

The Pœtic Construction of a World before Time

BORIA SAX

REAKTION BOOKS

To the trees that live in what I call 'my forest',

though it is not mine but theirs.

To the animals, plants and fungi that live in their boughs,

crevices, hollows and shadows.

Published by
Reaktion Books Ltd
Unit 32, Waterside
44–48 Wharf Road
London N1 7UX, UK
www.reaktionbooks.co.uk

First published 2023
Copyright © Boria Sax 2023

All rights reserved

Endpapers: Photo by Camille Brodard on Unsplash

No part of this publication may be reproduced, stored in a retrieval system or transmitted, in any form or by any means, electronic, mechanical, photocopying, recording or otherwise, without the prior permission of the publishers

Printed and bound in India by Replika Press Pvt. Ltd

A catalogue record for this book is available from the British Library

ISBN 978 1 78914 790 2

CONTENTS

View of the Shawangunk Kill on the Sax property.

Introduction: Forests and Memory

Under a spreading chestnut-tree
The village smithy stands . . .
HENRY WADSWORTH LONGFELLOW, 'The Village Blacksmith'

My grandfather, Bernard Sax, emigrated from Russia to the United States in 1914. He worked for a few years as an upholsterer, and then made his fortune working for the new Bolshevik government in Russia, selling antiquities looted from Tzarist palaces. Together with his wife, Bluma, he purchased some abandoned farmland so inexpensively that it was almost free. The land was for a little community of Russian Jews, largely Communist, as a buffer between them and a threatening world. They were like a flock of birds, blown off course during a storm, suddenly in unfamiliar territory, afraid of predators and seeking the security of a forest cover.

For me as a child, those woods seemed to go back endlessly. After a few steps amid the trees, time and distance seemed to lose meaning, though the sight of a stray bullet or a beer can on the ground might remind me that 'civilization' was not really so far away. Over the decades, there were occasional timber harvests. Poachers, lovers and neighbours out for a stroll passed through the woods, but, in about fifty years, I may have been the only one who even tried to explore them repeatedly. A portion of that land, a little over 80 acres, has come down to me, and it is as lovely and unprofitable as ever.

As you come to know a forest, a few trees start to stand out from the rest. Since prehistoric times, trees have been used as landmarks and to memorialize events in the past, though many of the associations may be the work of legend. Among these are the Bodhi Tree, where the Buddha meditated and received enlightenment; the Ankerwycke Yew, where King John signed the Magna Carta; the Major Oak, where Robin Hood and his men assembled; the Royal Oak, where Charles II of England hid from Cromwell's soldiers; the Breston Oak, planted by Henry IV after he signed the Edict of Nantes.

This is not only done with historical events. Since ancient times, it has been a custom for lovers to carve their names or initials, often surrounded by a heart, in the bark of beech trees. The practice is mentioned by Ovid, Ludovico Ariosto and William Shakespeare, among others.[1] Thomas Hardy concludes his poem 'During Wind and Rain':

> Ah, no; the years, the years;
> Down their carved names the rain-drop ploughs.[2]

The names will then grow and decay with the tree, subject to wind, weather, insects and lightning but perhaps destined to endure for a long time.

A deed to part of my land, dated 1933, cites a survey made in 1845. This opens by tracing the boundary of the property, 'Beginning at what is called "the pear tree"'. The survey goes on to mention another arboreal marker, 'a chestnut stump near the bridge'. There are additionally two references to specific white oaks.[3] All of these trees were so well known to local people that the demarcations could carry legal authority. I have looked in vain for the pear tree or any remains of it. Nevertheless, the forester who manages my property, Anthony Del Vescovo, tells me that it is still possible to walk the boundary given in the deed.

The forest preferred in the paintings and poems of European Romantics is one that seems almost primeval yet contains reminders of past civilization. Beside huge trees are overgrown ruins, usually of a once-imposing structure such as a church, castle or classical temple. Often that will be only a single wall or a column. An artist might show the moonlight gleaming through the bare lattice of what had once been a stained-glass window. The woods of the American Northeast fit this formula in ways. From a slight distance, the eastern forests may look like an untouched wilderness, yet there are many stone walls that once separated fields. There are, however, far fewer crumbling remains of buildings than in European woods, because early colonists relied far more on wood, which seemed to be inexhaustible, than on stone as a building material. As a result, many American barns, sheds, forts and homes could disintegrate, leaving hardly a trace.

Just as images by European Romantics often contain reminders of human conflict, those in America are touched by human greed. One

Jean-Honoré Fragonard, *The Souvenir*, c. 1776–8, oil on panel.

American Valentine, postcard from the late 19th or early 20th century.
Beeches with graffiti in New York State.

might like to think ruins bear witness to a tragic struggle for survival against overwhelming odds, but that is seldom actually the case. From the sixteenth until the eighteenth century, European colonists claimed the land as their own, driving out the Native Americans. Then, in the nineteenth and early twentieth centuries, they abandoned their farms to move westward in search of greater wealth. The forest quickly reclaimed deserted farms. The state where I live, New York, is known for its big city, but it is currently about 65 per cent forested, more than three times the rate at the end of the nineteenth century.[4]

Written records of forestland in the American Northeast are remarkably scarce. The New York Botanical Garden, which I visit often, contains an area known as the Thain Family Forest, which is advertised as the largest remaining 'virgin forest' in the New York City Area. The term itself is now controversial. It once meant a vast area of trees untouched by human beings, a bit like the mythic Eden. Tour guides have told me that the Botanical Garden defines 'virgin forest' as meaning that the area has never been clearcut as far as anybody knows. Even the Botanical Garden, which has vast resources and is among the most extensively visited places in New York, perhaps the world, is unable to tell with any certainty whether the land on which it rests has ever been clearcut in the past. The many landowners in New York State that I have discussed this with have been able to find out very little or nothing of the early history of their land. How severed from the past we Americans have become!

And why this paucity of records? One reason is that land ownership in the Old World was regarded more as a legacy, while in the new one it was more of a commodity, to be traded when the right opportunity arose. The inheritance of estates was a practice that many Americans associated with the aristocratic order, which they had come to the New World to escape. Just as they were not likely to plant trees for their great-grandchildren to enjoy, they usually would not record detailed histories of their property.

Another reason is what is called 'plant blindness'. That does not mean being as blind as a plant, for plants respond quickly to light and are not blind at all. The term was first coined by James H. Wandersee and Elisabeth E. Schussler in a guest editorial that appeared February 1999 in *The American Biology Teacher*. One of the definitions the authors give is 'the misguided anthropocentric ranking of plants as inferior to animals

Photograph from the early 20th century of an American family posing in a forest in front of a monumental tree.

and thus, as unworthy of consideration'. They state that people regularly fail to notice plants, appreciate their qualities or recognize their importance for human beings.[5]

The authors were mostly concerned about plants being overlooked in science classes, but the concept of plant blindness has implications for history as well. Forests become a blur of brown and green that people think of as outside of time. Until fairly recently, changes in forests were not often conscientiously recorded, largely out of a sense that forests would return to a primal, eternally virginal state that the influential American horticulturalist Frederic Clements called a 'climax forest' in the early twentieth century. He compared the development of a forest to the growth of an organism, but he did not see it as subject to old age and death.[6] Instead, like a god, it might remain forever in its prime.

In publications that are well over a hundred years old, I have uncovered a few brief allusions to a mill on my property in the eighteenth century, though they do not specify whether it was a saw mill, a grist mill or some other kind. There is an area by the confluence of two streams where the water pours over rocks, which would be an ideal place for a large mill. There is also a long slope downwards from the adjacent road, where settlers might easily have rolled logs down or carried grain to the mill. Every time I visit the property, I look around that area in the hope that a storm, a high tide, a fallen tree or pure chance may have revealed some relic of the structure such as a millstone or the foundation of a shed. But, so far at least, no trace of the mill has been discovered.

Nevertheless, more history is written in the land than in documents and books. Native American artefacts such as arrowheads have been found on my property, as have many shards of pottery that are very difficult to date. Over a hundred metres of stone walls wind through it, which show that it was used for farming. The remains of two cement milk coolers, fastened to the ground with heavy chains, tell me that it was once used as a pasture.

I have come across deer skulls placed on branches of trees, so they look like goblins from a short distance away. Was this some obscure folk custom? Was it a practical joke? If the skulls were meant to scare deer away, that surely failed. If they were meant to scare trespassers, it may sometimes have worked. I don't know who left the skulls there, but I do have a guess: a burly farmer that once worked as a caretaker of the property for my grandmother. His manner was very polite, even courtly, yet with an excessive control that at times hinted at potential violence. He liked to startle city people by suddenly taking out his gun and shooting mice for the pet owl he kept at home. After his death, I learned that he had very plausibly been accused of murder, but the case was dropped when the bullet used mysteriously disappeared from the office of the local sheriff. Such are the secrets of the woods.

A wind passes through the forest, and each leaf becomes a memory. Accounts of America by very early settlers tell of an abundance of life so rich that it seemed miraculous. You needed only to place your hand in a stream and fish would swim into it. Deer and turkey were not only plentiful but seemed to offer themselves to hunters. Flocks of birds were so numerous that a nearly random shot into the air might bring them down.[7]

The bounty was no doubt exaggerated, perhaps out of the American love of hyperbole that still fills our advertisements or to entice new colonists. But the colourful descriptions had a basis in experience, and much of the credit for it must go to how the Indigenous peoples, intentionally or not, managed the forest. Most landscape historians believe they deliberately lit forest fires, not only to clear land for villages and agricultural fields but to manage game,[8] although that has been questioned.[9] Blazes, whether from lightning, accidents or intentional creation, definitely cleared the undergrowth in forests and gave the landscape a park-like appearance.

Eventually, as the soil began to be exhausted, the Native Americans would move on, and the area might be reforested or taken over by another group. This created a sort of patchwork of unevenly aged forests, meadows and transitional areas, in which a vast range of animals and vegetation might thrive. In the early twentieth century colonists thought of the native peoples as essentially a force of nature in a forest that had remained unchanged from time immemorial before the arrival of Europeans. Their use of clearings for agriculture in the northeastern part of what is now the United States, however, appears to date back only about five hundred years before the arrival of Columbus.[10]

The Native Americans, like Europeans, represent only one chapter in the long history of forests in the Northeastern United States. After the glaciers had retreated, about 12,000 years ago, the initial forest consisted of pines and firs. About 2,000 years later, birches became common,[11] followed by oaks, maples, beeches and hickories. Chestnuts arrived only about 3,000 years ago,[12] but became for a while the most dominant tree in the forest canopy, only to be almost completely wiped out by a pathogen imported from East Asia at the start of the twentieth century.

My land is on part of the Atlantic Flyway, a migratory path for birds. Their basic pathways were set around the end of the Pleistocene. Clearings used by Native Americans probably helped them navigate the difficult journey by providing places where grassland species especially might rest. Today, migration has become far more difficult, due to many factors including disorientation caused by light pollution, noise pollution and electric grids, as well as habitat destruction and climate change.

A tree grows by adding a ring to its diameter every year. A dark line is created by the growth in late summer when the new cells become more compact. When water, nutrients and light are abundant, the growth will be greater and the rings will expand. When the tree has been damaged by calamities such as fires, a scar will be visible. Wind, patterns of sunlight, weight of nearby branches and other factors can make the rings asymmetrical. The pattern of growth can tell scientists a good deal not only about the tree but about climate, weather and other conditions in the forest.

Animals seem to mirror mostly transient human emotions such as amusement, fear or curiosity. Trees, by contrast, seem to tell us something about abiding passions and, more broadly, about the human condition. They have personalities, in ways more vivid than those of human beings. Their histories are told in scars, twists, breaks and changes in the direction of growth. They are about determination in the face of adversity. As Hermann Hesse wrote in his essay 'Trees', when we look at the stump of a newly felled tree, 'in its annual rings and deformities are faithfully recorded all the struggle, all the illness and suffering, all the joy and flourishing, the lean years and the rich years, attacks withstood and storms outlasted.'[13]

Maurice Maeterlinck writes of a hundred-year-old laurel tree in a gorge of the Loup River in the Cannes region of France: 'It was easy to read on its twisted and, so to speak, writhing trunk the whole drama of its hard and tenacious life.' A seed had landed in a crack in a perpendicular rock. As a thin stem, it had grown out, pointing downwards towards the water, but later the stem had turned up at a sharp angle to face the sun. Meanwhile, 'a hidden canker gnawed deep into the tragic arm that supported it in space.' The tree sent out two new roots, well above the bend in its trunk, which fastened it securely to the granite wall. Maeterlinck asks, 'What human eye will ever assist at these silent dramas, which are all too long for our short lives?'[14]

The arboreal composition of forests, as well as the frequency of fires, can be estimated with considerable precision from the sediments containing pollen grains and ashes that accumulate in the bottoms of lakes. There is no comparable way to measure the comparative density of fauna in times gone by. But, since the relative numbers of different trees varied greatly from one era to the next, it is likely that those of animals, which are dependent on them, did as well. At any rate, I personally have seen a substantial decline in wildlife. In my childhood, you would see a turtle perched on nearly every large rock in the river, but for well over a decade, I have not encountered a single one.

There has been a steady decrease in the diversity of North American forests since the coming of Europeans. The reasons are many, including massive clearcutting and excessive hunting. Forests are constantly fragmented by subdivisions, highways, agriculture and so on, isolating populations of plants and animals so they cannot easily adjust to change. The trees have been attacked by a seemingly endless array of imported parasites and pathogens, including the gypsy moth (arrived 1869), chestnut blight (*c.* 1900), beech scale (1920), Dutch elm disease (1928), the butternut canker (1967) and the emerald ash borer (2002). The forests today are never on the most fertile land since that has been reserved for agriculture. Passenger pigeons, once so numerous that a passing flock could darken the sky for days, fertilized the soil with great quantities of dung, but these birds were hunted to extinction in the nineteenth and early twentieth centuries. The considerable beauty of the forests that remains to us is touched by a sense of loss.

For millennia people have projected their fears and hopes onto the forest. They have then endeavoured to obscure, deny or ignore their own contributions, giving nature all the credit or blame. The forest is a monstrous double of humankind, completely alien in some respects and profoundly human in others. Forests reveal the myriad ways in which we think of nature, from terrifying to bucolic. We view forests with a combination of intense fear and longing; we alternately destroy and venerate them.

Foresters with a background in history can tell a great deal about what happened on the land in the past just by examining the trees. This includes not only specific information about human activity but fires, floods, hurricanes and so on. The forest seemingly obliterates the past yet also subtly preserves it in forms such as pottery shards, pollen grains, ruins, paths, introduced vegetation, scattered records and scars on bark.

My forest is heir to Native Americans, settlers, farmers, Communists, turtles, migratory birds and deer. In remembrance of all these tangled legacies, when I take my place alongside them, I would like it to be a wildlife preserve.

1

Wood and Leaves

Language is fossil poetry.
RALPH WALDO EMERSON

In the state of Utah, there is a 106-acre stand of genetically identical quaking aspens known as Pando, which is grown from a single root network. It dates back to the end of the last ice age, about 14,500 years ago. When one trunk falls, it opens a space in the canopy, and then sunlight encourages others to sprout. If you go by the DNA, the stand is a single plant, but, if you go by the number of stems, it is 4,700.[1] Each one has a distinctive profile, depending largely on its position with respect to the elements such as water and sun. In its long history, Pando has survived many upheavals, including fire, drought and the coming of Europeans. Now it is threatened by an abundance of deer, which nibble at new shoots. Not even Pando will last forever, but when it finally perishes, should a demise that is so gradual and so ambiguous be called death at all? And should we call Pando a forest or a tree?

Is a leaf part of a tree or an autonomous being? It may live for a long time after wind has torn it from a branch. What about a second trunk that has grown from a root? Is it the part of the original tree or a different one? What about two stems, perhaps of different species, that have grown together to form what looks like a single tree? Is it one tree or two? What about an acorn? Or a flower? And what about mycorrhizal fungi, which either start in the roots of a tree or wrap closely around them and are so intimately involved in the biology of a tree that it is hard to say how these partners are distinguished from one another?

About half of a tree is underground, in the form of roots. New shoots may sprout from the roots or from the stump. They may even sprout from branches of the fallen tree that are lying on the ground. Even if that does not happen, you would not call the tree 'dead'. It remains a host to countless forms of life, which, in many cases, are almost inseparable from it.

17

These may include birds, lichens, fungi, small animals and small plants. There is certainly no instant of death, but the individuality of the plant is ever so slowly absorbed into the entire forest.

When discrete identity is so uncertain, the old question as to whether organisms in the natural world are more competitive or cooperative no longer makes sense. They may be either, depending on where you decide each organism begins and ends. If you think of Pando as a group of separate trees, they may be competing for light. If one thinks of Pando as one tree with many branches, it is simply adjusting to changing circumstances.

The Intelligence of Trees

Trees don't have brains, at least not unless one considers the entire organism as a sort of brain. Both roots and branches are structured rather like neural networks. The roots, together with networks made of mycorrhizal fungi, are conduits not only for nutrients, water, carbon and minerals but for information in the form of chemical signals. This is passed between a tree and its offspring as well as to other trees, even those of different species. If a tree is attacked by aphids, for example, it can tell surrounding trees, which will immediately ready their chemical defences. Trees appear animated and purposeful in time-lapse photography, in which months or even years may be condensed into minutes.

In the words of contemporary botanist Steven Mancuso, 'If plants had eyes, ears, a brain, and lungs, we would not question whether they could see, hear, evaluate or breathe. Since they do not possess such organs, an effort of imagination is required to understand their sophisticated capabilities.'[2] When a butterfly lays eggs on the leaves of many plants, the recipient secretes a pheromone to attract wasps, which will eat the larvae, demonstrating at once the ability to both respond instantaneously and plan ahead.[3] As a strategy for survival, the behaviour itself is clever, but is the plant clever? What makes us hesitate to say yes is the lack of the sort of individual self to which we might attribute intelligence. According to Mancuso, 'even the definition of "individual" that we use for animals has little relevance to the world of plants.' Unlike animals, plants can split in two or more parts without any of them dying, and plants do not each have a unique genetic signature.[4]

Animals can escape threats from storms to predators primarily by changing their location. Plants, because they have roots, are unable to do this. Instead, they have developed a great sensitivity to nuances in their environment, including sunlight, availability of water, composition of the soil, warmth, atmosphere, chemicals and physical contact. These help to determine the rate, pattern and direction of their growth, as well as to activate chemical defences.[5] Acacia trees in Central America secrete nectar to attract leaf-cutter ants, which protect the trees from pathogens. Occasionally, plants respond to stimuli in a very immediate way, for example morning glories that open in the morning and close at night. In addition, plants have a modular structure, which enables them to replace lost parts with relative ease.

The bodies of animals, especially human beings, are hierarchically organized and centrally controlled through organs such as the brain and heart. This is also the sort of pattern that we reproduce in bureaucratic organizations, where each person is assigned a certain role, status and accompanying powers. But it is hard to say how much of that difference between plants and animals is an illusion of perspective. On closer examination, the human organism may not appear so unified. About 90 per cent of the cells in the body do not contain human DNA but belong to microorganisms.[6] As for the mental self, Descartes saw that as indivisible,[7] but many other theorists have divided it into parts, such as conscious, semi-conscious and subconscious.

In ways, human achievements may also be more collective than we usually think. Western tradition since the Renaissance has emphasized individual accomplishments, and laws make it possible to patent them. Nevertheless, fundamental devices such as the needle, the spindle, the drum and the wheel cannot be traced back to any one inventor. Later inventions such as gunpowder, the lightning rod and the steamboat originated simultaneously in more than one place. Inventions such as the photograph and the mobile phone came gradually, in so many stages that singling out a particular inventor is fairly arbitrary. This is also true of scientific discoveries. Calculus was developed simultaneously by Leibniz and Newton, natural selection by Wallace and Darwin. Today, most scientific papers have not one author but many co-authors, perhaps about seven or eight, while Wikipedia has millions.

Vegetative organization has many parallels among animals, which form swarms, flocks, herds and so on. Some of these, such as swarms of starlings, do not have leaders but navigate collectively. In humankind as well, the division into individuals is far from absolute. According to St Paul, man and wife become 'one flesh' (Ephesians 5:31). There is an ongoing debate as to when the foetus is part of a pregnant woman and when it becomes a separate organism. Units such as tribes, nations, cultures and corporations can be regarded for some purposes as collections of individuals, but in other contexts as organic wholes. They can hold property, publish manifestoes or engage in feuds.

One way to conceive of a tree or forest is as a place of perception without a beholder, thoughts without a mind and reveries without a dreamer. This helps to make the forest appear primeval, an embodiment of the primal chaos at the beginning of the world. It hovers strangely between divinity and nothingness. Life and death merge as organic material in the forest is constantly recycled and forms of life are perpetually combined with, separated from, absorbed into and incorporated within others. The countless leaves in a forest can blend for a while to create a single sound, usually a gentle roar that rises and falls with the wind.

But plants are, or at least appear to be, 'selfless'. Can you have a story without a hero? Can you have drama without characters? In ways, the perception of plants seems limited by their lack of individuality, but in others it becomes more universal. Nothing is just about them. Everything is about the world. Their feelings, if they have any, may have a purity that ours, and even those of other animals, lack, if trees are untouched by vanity or jealousy. According to the philosopher Michael Marder, 'plants embody the kind of detachment human beings dream of in their own transcendent aspiration to the other, beauty or divinity.'[8]

But perhaps trees, not so unlike human beings, really have a sense of self that constantly changes as they grow. And perhaps they construct this in ways that we can barely begin to imagine. Paradoxically, the profiles of trees are generally far more distinctive than those of human beings. When people are painted or photographed walking among large trees, the contrast often makes human beings appear monotonously similar to one another. Our upright stance, which has often been a source of human pride, shows little variety compared to the ways in which tree trunks can lean in any direction, twist or divide. Even when farmers have planted them into neatly spaced rows of orchards, trees never closely resemble one another.

In the latter twentieth century, scholars became increasingly mindful of the vast range of perception and feeling experienced by animals. One common response was to extend the structures of society beyond the domain of humankind, especially by granting animals rights. But that entailed the extension of modern individualism as well. We face a similar problem now, as we come to understand that this richness of perception may be shared not only by animals but by plants, yet it is still more difficult, probably impossible, to extend that individualism to their domain. Advocates for animal rights constantly blur the boundary between human beings and animals, but they simultaneously endeavour to reinforce that between animals and plants. Both frontiers are becoming less sharply defined today. Some activists and scholars have attempted to overcome this difficulty by appealing to the 'rights of nature',[9] but, when the concept is understood that broadly, are we really talking about rights at all?

These phenomena raise philosophical, social and even legal questions that are far beyond the scope of this book. The tension between rights and privileges of individuals and of groups probably runs through every human society. I do not wish to pronounce on the ultimate nature of individuality, only to note analogies between the societies of forests and human beings. Each tree is an individual or at least as close as anything the plant kingdom can offer. The forest is a collective, perhaps roughly comparable to a people or nation.

Chaos and Primeval Matter

A forest is the primeval darkness that we place at the beginning of time. It is full of wood that may become dwellings for people or fuel for fires. It is full of unseen beings, which are not quite human. It contains all potentials, yet they are unconsummated. In his *Aeneid*, Virgil imagined Rome as densely forested at the time of the city's foundation. The first people, he tells us, were born from the trunks of oaks. They lived by foraging and hunting, using branches as primitive weapons, and they knew neither manners nor the arts of civilization. The god Saturn, who had been deposed by Jupiter, came to them, gave them laws and inaugurated a golden age.[10]

People emerging out of trees was a decorative motif in Roman art and architecture. Along with them, Romans depicted figures of fantastic animals such as sphinxes, griffins and tritons emerging out of the leaves and stems.[11] This suggests that forests stand at the beginning of the world. This creation myth would be depicted in Gothic, Renaissance, Baroque and Victorian art. I love to walk through old neighbourhoods in New York City and observe the fantastic figures emerging from foliage in carvings on the facades of buildings from the building boom at the beginning of the twentieth century.

Roman bas-relief of boys
emerging out of foliage
as warriors and other
figures, as in Virgil's
creation myth.

Renaissance relief of an
angel and other figures
emerging out of foliage.

The idea that human beings first emerged from trees is found in the
mythologies of many other cultures as well. According to Norse legend,
the god Odin made the first man from an ash tree and the first woman
from an elm. One creation myth of the Lenape people, who lived in
what is now the American Northeast, tells that the first man sprouted
from the root of a tree; the first woman sprouted when the tree bent
over until the top touched the ground.[12] In a Zoroastrian legend from
Iran, the first human couple began as a tree with a double trunk. When
the plant had reached maturity, God separated the two parts and
endowed each with a soul.[13]

In some cultures, there are myths of a first, failed creation of human beings out of wood. These may well be from very early creation myths, which were partially repudiated and then absorbed into later ones. *Popol Vuh*, a scripture of the Quiche Maya of Guatemala and Mexico, tells that the gods made the first man from a cork tree and the first woman from a willow. Their race proved incapable of learning the arts of civilization or honouring the gods. Most of these people were destroyed by storms and floods and the remaining ones are monkeys today.[14] The identification of forests with the primal material of creation is a motif that has run through the culture of the West – and, to an extent, the world – from very early times.

Our word 'wood' can refer both to a forest and to ligneous material. The Greek cognate is *hyle*, which has the same double meaning. In addition, *hyle* also designates chaos and primeval matter.[15] The sort of philosophy we call 'materialism' is, if we strip away the accompanying abstractions, something like the image evoked by Virgil, in which human beings, together with many fantastic creatures, first emerge out of the woods. *Hyle* has usually been translated with the Latin *silva*, which was used widely throughout the Roman Empire and remained a common near synonym for 'forest' well into the early modern period.[16]

The forest is the domain of vegetation. The process of growth, which distinguishes living things, is most easily identifiable in plants and, therefore, in forests. For plants, as we have seen, it is almost the same thing as birth. The Greek word *phȳsis*, roughly the same as our 'nature', derives from the Indo-European *bhu*, meaning procreation, germination, growth and birth, especially as pertains to vegetation. The Latin equivalent is *natura*, which originally meant 'birth' and, understood only a bit more broadly, also refers to the power of growth.[17] It is not only Western tradition that accords this primal significance to wood. In Chinese alchemy, wood is one of the five basic elements out of which all things are composed, alongside earth, metal (or gold), water and fire. Each of these components is defined by a process,[18] and in the case of wood it is growth, which is as fundamental as the way fire burns or water flows.

The association of forests with primeval chaos is shown by the way in which, according to legends, it is frequently the dwelling of monsters and prodigies. These include many dragons, ogres, werewolves, giants and sorcerers. According to medieval legends, even such refined knights as Sir Tristan, Sir Lancelot and Sir Ywain, when they live in the forest, go mad and become wild men.

The Forest and Identity

Judaism, Christianity and Islam, which see the self as unitary, all originated in arid geographical locations with relatively sparse vegetation. Buddhism and Jainism, which see the self as an illusion, first developed in the rainforests of India. The forest is the place of nature at her most abundant, with a concentration of presences, stories and meanings. A vast range of living things from trees to birds constantly signal to one another. The intricate play of light and shade as sun is reflected among leaves and diffused by moisture suggests fleeting intuitions. Trees, especially old ones with gnarled limbs and twisted trunks, express a great deal without even moving. The self seems to fragment as one passes through the forest, alternately identifying with the various animals and plants.

As they draw us into the community of creatures, forests also work against human society. When even small groups of people enter a forest that has no paths, they must constantly walk around trees, and so they are in danger of losing sight of one another. Unless the forest is on the site of a former pasture or settlement, the ground will also probably be irregular. It will have mounds where old trees fell over, lifting soil with their roots. Human habitations are mostly built along straight, perpendicular lines, but the forest is dominated by irregular, organic curves. If they are too distracted either by the beauty of the woods or by practical tasks, people are likely to become lost.

As a person walks in the forest, she or he will likely relate to the innumerable forms of life in very different ways, including as a predator and as potential prey. This constant change of perspective entails a perpetual adjustment, which may be understood as a sort of metamorphosis.[19] For the Tzeltal Maya, who live in the heavily forested region of Chiapas, Mexico, every person has between four and sixteen souls. One of these has a form appropriate to his or her heritage. The others may take almost any form, from hummingbirds or lightning bolts to Catholic priests. These souls may be scattered over the earth but have doubles within the heart. A person does not necessarily know what form his or her souls take, though a very few encounter their souls among the creatures of the rainforest.[20]

Anthropologist Eduardo Kohn has analysed this vision of the self in detail with reference to his work with the Runa Puma, a forest-dwelling people in the upper Amazon of Ecuador, in his book *How Forests Think*.

Building on the work of American philosopher Charles Pierce, Kohn maintains that all knowledge and communication, including that of species other than the human, is mediated by signs. Symbolic language is, in his opinion, confined to people; in fact, it marks the boundaries of the human realm. But this is only one means of communication, and messages of considerable subtlety are constantly exchanged by means of iconic (naming) or indexical (associative and classificatory) signals among the countless living things that make up the forest, where one thinks, like other forms of life, in images. In responding to each, one constantly alters one's personality. Identity is a shifting point of orientation, determined by constantly changing relationships with other objects and living things.

Kohn was told by one of the Runa Puma that he should sleep with his face upwards so that, should a jaguar come, he could look the animal in the face, thus inhibiting it from attacking him. Were he to sleep face down, the jaguar would take him for meat. Thus posture conveys a change between the identities of predator and prey, which may be noticed by many members of the forest community.[21] For Indigenous people of the Amazon, subjectivity is universal, so there is no absolute death. Individuality lies in the body, which becomes something like a signifier. Its meaning depends on context and is understood through analogies. The actions of people are part of a language with which the forest thinks.

Sound Symbolism

In *The Order of Things* (French edition, 1966), the historian Michel Foucault writes that the power of signification was not originally confined to words: 'The names of things were lodged in the things they designated, just as strength is written in the body of a lion, regality in the eye of an eagle, just as the influence of planets is marked upon the brows of men: by the form of similitude.'[22] To describe something was to locate it in the intricate matrix of signatures, analogies, sympathies and correspondences that seemed to make up reality.

Foucault places the change in the function of language around the start of the seventeenth century,[23] the era of Shakespeare. In the play *As You Like It*, the playwright contrasts the new use of language, as something apart from reality, with the traditional one, where significance is embedded in the world. When Duke Senior and his companions have gone into exile in the Forest of Arden, he says:

> And this our life, exempt from public haunt,
> Finds tongues in trees, books in the running brooks,
> Sermons in stones, and good in everything. (2:1, 562–4)

In the court or the city, meaning lies only in human words, but in the woods it pervades everything. Non-human voices, which are elsewhere drowned out by human noise, emerge.

Foucault regards the regulation of meaning to language as characteristic of the modern way of thinking, which may be drawing to a close.[24] That is partly true, yet he divides up human experience too neatly by historical eras. While the emphasis has shifted, both ways of understanding language have probably been around at least since people first began to draw abstract signs in clay tablets. People of the Renaissance already looked back to an even earlier age, a time in antiquity when language was even less a realm apart from the world. In mythic terms, this could be the language of humankind in which Adam named the animals (Genesis 2:18–20) or of human beings before the Tower of Babel (Genesis 11:19). According to Judeo-Christian legend, in Eden the first man and woman could talk to animals, an ability that they lost when an angel with a flaming sword drove them away. The Tower of Babel was a sort of second fall, where the primordial language divided into tribal ones. The first story may be about the advent of farming, the second about urbanization. Both bring increasing alienation from the natural world and a limitation on human speech.

This is not just a nostalgic fantasy. The ethnolinguist Brent Berlin has argued that, contrary to what Ferdinand de Saussure and Jacques Derrida believed, the relationship between objects and signs is by no means arbitrary. Many words sound like what they describe, such as 'crash'. But even more important than auditory similarity, known as onomatopoeia, is phonaesthesia or sound symbolism, which is the way certain words have patterns of energy that suggest the thing they designate.[25] The word 'lizard', when said out loud, flows in a way that is very suggestive of a lizard twisting its body as it runs across a rock. This quality contributed greatly to the origin of language. As words were increasingly detached from a context in the natural world, they have lost some phonaesthesia, though by no means all.[26]

We are increasingly recognizing that both animals and plants are constantly communicating, sometimes across lines of species, through chemical signals, electrical impulses, changes in colour, scents, calls and in many other ways, some of which we can hardly begin to imagine. They are full of meanings, both corporeal and relatively intangible, and we at least sense this when walking through the woods. Sound symbolism is not confined to human tongues but may be found in sounds in the forest from the growl of a bear to the song of a thrush.

To summarize, the difference between human beings and animals is not, as Descartes and many others have thought, that only people have language or even the capacity for abstraction. It is that for humans, especially in the modern era, meaning, at least partially confined to language, stands apart from the rest of the world. For animals and perhaps plants, meaning is immanent in objects and the relations among them, much as it is in similes, allegories and implicit metaphors that are conveyed through poetic images. This renders events like the flight of birds, which the Homeric Greeks interpreted as omens, heavy with significance.

Meaning before Words

For people who live in intimate contact with the forest, there is a profusion of meanings, which can be overwhelming. From Dante's time until today, people in Western culture, who have increasingly little contact with forests, have constantly suffered from an absence of meaning, which can lead to despair. Dante is remembered as a supreme master of language, yet his masterpiece, *The Divine Comedy*, begins with a total failure of words:

> *Nel mezzo del cammin di nostra vita*
> *Mi ritrovai per una selva oscura,*
> *Chè la diritta via era smarrita.*

> *Ah quanto a dir qual'era è cosa dura*
> *Esta selva selvaggia e aspra e forte*
> *Che nel pensier rinnova la paura!*

> In the middle of my life,
> I found myself in a dark wood
> For the direct path had vanished.

> Ah, how can I tell you what it was like or how long it lasted,
> that forest, so savage, bitter and intense,
> When, with the memories, the terror returns?[27]

Dante in a gloomy wood, illustration by Gustave Doré for *Dante's Inferno* (1887).

Dante may never have seen a dark forest, for his native Tuscany was very sparsely wooded. Some scholars believe he may have been inspired to write, or even partially composed, his *Divine Comedy* while walking through the pine woods of Ravenna. These had been exploited for timber since at least Roman times. We have pictures showing these woods in the background by Botticelli, Uccello and other painters of the Renaissance. They are highly cultivated and have enough open space for several horses and riders to easily pass among the trees.[28] The dark wood was not an actual place but the antithesis of the emerging Renaissance Humanism, a tradition that had failed Dante.

Paolo Uccello, *The Hunt in the Forest*, 1470s, tempera, oil and gold on panel. This picture shows the Ravenna Woods, where Dante was reportedly inspired to write the *Divine Comedy*. The trees are carefully tended, with dying branches cut off. It is sufficiently open for a huge party to assemble without difficulty.

The Latin of Dante's day had a formal elegance, just as it does today, but it was not very well suited to expressing raw emotion. Dante had to discard the language of learning and write in Tuscan, the language of everyday life. Because it was primarily a spoken rather than a literary tongue, Tuscan was full of associations with lived experience, from ordinary routines to political upheavals, which Latin had in Virgil's time but had lost when it ceased to be spoken. The vernacular had remained relatively embedded in both the social and natural worlds. The dark wood was a primal state prior to language, which was something that Dante had to largely reinvent to write his epic. His writing standardized what had previously been a local dialect, and Tuscan became what we know as 'Italian' today.

To describe his experiences, Dante had to efface the boundary between the Christian present and the pagan past. He let himself be guided by the pagan poet Virgil, who had written of the forest that stood at the foundation of Rome, though even Virgil speaks in Tuscan rather than Latin. To fit Virgil and other ancient poets within the late medieval world, Dante needed to represent their world as part of hell. Dante added a Garden of Elysium, an earthly paradise in hell for the just pagans, but not even Virgil is allowed to enter the more exalted parts of the cosmos.

In summary, to enter the dark wood is, in a sense, to go back in time. Dante returned to an era where words were not yet sharply separated from the things they designated or the meanings they conveyed. The forest is a place where meaning, rather than being confined to signifiers arranged neatly on a page, pervades the landscape entirely. Life and death, while perhaps terrifying, become meaningful, and Dante could find new inspiration.

Why do leaves in a forest make a rustling sound in the wind? I know of no way in which this has any very specific function. One can speculate that perhaps the sound could, say, send information to the forest community about the impending weather. One can also attribute the phenomenon to chance. At any rate, the sound of leaves is very restful and full of suggestive power. Perhaps the language of the forest eludes precise translation.

2

The Spirituality of Trees

The man, who was beginning to see, replied, 'I can see people;
they look like trees to me, but they are walking about.'
Mark 8:24 (Jerusalem translation)

When the Israelites are being held captive in Egypt, Moses and his brother Aaron have an audience with the pharaoh. Aaron, at the direction of Moses, throws down his staff, and it turns into a snake. The magicians of the pharaoh do the same, making their staffs turn into serpents as well, but Aaron's snake devours the others (Exodus 7:8–13). The staff of Aaron is essentially a magic wand. To make the Egyptians let the Israelites leave, Aaron, at the direction of Moses, stretches out his staff and changes the water in a river into blood. When that is insufficient, Aaron uses his staff to create nine additional plagues (Exodus 7:14–12:36).

Later, after their deliverance, power struggles emerge among the Israelites. Moses has each of the twelve patriarchal families bring him a branch, saying that the clan whose branch blossoms will be their leader. The staff of Aaron, which represents the house of Levi, immediately sprouts not buds but flowers that are already open and almonds (Numbers 17:8). By tradition, the Messiah is to come from the house of Levi, and Christians have interpreted the flowering staff as an anticipation of Jesus. Medieval European artists would depict this genealogy as the 'tree of Jesse', father of David. It would show the tree as sprouting from the side of a man lying on the ground, with the various offshoots of the family as branches, culminating with Jesus Christ at the top. In the latter nineteenth and twentieth centuries, this arboreal structure became the Tree of Evolution, in which the branches hosted not people but species and at the pinnacle was humankind.

Snakes, because of their curved bodies and their frequently green or yellow colour, are often identified with vegetation. People sometimes view them as mediators between the realms of plants and animals. One

'Unicorn of the Annunciation', illumination from a Book of Hours, Netherlands, *c.* 1500. In the background is the flowering rod of Aaron, a symbol here of resurrection.

Absolon Stumme, *Tree of Jesse*, 1499, tempera on panel.

Christian von Mechel, after Hans Holbein, *The Fall*, 1760, engraving. The form of the serpent blends almost completely into the branches of the tree.

tree is a repository of knowledge, which it offers by means of its fruits. Even that tree does not use spoken words, but the fruit itself seems like a sort of language. Artists would often show the serpent entwined about the tree as though they were one. The snake is usually shown offering an apple to Eve.

Hybrids and Anomalies

People in Western culture have conventionally attributed apparently purposeful behaviour in humans to intelligence; in animals, to instinct; and in plants, to a purely mechanical process. In *De anima* (On the Soul), Aristotle distinguished three varieties of soul: the nutritive soul, which enables growth and reproduction and is possessed by plants, animals and human beings; the sensitive soul, which enables perception and locomotion and is possessed by human beings and animals; and the rational soul, which enables thought and is the exclusive possession of human beings.[1]

The boundaries that separate bestial, vegetable and human life are among the most fundamental foundations of Western culture. They are so deeply integrated into our traditional moral philosophies and legal systems that transgression of them can threaten to throw everything into chaos. It can inspire perpetual existential insecurity, since all creatures, especially human beings, may risk being deprived of any assured place within the cosmos.

According to anthropologist Mary Douglas, people across cultures perceive anomalies, phenomena that do not fit neatly into accepted systems of classification, as pollution, which they then deal with in a range of ways including avoidance and ritual purification.[2] She writes, 'Holiness is keeping distinct categories of creation.'[3] In the books of Deuteronomy (14) and Leviticus (11), these categories are affirmed with an elaborate series of prohibitions and directives. Living things that do not conform to divisions are considered abominations. A pig, for example, is unclean because it has cloven hooves like cattle but does not ruminate, violating a usual pattern. Israelites may not eat this animal or even touch its corpse (Leviticus 11:7–8).[4]

Nevertheless, violation of taxonomical boundaries, in the form of either hybridization or metamorphosis between different classes of living things, seems just about impossible to avoid. There have always been plenty of hybrids and anomalies – living things that do not seem to fit neatly into this threefold division. Animals from monkeys to octopuses have often startled people by showing an intelligence that seemed the exclusive property of human beings, while people have acted in ways that, for one reason or another, impressed other men and women as 'animalistic'. Human identity is volatile, multifaceted, precarious and prone to mental hybridization.

There are also beings that seem to occupy the boundary between animals and plants. A few plants have characteristics that we normally think of as exclusive to animals, such as responding immediately to touch or eating flesh. The sensitive plant (*Mimosa pudica*), a shrub native to the tropical regions of the Americas, responds immediately to even a light touch of a finger by closing its leaves and drooping. Because of its seeming delicacy, it was sometimes used as a representation, or caricature, of Victorian womanhood. Then there are carnivorous plants, ones that eat insects, lizards, plants, frogs and even rodents. Like hunters, they lure prey with nectar, pretty colours and attractive smells, and then they close around it with a sort of jaw. In the sea, forms of invertebrate life are so

J. J. Grandville, 'Sensitive', hand-coloured wood engraving from Taxile Delord, *Les fleurs animées* (The Flowers Animated), vol. II (1847).

varied that the distinction between plants and animals is far from being intuitive. Scientists now consider corals to be animals, yet they remain stationary and grow in patterns that appear vegetal. For hundreds of years, fungi were considered plants, but now they are placed in a phylum of their own and are regarded as closer to animals.

Anomalies of this sort are also common in legend, though a bit less so in Abrahamic religions. The snake of Eden is the only animal in the Torah or Old Testament that talks of its own volition. The staff of Aaron, together with those of the Egyptian sorcerers and Moses, is the only clearly delineated hybrid of plant and animal life. According to Douglas, Christianity spiritualized the concept of holiness, so that it was possible to disregard the material circumstances.[5] But, rather than simply ignoring anomalies, Christianity often glories in them, regarding them as miracles that prove the power of God. The central idea of Christianity is perhaps the greatest conceivable metamorphosis. God is transformed into a human being who can suffer mental anguish, physical pain and death.

There is also a strong identification of Christ with flora and foliage. As James George Frazer argued in *The Golden Bough*, Christ is heir to vegetation deities such as the Phrygian Attis, the Egyptian Osiris, the Babylonian Tammuz and the Canaanite/Greek Adonis.[6] Like a flowering plant, he dies and is reborn. In the Eucharist, his body is transformed into bread, a product of wheat, and his blood into wine, a product of grapes.

Plants in Folklore

In folk literature around the world, plants, especially flowers and trees, are sentient and open to persuasion. Native American author Joseph Bruchac has written, 'Just as, in Native stories, human people and animal people are able to communicate freely with each other and even walk in each other's worlds, so too the plants are able to speak with human beings and enter their lives in a variety of ways.'[7] This interaction has been better preserved in Native American traditions than in most, but it is also found in the fairy tales of Grimm and, if one goes back a little in time, just about everywhere. Many Jewish, Christian and Islamic legends are just as animistic as those of Native Americans. Even though they may deny their capacity for reason, people still talk to pets and house plants. In the modern era, animism found a refuge in less closely monitored aspects of Western culture such as literature for children. This fluidity of categories is the default mode of human perception and never very far from the surface. Despite attempts to suppress it, this quality constantly resurfaces everywhere from ancient Israel to modern Europe.

A character in folklore might move back and forth among fundamental categories, starting as a human and becoming, perhaps only for a brief time, a god, bird or tree. Even in the relatively rationalistic cultures of the Greeks and Romans, there are plenty of tales of transformations. Ovid, among others, wrote an entire book of them, *Metamorphoses*. To name just a few from a very long list, the elderly couple Baucis and Philemon become a pair of intertwining trees, an oak and a linden; the hunter Acteon becomes a stag chased by his own hounds; Arachne, a superb weaver, becomes a spider; Aeneas, a Trojan warrior and founder of Rome, a god. There are also many intermediate figures who may be human yet partly god, such as Hercules; partly animal, such as centaurs or satyrs; and partly plant, such as the nymph Daphne, who becomes a laurel tree yet retains a 'human' sort of awareness. There are also figures that, though not possessed of human attributes, combine features of various animals such as a horse with wings.

There are several creatures in folklore that blend the characteristics of plants with those of people or other animals. In European folklore, one is the mandrake or 'mandragora'. This is a root that grows in the form of a little man or woman. When plucked from the ground, it lets out a scream that is harsh enough to kill whoever hears. The plant may,

Drawing of a mandragora in a medicinal herb book (*Arzneipflanzenbuch*), possibly from Augsburg, 1520–30.

however, be obtained if you go out on a dark, moonless night and stuff your ears with wax. You then tie one end of a string to the plant and the other to the tail of a dog. Then, at midnight, place your back to the wind and blow a trumpet to assure that you will not hear the scream. At the same time, whip the dog so that it starts to run away, pulling the mandragora up with its tail. The dog will die, but you will have the plant.[8] Another hybrid between plants and animals is the barnacle goose, which grows on trees like a fruit and then falls to the ground at maturity. This legend was widely reported in the Middle Ages and even found its way into John Gerard's *Herbal*,[9] first published in 1597, which was often regarded as the foremost authority on plants.

In many old English and Scottish ballads, trees and other plants are not only amenable to persuasion but compassionate and wise as well. In 'The Cherry-Tree Carol', Mary is walking with Joseph in a garden, and she asks him to pick cherries for her. Thinking she has been unfaithful to him, Joseph at first refuses, and then:

> Mary said to the cherry tree,
>   'Bow down to my knee,
> That I may pluck cherries,
>   By one, two, and three.'

> The uppermost sprig then
>   Bowed down to her knee:
> 'Thus you may see, Joseph,
>   These cherries are for me.'[10]

In several ballads lovers are separated in life but reborn to be united as plants, often a vine and a tree, which grow from their graves and find one another. In the Scottish ballad 'Prince Robert', a young man is poisoned by his mother, who does not approve of his marriage. His bride comes to him but arrives only in time for his funeral, and his mother will not even give her his ring. She dies shortly, and then:

> The tane (one) was buried in Marie's kirk (church),
>   The tother in Marie's quair (choir),
> And out of the tane there sprang a birk (birch),
>   And out o the tother a brier.

And thae twa met, and thae twa plat (wound together),
The birk but (stem) and the brier,
And by that ye may very well ken
They were twa lovers dear.[11]

In a similar story from Chinese folklore, the emperor wants the wife of Hanpang, his secretary, as a concubine. After the couple refuse his request, the emperor orders Hanpang thrown in prison, where he soon dies. His wife continues to reject the advances of the emperor and, when he persists, commits suicide by jumping from a cliff. Her last request is to be buried beside her husband, but the emperor refuses. The husband and wife are buried separately, but large cedars grow from each grave and intertwine, becoming known as 'the tree of the faithful lovers'.[12]

Perhaps the most liminal plant of all is the Waq Waq tree of medieval Arab myth. It is found on a remote island in Asia. From its branches grow heads, in some versions of the tale the heads of men and women, in others of many fantastic animals. In yet other versions, it grows miniature human beings, which fall to the ground as they mature.[13] It is a being that transgresses all categories that divide living things, especially the boundaries between humans, plants and animals.

The World Tree

The Vikings thought of the cosmos as a world tree, and it is described in detail in the *Poetic Edda*. It is possibly an ash, but, unlike other ash trees, it is always green. The three Norns, wise women who control the fate of human beings, sit at the base of the tree. Below it is also the well of destiny.[14] One root reaches into the underworld, ruled by the goddess Hela. A second root reaches into the land of the frost giants and a third into the realm of gods. There are numerous snakes beneath the tree. The serpent Nidhogg gnaws at its roots. An eagle is perched at the crown. The squirrel Ratatosk moves back and forth among its branches between the eagle and serpent, carrying messages and stirring up strife. Four harts move among the highest branches, eating the leaves.[15] As Ragnarök, the apocalyptic battle between gods and giants, approaches, the tree will shudder, releasing monsters,[16] a bit like suppressed thoughts rising to the surface as a crisis approaches.[17] The tree is not insensate, since the two human beings, a man, Life, and a woman, Lifthrasir, will survive the last days by hiding in a wood, probably the branches of Yggdrasil.[18]

Tree on the Island of Waq Waq, Golconda, India, early 17th century,
ink, opaque watercolour and gold on paper.

John Augustus Knapp, *Yggdrasil*, late 19th or early 20th century, tempera on canvas.

There is a lot here that challenges the imagination. If the roots reach into the abodes of gods and giants, does this mean that both live underground? If six stags are in the canopy, does that mean they walk on branches? Or are they giant stags with their feet on the ground? But then, we might ask, 'What ground?' Where is the earth? Where is Yggdrasil? It seems to embrace all worlds and yet exist in none. The Vikings probably did not attempt to picture Yggdrasil at all, just as modern physicists do not visualize their models of the universe. The Vikings simply walked beneath trees and observed the play of light and shadow. They listened to leaves rustling in the wind and to the sounds of birds. They could easily observe that many trees can sprout new shoots from their roots, and so a tree need not be confined to a single stem. Yggdrasil, like Pando, is as much a forest as a tree. If you went looking for Yggdrasil, where might you find it? Either everywhere or nowhere at all.

The world tree is a motif found in myth and folklore throughout much of the world, and the trees show a bewildering variety. For the Ottoman Turks, the Tree of Life has a great profusion of leaves, and a human fate is written on every one. Whenever a person dies, a leaf falls from the tree. For several Siberian tribes, the souls of the unborn perch on the Cosmic Tree like birds until they are summoned by a shaman.[19] The Tzeltal Maya of Chiapas, Mexico, believe the Ceiba Tree is the centre of the cosmos. Infants who died at birth ascend the tree to heaven, nourished by its fruit and protected by its branches.[20] Such colourful beliefs need to be understood with a bit of caution – even with an intimate knowledge of the culture, it can be impossible to know how much is poetic, metaphoric or literal – but they document how intimately trees are integrated into the rhythms of life and death.

These trees are, like Yggdrasil, bonds that unify several parts of the cosmos, including heaven, earth and the underworld. Simply on the basis of scale, they are all as much forests as trees. But, in a sense, every tree is a forest. The branches grow from the trunk as well as from one another much as the foundation rises from the ground. Even isolated in a city square, a tree is united with others in ways that are not visible to human beings. Perhaps the Vikings thought of every tree as a branch of Yggdrasil.

The central image in Christianity is the cross, which has the general shape of a tree with a spreading canopy. Vladimir Bibikhin points out that the cross itself takes on the features of a deity and seems to merge with the person of Jesus.[21] The two merge almost completely in *The Dream*

Folio from the *Salzburg Missal*, 1478. Here, the Tree of Knowledge and Tree of Life are one. The half on the right brings death, but that on the left brings eternal life. It will provide wood for the True Cross, which appears in its branches.

of the Rood, an Old English poem from the eighth or ninth century. The cross tells the reader that it grew as a tree and was cut down by enemies, dragged to a hilltop and placed upright. It suffers the nails, spear thrusts, mockery and all the agonies of Christ. The cross is then cut down and buried, but, like Christ, resurrected. It is exalted above the other trees of the forest and has the power to save men and women.[22]

In the European Middle Ages, there were many tales of the Holy Cross and miracles connected with it. Several are recorded in *The Golden Legend*, a collection of lives of the saints, published by Jacobus de Voragine in about 1255–66. A bit like a contemporary folklorist, Jacobus often gives several versions of a single incident, but, whichever account one prefers, the cross emerges as a world tree. To summarize the story briefly without giving all the variants, when the original Adam is dying, he sends his son Seth to the gates of paradise. The angel gives Seth a branch from the Tree of Eternal Life, telling him that, when the branch bears fruit, his father will be healed. When Seth returns, Adam is dead, and so Seth plants the branch on his father's grave, where it grows to become a tree. Solomon later has the tree cut down to use in building his house in the forest, but it never fits, for the board is always too short or too long. Instead, he makes it into a bridge, and when the queen of Sheba visits him and walks across, she has a vision of the Crucifixion. Solomon is distressed and has the wood buried deep in the earth, but it eventually rises to the surface of a

Piero della Francesca, *The Arrival of the Queen of Sheba*, c. 1452–7, fresco, Basilica di San Francesco, Arezzo, showing the Queen of Sheba venerating the beam that will later form the True Cross.

pond, where it is used to make the holy cross on which Christ is to be crucified. After the Crucifixion, the wood is buried once again but then rediscovered by St Helena, mother of Emperor Constantine. The cross is tested by holding it over the dead body in a passing funeral procession, and the corpse immediately comes to life. Helena decides that the cross had too much power for any single person to possess, so she has it cut in pieces and sent to churches throughout the world.[23]

The Longing for Heaven

One of the first people in the modern era to seriously argue that plants had reason and emotion was the Belgian essayist and playwright Maurice Maeterlinck, who, in his book *The Intelligence of Flowers*, first published in 1913, even attempted to reconstruct their point of view. People often think, rightly or wrongly, that our status as spiritual beings confined to a material world gives humankind a special, and largely tragic, fate. Maeterlinck believed that was shared by plants:

> The essential organ, the nutrient organ of the plant, its root, attaches it to the soil. If it be difficult to discover among the great laws that oppress us that which weighs heaviest upon our shoulders, in the case of the plant there is no doubt: it is the law that condemns it to immobility from its birth to its death.[24]

According to Maeterlinck, the life of plants, like that of men and women, is a perpetual struggle against the constraints of the physical world, as shown in the unceasing growth away from the soil. This, of course, seems especially applicable to trees, which often attain vast heights while remaining rooted in the earth. This is also, in his opinion, the source of their creativity in matters such as engendering flowers and disseminating seeds. The interpretation compares plants not to the functions of the human body but to the aspirations of the human soul. To sum this up in an image, we might say that their life, and all life, is a rebellion against a seemingly indifferent cosmos.

Perhaps Maeterlinck forgets that plants do not always aspire towards the heights and grow as much under the ground as above. In some ways, his idea is very much a product of its time. Like traditional Christians, his trees are striving to enter heaven. Like men and women of Romanticism and the Enlightenment, they are in perpetual revolt against restraints. But, even if Maeterlinck may have been anthropomorphizing, there are elements here that are close to universal. For those ready to concede plants a sort of sentience, trees seem to have an elemental spirituality that people may have shared before the profusion of religions, sects, philosophies and ideologies that clutter our spiritual life.

Terracotta wall panel depicting Enkidu, Ur, Iraq, late 3rd or early 2nd millennium BCE. Already, the figure of Enkidu shows many of the characteristics that will be associated with the 'wild man' for thousands of years to come. He is almost naked and has a bushy beard, and his protruding ears and erection suggest an animalistic nature.

3

Mythic Beings of the Forest

*For six days and seven nights they lay together, for Enkidu had
forgotten his home in the hills; but, when he was satisfied,
he went back to the wild beasts. Then, when the gazelle saw him,
they bolted away; when the wild creatures saw him they fled.*
The Epic of Gilgamesh (Sandars translation)

John Burroughs, the most popular naturalist in nineteenth-century America, asked, 'Do such books as mine give a wrong impression of nature, and leave readers to expect more from a walk or a camp in the woods than they usually get?' He reminded people that time spent in the forest, like all experiences, requires interpretation. He himself often did not know how much pleasure he had from a walk in the woods until he sat down at his writing desk. Only in the process of composition did he discover just what had happened and how he felt.[1] The increasing estrangement from the natural world has sometimes left people with unrealistic expectations for a walk in the woods. They want instant epiphanies at least, and feel disappointed when these are not forthcoming.

The Western concept of the forest is intimately tied to that of nature, and the West has constantly oscillated between extremes of venerating and demonizing both. Cultures such as those of Native Americans that do not distinguish as sharply between the realms of nature and civilization may have no concept that is a very close equivalent. Anthropologist Philippe Descola writes, 'For the (American) Indians, the forest is an extension of a human house, and in it they engage in ritual exchanges of energy with animals and with the spirits that rule there.'[2] Nevertheless, the woods still are a place of heightened spirituality. Among the Woodland people of the Northeastern United States and Canada, as well as many other native peoples of the Americas, young people would go alone into the woods on a vision quest to interact with their guardian spirit. For the Hindus as well, both village and forest are the abode of humankind. They are both subject to the same hierarchies. Brahmins often feel called at an advanced age to give up their possessions and live as ascetics in the woods, not as a renunciation but for renewal through more intimate contact with the rhythms of the natural world.[3]

As experienced in the forest, living things are glimpsed fleetingly, while moving from one place to another, with the field of vision partially blocked by trees. They are heard amid a background of other sounds, often muffled by surrounding leaves. There are also odd scents, overgrown pathways and indistinct tracks. New creatures are then reconstructed from these sensuous bits and pieces, filtered through the human imagination. The proliferation of fantastic creatures of legend in the forest is found in most or all cultures of the world.

For people who live in settlements surrounded by woods, a few basic perceptions may be universal. Belief that trees are the homes of spirits is common among Indigenous peoples of Asia, Europe, Africa, the Americas and elsewhere.[4] A woodland is where spirits predominate, a supernatural community that may be benign, threatening or indifferent. The hamlet or village is, by contrast, primarily the domain of human beings.[5] In most or all human cultures, forests represent something primordial, either as an aspect of society or a relatively autonomous realm.

The most conspicuous among the mythic inhabitants of the forest are figures of terror, which give a tangible form to the amorphous fears that the forest can inspire. Around the world, sighting such figures in or near a forest has often been able to create panics that lead to the evacuation of entire villages. Among these monsters is the Wendigo, a Native American giant feared by many tribes in North-Central Canada and parts of the United States. The Wendigo is usually human in form but almost incomprehensibly large, and its favourite food is human beings.[6] The Nandi Bear of Kenya, another creature of legend, eats only the brains of humans. It hides amid the leaves on a low branch of a tree and, when a victim walks by, opens the top of his head with a single blow, eats the brain and leaves the empty skull.[7] A vast array of monsters reportedly were present at the witches' sabbaths reported in Renaissance and early modern Continental Europe in and around forests.

Then there is the master or mistress of animals, a figure that protects the creatures of the forest. Most of the time, s/he will allow some hunting and gathering in the forest but punishes anyone that takes too much. A single deity may protect all or just a single species. In the Brazilian rain forest, the protector of animals and plants is Curupira, who generally has a humanoid form but with his feet facing backwards in order to confuse hunters and gatherers. He takes the form of various animals to watch over people in the forest, and, if they are getting out of line, he may send them a warning by shaking a tree. He will punish those who are disrespectful or greedy by misleading them or taking away their shadows. In addition, the lore of the Brazilian Amazon includes other deities that specifically protect fish, palms, rubber trees and turtles.[8]

Japan is rare, arguably unique, in having continued in the practice of its indigenous, animistic religion even as it entered the modern world. The Japanese consider forests a dwelling place of spirits that need to be respected and conciliated. At least since the eighteenth century, Japan has done more to protect its forests than any other country in the world.[9] This does not mean, however, that the Japanese have traditionally regarded the forests as unequivocally benign. There are plenty of legends of oni, giant spiders and other goblins that live deep within the forest,

'The groves were God's first temples – avenue of noble cryptomerias at Nikko', 1904, photograph. From early times, the Japanese have regarded their forests with reverence.

many of whom eat travellers that stray into their domain. Many samurai are renowned for slaying these monsters, but the ravages of such creatures are not blamed on the forest itself. Even goblins are given a place to live so that they will not invade the human world.

The supernatural figures of the forest are far too numerous and diverse for me to attempt any comprehensive categorization. They include a virtually endless array of werewolves, elves, wild men, swan maidens, satyrs, moss people, ghosts, ogres, rusalki, dragons, trolls, spirit animals, witches, fairies, orishas, yakshis, kami, oni and so on. I will give a few tales that illustrate their range and variety.

The Wild Man

A terrified trapper encounters a man of superhuman strength at the watering hole where animals come to drink, somebody who eats grass, runs with the beasts, fills in holes that had been dug to trap game and tears apart snares. At the advice of his father, the trapper goes to Gilgamesh, king of the Mesopotamian city of Uruk, and asks him to send a harlot from the temple of the goddess Ishtar to seduce the mighty stranger. The king grants the request. The trapper and the woman wait at the pond and, on the third day, the wild man appears. The harlot then undresses and approaches him, and the two lie together for six days and seven nights. When the man returns to his animal companions, they avoid him. He tries to run with them as before but can no longer keep pace, and his knees give way. As N. K. Sandars put it in her translation of the tale, 'Enkidu (for that was his name) was grown weak, for wisdom was in him, and the thoughts of a man were in his heart.'[10]

He has no choice but to return to the woman, who teaches him to drink wine, eat bread, anoint himself with oil and wear human clothes. She arranges for a barber to cut his long hair. Instead of destroying traps, Enkidu learns to hunt lions and wolves that attack the flocks of shepherds. He also gains the ambitions of a human being and resolves to challenge Gilgamesh himself. When the king is entering a temple to lie with the bride of another man, Enkidu blocks the way. The two fight furiously for a while and then become the best of friends.[11] This is the opening of the *Epic of Gilgamesh*, and the partners go on to experience triumph and tragedy, which I will speak of in the next chapter.

We do not have a complete or definitive version of the epic. The closest thing is the earliest discovered manuscript, dating from the seventh century BCE and found in the palace of the Assyrian king Ashurbanipal during the early 1850s. It consists of twelve tablets, the first eleven of which tell a cohesive tale, and the last of which consists of marginally connected texts. These are known as the 'standard version' and provide the foundation for subsequent attempts at reconstructing the story. There are many gaps where the text is unreadable. Many of these are filled in with material from fragments of an Old Babylonian version from the early second millennium. The epic emerged in something close to its final form around 1300 BCE, when it was edited to form a single narrative by the Babylonian scribe Sîn-lēqi-unninni.

There are also five tablets telling stories of Gilgamesh in the Sumerian language, which go back to the latter third millennium BCE. These provide early versions of the stories in the Babylonian and Akkadian tablets as well as a few additional tales. There are also accounts of Gilgamesh in Hittite and other ancient languages, and new fragments are regularly being unearthed. Taken together, the various versions span a time almost equivalent to that between the fall of the Roman Empire and the present. The stories probably go back additional centuries in oral traditions. They are filled with the themes that are the foundation of our literary traditions, such as love, death, friendship and human destiny.

Enkidu, in the beginning of the story, is the first 'wild man' in literature, and he introduces a basic profile that has remained remarkably constant in some respects throughout history. Like so many wild men in art and literature, he is hairy, wears little or no clothing, drinks from streams and eats foods of the woods without preparation. A remarkable number of celebrated tales are derived from that of Enkidu and the harlot, starting with the biblical Adam in the second of the two biblical creation stories (Genesis 1:7–25). Like Enkidu, Adam was created individually from earth with no female companion or counterpart. Just as the harlot was brought in to seduce Enkidu into adopting human ways, Eve was created to be a companion to Adam. In both cases, a female presence led to expulsion from a natural paradise.

Also in the Bible, the outlines of the tale of Enkidu and the harlot are apparent in the story of Samson and Dalilah (Judges 13–6). Like Enkidu, Samson was a man of incredible strength. At the direction of the Philistines, Dalilah seduced him. As the harlot did with Enkidu, Dalilah arranged to have Samson's hair cut, at which he lost most of his strength. The story of Enkidu is also apparent in the medieval lore of the unicorn, a mythic animal resembling a horse or goat with a huge horn in the middle of its

Walter Crane, 'Am I so very ugly?', illustration from *Beauty and the Beast* (1874). Amid all the paraphernalia that the Victorians associated with 'civilization', the Beast's animalistic features seem especially pronounced. The sword at his side and the hat over the area of his crotch also subtly suggest that, for all his grooming, the man has not entirely overcome his bestial nature.

forehead. Like Enkidu, the unicorn was too fierce and powerful to be captured by force, yet it would become tame in the presence of a maiden and lay its horn in her lap, allowing itself to be captured.[12]

The story of Enkidu and the harlot, told from a female point of view, is also the foundation for the popular fairy tale known as 'Beauty and the Beast', best known from the English-language version written by Jeanne-Marie Leprince de Beaumont published in 1756.[13] To summarize very briefly, a young woman goes to the castle of a terrifying, half-human monster deep in the woods, where she initiates him into human civilization, much as the harlot did with Enkidu. By earning her love, he is able to cast aside his bestial form and become fully human. Folklorists had widely assumed that the tale was fairly modern, but Sara Graçe da Silva and Jamshid J. Tehrani, by tracing various versions back in time, have estimated that the tale is about 2,500 to 6,000 years old.[14] The mean between the two dates is 4,250 years before the present, which is a time when Enkidu's tale was very popular. Da Silva and Tehrani did not make the connection, but the story doubtless comes from *The Epic of Gilgamesh* or a closely related source.

The wild man of the forest became an obsession in medieval Europe which has continued up to the present day, in tales, masquerades, illuminated manuscripts and just about every facet of culture. He is sometimes identified with the fauns and satyrs of Greco-Roman mythology. He is often pictured in heraldry, especially in Scotland, with his iconic long hair, beard and a simple garment of fur. In Shakespeare's play *The Tempest*, he appears as the character of Caliban. Occasionally, he has been accompanied by a 'wild woman' but is usually alone.

Enkidu may be the oldest known source for the folkloric motif of the wild man, but he is still only one of many. The history of the figure cannot be traced in a purely linear way. The motif is probably a composite of several traditions that originated in different places, converged and repeatedly intersected. In many instances, including that of Enkidu, wild men of legend may have been inspired by sightings of apes. Nevertheless, images of the wild man are remarkably consistent throughout the world. He is covered with hair or fur. He is either naked or dressed only in a crude garment of animal skin, and he has an intense scent. He has superhuman strength and is usually, though not always, larger than a normal man. Occasionally, he has the characteristics of a specific animal such as a goat.

Anonymous, after Pieter Bruegel the Elder, *The Wild Man; or, The Masquerade of Orson and Valentine*, 1566, woodcut. The wild man was a favourite figure of medieval to early modern heraldry, masques, carnivals and entertainments. Here, somebody has dressed up as Orson, the wild man from a popular romance.

In the tradition of Enkidu and the biblical Adam, the undomesticated person is always thought of as male. This is especially noteworthy because it reverses a habitual pattern. When humankind has been personified, it is usually as male, while nature is personified as feminine. 'Man' or 'mankind' is constantly credited with great discoveries from agriculture to nuclear fission. The spirit associated with forests and meadows is called 'Mother Nature'. Here, by contrast, society is feminine, personified as the harlot in the tale of Enkidu or as Eve in the first biblical creation myth. Nature is masculine. This tradition continues in the tales of rugged, isolated males that make their living in the depths of the woods such as Daniel Boone and Davy Crockett. Popular images of the wild man have also influenced early depictions of the Neanderthals.

Much of the time, when wild men are reportedly sighted, one or two accounts can be enough to start panic on a local level. I can recall hearing, as a child in upstate New York, accounts of the 'horse man'. Like other wild men, he was hairy, and he supposedly neighed as a horse as he ran. He was said to attack children, and the stories were scary enough to make me stay indoors for a while. Similar panics on a larger scale have been inspired by figures such as the skunk ape in Florida or the orange-eyes in Ohio.

In a few cases, accounts of these half-human figures have been considered plausible by cryptozoologists and even mainstream scientists.

John Peter Simon, after Henry Fuseli, engraving depicting a scene from Shakespeare's *The Tempest*, 1797. Caliban, on the right, is essentially a wild man.

Orangutan illustration from George Shaw, *General Zoology; or, Systematic Natural History*, vol. 1, part 1 (1800). Europeans often confused newly discovered apes with native peoples and imagined them as something like the wild men of traditional lore.

Considered on an international scale, some of the best-known figures of this sort include the legendary yeti (Himalayas), yeren (China), sasquatch (North America), almas (Siberia), nondescript (Guiana) and orang pendek (Sumatra).[15] When the orangutan was discovered by Europeans in the rain forests of Southern Asia during the seventeenth century, they adopted the Malay name, which literally means 'wild man' or 'man of the woods'. It was probably originally used by urban people of Malaysia or Indonesia to designate forest dwellers whom they considered uncivilized.[16]

The Sylvan Immortals

The goddess Guanyin has assigned the Buddhist monk Tripitaka Tang the task of journeying from China to India – through unknown territory filled with demons and wild animals – to retrieve Buddhist scriptures and save China from chaos. He has three preternatural disciples who serve as helpers and bodyguards – a monkey, a pig and a water spirit. The four companions have just completed an arduous journey through brambles when they encounter an old man, who is accompanied by a servant with scarlet skin, a bright red beard, a green face and tusks. The old man welcomes the travellers and offers them refreshments. When the pig is starting to take a cake, the monkey recognizes the strangers as demons. Before he can strike the old man with his staff, the fellow changes into a wind and whisks the monk away.

The monk suddenly finds himself before a house surrounded by mist and bearing the sign 'Shrine of the Sylvan Immortals'. The old man politely introduces himself and three companions, who are all over a thousand years old. The five go inside, recite poetry, share refreshments brought by the scarlet attendant and engage in an eminently civilized discussion of Buddhist and Daoist philosophy.

Eventually, the monk worries that his companions must be searching for him. He tries to excuse himself when in walks a maiden holding a branch with apricot blossoms, accompanied by two attendants. When the monk rejects her amorous advances, the four elderly gentlemen offer to avoid any impropriety by marrying the monk and the young lady. At this, the monk becomes angry and tries to leave, but the others block his way. They all tussle until dawn, when the monk hears the calls of his travelling companions. The four old men, the girl and their attendants instantly vanish.

Looking around, the monk and his disciples find the sign with the words 'Shrine of the Sylvan Immortals'. Near it are four ancient trees, which had been the old men – a juniper, a cypress, a pine and a bamboo. There is a maple, which had been the scarlet attendant. Finally, they see an apricot tree, which had been the young girl, surrounded by plum trees and cassia plants, who were her servants. The monk says that the trees have not hurt anyone and wishes to leave them alone. The monkey, who is more worldly and often seems to be the one really in charge, insists that they might do people great harm. The pig knocks over the trees with a rake and blood pours from the roots.

This tale is from the phantasmagoric Chinese novel *Journey to the West*, attributed to Cheng'en Wu and first published around the start of the sixteenth century CE.[17] So far as I have been able to ascertain, there is no other source for the story. It is hard to know how much of the tale is folklore and how much is literary invention. Written from a Buddhist perspective, the novel is usually respectful but at times very irreverent towards Daoism. There are eight anthropomorphic trees in the story, and they may be satiric representations of the Eight Immortals of Daoist lore.

On reading the story, we will probably wish that the monk had been more forceful, not allowed the irascible monkey to overrule him and insisted on leaving the trees alone. The monk later seems to have come to that conclusion as well, since he begins to assert more authority over the monkey. A few readers might even wish that the monk had stayed and married the apricot maiden, though who can guess what might have happened then? The tale is a perfect illustration of the recent discoveries showing that trees are constantly exchanging messages and even have a sort of community. The monk is an observer who enters arboreal society but then is drawn into it further than he cares to go. Perhaps the message of the story is that, although trees may appear like us in many ways, they are not truly human in the end.

The story illustrates the Chinese ambivalence toward forests. The transformation of the Chinese countryside through such means as aggressive deforestation, unrestrained hunting and diversion of water created, as a reaction, an intense love of landscapes.[18] In ways not so unlike those of the West, the forbidding settings were places to which

Kawanabe Kyousai, *Journey to the West*, 1864, colour woodblock print.
The tall figure directly in the centre is the monk Tripitaka, who has undertaken a perilous journey from China to India. At the top, directly to his left, is his patron, the goddess Guanyin. To his right are his three disciples, a monkey, a pig (depicted here as an elephant) and a water spirit. Most of the action in the novel consists of the monkey's battles with various demons, and a couple of these (Kinkaku and Ginkaku) are shown in the left section of the print.

scholars who were disillusioned with life at court would retreat to lead a life of contemplation. Artists painted vast scrolls showing landscapes of forests, mountains and rivers that seemed to go on indefinitely, with only occasional pagodas and isolated figures to remind the viewer of humankind. These were, however, ideal rather than actual scenes.[19]

The story also shows us how what may seem a dramatic scientific advance to us would have been far less radical to people in many other times, places and cultures. It is always hard to know just how far we should go with anthropomorphism, and forester Peter Wohlleben, who looks after an ancient beech forest in Germany, pushes the limits in his bestselling *The Hidden Life of Trees*. He writes about how trees care for their young, their elderly, their ill, their close relatives and even strangers in their realm. One dramatic illustration is his discovery in the forest of a beech stump of a tree cut four or five hundred years ago yet still kept alive by its neighbours, which send nutrients through their roots and mycorrhizal fungi.[20]

Essentially, he sees trees as a sort of idealized, old-fashioned village with friendships and occasional enmities, where age and custom are respected. It is hard to say to what extent he believes this and how much is simply due to the use of anthropomorphic language. Among other problems, this view presupposes a very human sort of individualism, which, as we have seen, is not very appropriate for trees.

The 'Evil' Forest

Sub-Saharan Africans traditionally take a view of the forest that is surprisingly close to that of European folklore. According to Descola, Africans 'regard it simply as a wild, dark, dangerous place, to be avoided as far as possible . . .' and 'the absolute antithesis of inhabited space'.[21] In traditional Central African belief, spirits lived in forests, bodies of water and the sky but generally not in villages.[22] They were dangerous but, like the forest spirits in European lore, also helpful on occasions.

In his novel *Things Fall Apart*, Igbo storyteller Chinua Achebe writes of his native Nigeria during the late nineteenth century, 'Every clan and village had its "evil forest". This was where the villagers buried people that had died of diseases such as leprosy. It was also 'the dumping ground for the potent fetishes of great medicine men when they died'. Once in the novel, the forest even becomes a place of human sacrifice. The evil forest was therefore 'alive with sinister forces and powers of darkness'.[23]

Nevertheless, it never occurred to the villagers that the evil forest should be cut down. They needed the forest as a sort of landfill for all things that the people of the village wished to banish from their lives. By depositing everything they abhorred in the forest, they carried out a perpetual work of purification. Apart from its physical extension and comparatively small scale, this forest resembled the dark wood of Dante's *Divine Comedy*. As previously noted, the boundaries of the dark wood are not clear, but it seems to encompass hell, which serves a similar purpose in traditional Christianity. The netherworld is not only an abode of demons and damned souls but a place where all things that believers wish to exorcise, such as uncontrolled fire, are taken.

Such similarities may partially explain the rapid acceptance of Christianity by Central African villagers. It is probably a reason why the Church of Nigeria now dwarfs the Church of England in both number of members and religious intensity. Assuming that Achebe's portrayal of traditional village life in Central Africa is accurate, it also shows how an intense dualism, contrary to what many people today believe, does not necessarily lead to the destruction of the natural world.

In the novel, missionaries came and requested a place to build a church. The villagers give them land in the evil forest, assuming the newcomers would last only a very short time. Instead, the missionaries, whose religion is more otherworldly, cut down part of the forest to build their house of worship. The church quickly grows by attracting those who had low status in the village, thus undermining the tribal hierarchy. The protagonist of the novel is a warrior named Okonkwo, who adheres to traditional ways with a militant rigidity. In the end, he commits suicide by hanging himself in the evil forest.

But the forest does not seem entirely 'evil' in the Christian sense, and it may be that the author was using the word with just a touch of irony. At one point in the novel, a young woman is brought into the forest to be cured of a grave malady. At another, the forest speaks through the mouth of a shaman. The forest resembles those where the protagonists of fairy tales such as 'Vasilisa the Beautiful' or 'Hansel and Gretel' find great perils but, ultimately, may achieve deliverance.

A further stage in the development of the forest in Nigeria is depicted in *The Famished Road Trilogy*, a series of three novels by contemporary Nigerian author Ben Okri set in about the 1960s. Nigerians by that time were largely secular, Christian or Muslim. More traditional ways of thinking no longer had enough cohesion to constitute a system of belief, but they remained pervasive. The forest was no longer evil, and the spirits were just as disoriented as human beings.

In the book, the remaining forests are being constantly cut down to make way for settlements. This unsettles the forest spirits, who constantly try to enter the village, not to do harm so much as to find refuge. They are fascinated by human beings yet do not understand them. They try to adopt human form but make mistakes. The story is narrated by an *abiku* or 'spirit child' named 'Azaro', whose original home was in the forest surrounding an unnamed village. The *akibu* traditionally enters human wombs to be born but then very shortly returns to the supernatural world. Azaro learns, however, to love his mother, a hawker at the market, and his father, a manual labourer and boxer. When he refuses to depart from this life, the other spirits constantly follow him, entice him to return and even try to kidnap him. While resisting them, he becomes increasingly fond of the human world, despite its squalor and frequent brutality.

Unlike European elves and fairies, at least as these are usually described, these forest spirits do not have any consistent form. This is how the narrator describes his first glimpse of them at the beginning of the trilogy:

> I saw people who walked backwards, a dwarf who got about on two fingers, men upside down with baskets of fish on their feet, women who had breasts on their backs, babies strapped to their chests and beautiful children with three arms. I saw a girl amongst them who had eyes at the side of her face, bangles of blue copper around her neck, and who was more lovely than forest flowers.[24]

In the context of the novel, these are awkward and misguided attempts to assume a human form, perhaps comparable to human imitations of a lion or rhinoceros. They resemble Central African masks in their energy, their humour and their variety. Azaro, as a spirit himself, does not always find the other spirits especially strange or frightening, and he does not even distinguish very clearly between them and human beings. The story is not so much a continuous narrative as a series of brief, fantastic vignettes that take place in liminal places where the human and spirit worlds meet, such as a bar frequented by both on the outskirts of the town.

The novel shows how, as the forests are cut down, the urban spaces along their edges can assume much of their ambience. In young

Drawings of traditional Central African masks. These show a great range of fantastic creatures, largely unnamed, with a touch of humour.

adulthood, I often walked through the slums of Chicago, where one knew that one might be constantly watched by others, including potential thieves and muggers. At the time, I was rather heedless, yet not so much that I neglected to project a certain image. I knew that I needed to appear knowing and confident (even if I felt anything but). My posture had to be erect, and my face must reveal as little as possible. I had to look as if I knew my destination. If I got lost and stopped to check a map, people would likely notice that, and it could provoke an attack. This was an aspect of life in what we call the urban jungle. When I returned home and, exhausted by the pretence, flopped down on my bed, I could be myself at last.

4

Conquest of the Woods

Which came first, civilization or nature? In the Bible, it is the former. The primal landscape was a garden, not a jungle. This was under the dominion of Adam and Eve, the first human beings. It was a place of exquisite order that was lost when they defied a prohibition not to eat of the tree of knowledge. What we call wilderness was actually a fallen world. In most traditions, including the Greco-Roman, the opposite view prevails. Civilization came only after a time of primeval chaos. There were countless monsters that mixed the features of animals and human beings in inexplicable ways. There were violent wars between tribes of deities, which tore apart the heavens and the earth.

Paleolithic culture is known mostly through cave paintings, which focus on animals of imposing size, speed and power such as big cats and mammoths. Human beings only begin to appear in the later paintings, and they are usually only stick figures, which appear far less impressive than the great mammals. People ate those animals and might be eaten by them, in a sort of eternal reciprocity. To die through predation was usual, while to be eaten was nearly universal. It is a world, usually enshrined in myth, that hunters have looked back on nostalgically ever since.

This world gradually came to an end as the ice sheets receded, the forests advanced and human beings began to practise agriculture. In Neolithic times, as people became settled and 'put down roots', their former intimacy with animals was replaced by a mystical solidarity with vegetation.[1] Perhaps trees, with their enormous height, seemed more imposing than any animal. People began to think more in terms of cycles, which are more easily apparent in vegetation, of birth, infancy, youth, maturity and eventual death. They buried their dead, rather as they planted seeds, in the hope of eventual resurrection. Time was less an eternal present than a cyclical return.

Eventually, human beings entered into a symbiotic relationship with certain animals, which they nurtured and cared for like vegetation. First came the dog, a bit later the sheep, goat and bee. They were followed by the pig, cow, silkworm and many others. A few peoples have continued as hunter-gatherers up to the present. A far larger number, in fact almost all societies, have continued hunting and gathering but on a greatly reduced scale, more as a ceremonial practice or recreation than as a practical necessity. Yet what it enacts, or at least endeavours to enact, is a drama of mythic proportions.

The First Epic

Gilgamesh, the world's first epic hero, does not seem superhuman even in his greatest moments of victory. He is a sort of everyman, experiencing the full range of human responses, including triumph, defeat, terror, arrogance, humiliation, fear, love and despair. He is alternately mighty and helpless, wise and foolish.

In this chapter, I will focus mostly on the episode in which Gilgamesh and his companion Enkidu kill Humbaba (or 'Hawawa'), the guardian of the Cedar Forest of Lebanon. This is told in tablets five through seven of the Standard Version. We can see, in the successive versions, the development of the entire tale from something like a history to a myth. The Sumerian version, usually entitled 'Gilgamesh and Hawawa', is the most detailed and realistic.[2] Gilgamesh and his companion Enkidu journey with fifty followers carrying axes to a distant land in search of trees. They pass seven mountains but find none that are suitable. Finally, they come to a forest. Gilgamesh and Enkidu cut down a tree, remove its branches, cut it into logs, tie the logs and prepare them for transport. At this, Hawawa awakens, and hurls one of his auras, magical powers visualized as trees, at the intruders. Enkidu and Gilgamesh are initially dazed. When they recover, Enkidu, who already knows Hawawa, explains that their adversary is formidable but together they can prevail.

The two approach Huwawa's home, but, rather than attacking, they defeat him by trickery. When Hawawa appears, Gilgamesh offers his own sisters to the giant in marriage and goes on to offer many luxuries that come with urban life. With each promise of a gift, Hawawa surrenders another of his seven auras. He is then defenceless, and the intruders take him prisoner. Hawawa begs to be spared his life. He offers to serve Gilgamesh and build houses for him. Gilgamesh is moved to pity, but Enkidu says the monster cannot be trusted and cuts his throat. After killing Hawawa's seven children, they cut off Hawawa's head and take it to the god Enlil, who is displeased and says they should have treated the guardian of the forest with courtesy. Enlil takes the auras and distributes them to the field, river, thicket, lion woods and palace, giving the sixth to the goddess Nungal and keeping the last for himself.[3]

This Sumerian tale is especially important because Hawawa is the first appearance of a figure that often appears in the legends and literature of the forest. He is the embodiment of the woods, their soul, so to speak. He may also be a Near Eastern deity, probably Humban, the

Terracotta figure of Humbaba, Iraq, first half of the 2nd millennium BCE. The protruding ears, large mouth and broad chest suggest a bear.

Black bear in the author's forest in New York State.

Elamite god of the sky.[4] If this is so, the association with the heavens suggest that this may be an extremely early version of the well-known fairy tale 'Jack the Giant Killer' (also known as 'Jack and the Beanstalk' and classified by folklorists as ATU 328), one of the oldest of all fairy tales, which goes back an estimated 5,000 years.[5] Like Gilgamesh, Jack kills a giant with cleverness and trickery, and, in many versions, even accomplishes this by cutting down a tree.

I believe Hawawa/Humbaba is also a bear, probably a Syrian brown bear. Such bears inhabit the cedar forests of Lebanon to this day. Bears are the only other large mammal apart from man that share the human ability to walk completely upright. Even apes cannot accomplish this without awkwardly bending over. Bears are extremely strong and have a greater physical resemblance to people than any other animal. In Mesopotamian art, the figure of Humbaba is given ursine features. He has a human form but with claws, a hairy face and whiskers.[6] Often, his ears stick out on the sides like those of a bear. The features of his face are large and his teeth are sharp. His chest is usually large, like a bear's, while his lower body is relatively small. Furthermore, as the lord of the cedar forest, Humbaba has the same position the bear has originally had in the lore of Europe and other places where it is indigenous – as the king of beasts.[7]

There is considerable circumstantial evidence for a widespread cult of the bear, which was already present in Paleolithic times, continued in the Neolithic era and may even survive in attenuated form among the

Ainu and people of the Arctic Circle to this day. In the caves and graves used by Neanderthals and early *Homo sapiens* are the bones of bears, placed in arrangements that seem too deliberate to be accidental and suggest possible veneration. In Montespan, France, is a cave containing what is possibly the oldest sculpture ever made, in the shape of the body of a bear with a hole where the head was intended to be attached.[8] For people of the northern hemisphere who lived in the vicinity of forests, the bear was a perpetual danger, and it was hunted relentlessly. As the bear was a very formidable predator, this required the resources of royalty and nobility, and it was generally conducted with the same combination of dread and admiration that we see in the story of Humbaba.

Archeologist Elizabeth Douglas van Buren writes, 'In early Mesopotamian art, the Bear did not figure very frequently, but, when it was represented, it was always with a mystical significance which is now obscure.' Early graves of warriors had contained talismans of bears, but by the time of the Assyrian Empire, the bear had become just one more animal to be hunted.[9] Perhaps the killing of Humbaba represented a revolt against a cult of the bear that had continued from Paleolithic through to Neolithic times but was drawing to a close as the first urban centres were established.[10]

In the standard and Old Babylonian versions, the forest journey is less pragmatic. Gilgamesh decides to challenge Humbaba out of pursuit of glory rather than timber. The elders of his kingdom try to dissuade him by recounting the ferocity and power of his adversary. When Gilgamesh cannot be turned aside, they give the expedition their blessing.

He and Enkidu enter the forest without companions. Enkidu, who had started life as a wild man and already knows Humbaba, goes first. Both are terrified, but they urge one another on. This time, they attack Humbaba before he can put on the seven auras of protection. They triumph by force of arms rather than trickery, but they are only successful because the sun-god, Shamash, sends violent winds to blind Humbaba. So that there would not be witnesses to tell the other gods of their deed, they also kill Humbaba's seven sons. As soon as they have finished, they cut down the timber in Humbaba's sacred groves. Enkidu takes a great cedar for the door of the temple of Enlil, perhaps a peace offering to the angry deity.[11]

In none of the manuscripts is Hawawa/Humbaba simply an ogre. The admiration for him, which is implicit in the Sumerian telling, becomes more overt in the later ones. When Gilgamesh and Enkidu first come to the cedar forest of Lebanon, they could only marvel at its beauty. There are clear paths among lofty trees. The shade is pleasant, and there is the constant sound of birds such as pigeons, turtle doves and francolins. There are also the calls of monkeys, cicadas and many other creatures. Aromatic resin, which was used to make perfume, cascaded from the trees. When the trees have been cut down, Enkidu says regretfully that they had 'reduced the forest to a wasteland'.[12]

Like Prometheus stealing the fire of heaven or Adam and Eve eating the fruit of knowledge, this act of pillage begins, or at least helps to establish, civilization through a transgression. Since wood is an important building material, the tale suggests that even living in wooden homes could make people accomplices in guilt. This ambivalence was to accompany forests and those who live from them for decades, not unlike our mixed feelings about hunting or the consumption of meat. Already, forests were becoming stylized as a primeval condition prior to that of civilization.

The events after the heroes kill Humbaba and despoil his forest seem to take place in a fallen world. Humbaba is the first character in the epic to die. Enkidu and Gilgamesh kill Humbaba deliberately, so they are aware of death on some level, but they do not seem to appreciate its finality. They destroy a forest, as several subsequent civilizations have done, without appreciating the consequences. Prior to Humbaba's demise, death played no role in the epic, but afterwards it completely dominated the narrative.

Gilgamesh receives the renown that he had sought by killing Humbaba, but it leads to the destruction of both his partner and himself. His glamour attracts the goddess Ishtar, who asks him to marry her. Gilgamesh refuses, saying that Ishtar has destroyed all her previous lovers. Ishtar returns to the abode of deities and throws a tantrum until her father, An, god of the sky, agrees to release the Bull of Heaven (the constellation Taurus) on the earth. The bull drinks up lakes and rivers, creating a terrible draught, but Enkidu and Gilgamesh finally kill it. Enkidu tears off one of the creatures' forelegs and throws it at Ishtar, who then sues before the assembly of heaven. If she does not get her way, she threatens to bring back the dead so they will overwhelm the living. The divinities compromise, saying that Gilgamesh may live but Enkidu has to die. After his companion has suffered an agonizing death from plague, Gilgamesh embarks on a long, ultimately unsuccessful pilgrimage to find the secret of immortality.

Finally, Gilgamesh retires to his kingdom, which he surrounds with a protective wall of brick and stone, and this, rather than any conquest, becomes his enduring accomplishment. The act was a renunciation of the goal of conquering the wilderness and a resolution to protect the human realm. This is an environmental parable that is as relevant today as when it was written.[13]

We still speak of the human 'conquest' of nature. The ancient people of Mesopotamia might not have been able to express that idea in entirely abstract terms, but this is clearly what Gilgamesh accomplishes. Especially in the Sumerian version, the expedition to the forests of Lebanon is conceived as a war of conquest. Humbaba/Hawawa is an embodiment of nature, and the cutting down of the forest is the plunder of a vanquished kingdom. This is done with all of the fear, hesitation, ambivalence, frenzy and remorse that have accompanied the conquest of nature, real or imagined, up to the present.

The tale of Gilgamesh's forest journey has a mythic structure, which will be found in stories for millennia to come. The forest has often been personified as a single being, a soul inside the body of the woods. In tales recorded over centuries, a hero, driven by either hardship or the pursuit of glory, makes a journey into the depths of a forest and encounters the guardian of the woods. If she or he kills the spirit of the forest, the woods lose their terror, wildness and vitality. If she or he reaches an understanding with the spirit, it will be possible to live beside the woods in relative harmony.

The killing of Humbaba by Enkidu and Gilgamesh may have been followed by partial regret, but it was done without ceremony and followed by no commemoration. With their ruler gone, the woods lose a kind of wildness that could never again be attained, and people can do with them as they please. In such a way, bears would be ruthlessly trapped, killed and driven from all but the most remote woodlands of Europe during the millennia to come. They would also be mocked and forced to dance in chains at fairs by their conquerors.

The hunting of a bear also symbolized the taming of wilderness in early America. Pioneers such as Daniel Boone and Davy Crockett were famed for killing bears. American President Theodore 'Teddy' Roosevelt, an advocate for wilderness conservation, was similarly famous, according to highly romanticized accounts, for sparing one.

A Modern Humbaba

As a university teacher of literature, my favourite assignment to give students is to retell a story from the distant past in another era. What would Rip Van Winkle be like had he lived in the twentieth century instead of the late eighteenth? And what if, instead of going to sleep for ten years right before the American Revolution, he had dozed off before the Second World War? On waking, would he be puzzled by the Cold War between the United States and its former ally, the Soviet Union? And could he get used to the new medium of television quickly enough?

So how might one retell the story of Gilgamesh, Enkidu, and Humbaba in modern times? That has been done, though not consciously, by the American writer William Faulkner in his novella 'The Bear', included in the collection *Go Down, Moses* (1942). Though the *Epic of Gilgamesh* had been known for over half a century before Faulkner penned his story, there is no indication that the American author had been influenced by, or even read, the tale. He simply recreated it unknowingly, and the fact that he might do so, after a lapse of about 4,000 years, is a testimony to the way – despite all the new technologies, wars and other upheavals – some basic dynamics of human civilization have remained almost unchanged.

The story, set in late nineteenth-century Mississippi, is told from the viewpoint of a boy named Ike McCaslin, who is learning to be an accomplished woodsman, only to find the woods losing their wildness just as he perfects his skills. The forests have been protected by a huge bear known as Old Ben, and Ike is among the few brave enough to explore it. Old Ben is a figure of mythic proportions, and most people in town are content to leave the bear to his domain, provided he does not encroach on theirs. That changes when Old Ben kills some livestock. Old Sam Fathers, part Amerindian and part Black, puts together a hunting party to track Ben down and kill him. He is aided by Boon Hooganbeck, a sort of 'wild man' who sleeps with the dogs. Boon is huge, superhumanly strong, completely without fear and utterly childish. When bullets seem to have no effect on Ben, Sam sends a huge dog named Lion to attack. As Ben rips the dog apart with his claws, Boon jumps on the bear from behind and cuts its throat.[14]

Sam, the more worldly hunter, might be compared to Gilgamesh, and Boon certainly resembles Enkidu. But this time, unlike in the Mesopotamian epic, it is the former that must die. With Ben, his mysterious double, gone, Sam finds he has nothing left to live for. He collapses after the hunt and soon perishes. As for Boon, he grows less heroic and even more infantile as he goes from knifing bears to shooting squirrels. The area of the hunt is sold to a logging company, and what forests remain no longer seem primordial.

Finally, the killing of Humbaba by Gilgamesh and Enkidu reminds me of a little jingle from the television show *Walt Disney Presents*, which I heard so many times while growing up in Chicago that even now, in my seventies, it remains etched in my memory. The first verse tells how Davy Crockett was born on a mountain, was raised in a forest and had already killed a bear at the age of three. Then comes the refrain: 'Davy, Davy Crockett, King of the Wild Frontier'.[15] Crockett combines traits of the two Mesopotamian heroes, being a sort of 'wild man' like Enkidu and yet regal like Gilgamesh. Like them, he kills a bear to take over as ruler of the woods.

The growing absence of bears from our woods left an imaginative void, and humankind, like a colonial army, installed another monarch. For human royalty and aristocracy, the stag became the sole object of a sacred hunt in much of Europe during the twelfth and thirteenth centuries,[16] and then, a few hundred years later, in North America.

Jean Bourdichon, 'Vision of St Hubert', illumination
from *Grandes Heures d'Anne de Bretagne*, 1503–8.

5

The Royal Hunt

The horns of the stag in their make and growth resemble
the branches of a tree; and its substance is perhaps more of the
nature of wood than bone; it is, as it were, a vegetable grafted upon
animal, partaking of the nature of both, and forms one of those shades
by which Nature always approximates the two extremes.

GEORGES-LOUIS, COMTE DE BUFFON

Deer change colour according to the season, rather like leaves, and their antlers resemble branches of trees. Like trees, they follow a yearly cycle in their behaviour, rutting in late autumn and giving birth in spring or early summer. The antlers of a stag were held by the prominent eighteenth-century zoologist the Comte de Buffon to be a form of vegetation, since an antler 'retains all the marks of that vegetable form from which it derives its origin and resembles the branch of a tree in the manner it grows, expands, hardens, dries and separates . . . it falls off spontaneously after having acquired its full degree of solidity like the ripe fruit from a branch.'[1] The French word for both forests and wood is *bois*, which can also refer to antlers. The stag, in effect, *was* the forest.

Buffon also wrote of the stag, 'his light and elegant form, his flexible yet nervous limbs, his grandeur, strength and swiftness, his head rather adorned than armed with living branches, which, like the leaves of a tree, are renewed every year', making him the 'noblest' of forest animals. One might, then, have expected Buffon, who was intensely concerned about animal welfare, to object to the hunt of the stag. On the contrary, however, he saw that as the pursuit of the greatest men.[2]

The word 'deer' comes from Old English *dēor* meaning 'animal'. That is still the meaning of etymological relatives such as the German *tier* and the Dutch *dier*. It goes back ultimately to the Indo-European *dheusōm*, meaning 'a creature that breathes'.[3] The stag represented animals of the forest just as the king represented his people and his land. The high hunt became a universal drama, a confrontation of civilization with wilderness, with all the psychological complexity and ambivalence that entails. Buffon may have been writing as an early modern scientist, but he was articulating an ancient paradigm, one that may have changed little since Neolithic times. In the words of anthropologist Bertrand Hell, 'The hunt was more than a simple "noble" activity; it was ontologically linked to the civilizing function attributed to the king-hero.'[4]

In very remote times, the stag had become a symbol of the ruler, while the hunt for it was a cyclical, ritualistic regicide, intended ultimately to reaffirm his power. Especially in Northern Europe, the institution was Christianized, and the stag became a symbol of the killed and resurrected deity.

Nature becomes Wild

Archaeologist Jean-Dennis Vigne argues that the division between the realms of 'wild nature' and 'civilization' was constructed in Neolithic times. According to Vigne, the domestication of animals took place at roughly the same time as 'cynegitization', which is the displacement of animals into hunting preserves where game would be managed and eventually harvested. The primary animals involved in cynegetization were deer, and his major evidence for it is that deer are not only extremely widespread throughout Eurasia, but appear to have been introduced in Neolithic times on islands from the Mediterranean to the Hebrides, places they could only have reached if transported by human beings.[5]

Vigne believes that cynegetization, since it entailed an intricate division of labour, contributed to the division of humankind into classes. The actual hunt of deer, which is the culmination of all the activities, eventually acquired great symbolic significance as a display of status. Subordinate activities acquired a lesser rank in accordance with their importance. The relocation of deer started before recorded history, but the existence of royal parks set aside for the chase is attested by many peoples, including the Hittites, Babylonians and Assyrians as well as – much later – the Greeks and Romans.[6]

We tend to think of hunting as prior to domestication, both in terms of time and ontology. Hunting is 'natural' for those who approve of it and 'savage' for those who do not. Today we also think of hunting as masculine and gathering as feminine, yet that may be partly due to our projecting a more modern division of labour along lines of gender into remote times.[7] What if, as Vigne maintains, domestication of animals and hunting as we know it came at approximately the same era in prehistory? And how did human beings obtain meat before either had begun? It may be that people or their hominid ancestors in even more remote times perceived little difference between gathering, hunting and scavenging. All three might be dangerous. People might simply venture out in search of food and accept it in whatever form might be available.

Though seldom studied or even recognized, cynegetization is a very widespread form of human–animal relationship, which in ways rivals domestication in importance. Deer are the most widespread and dramatic example but far from the only one. Rabbits and fallow deer were imported into England by the Normans to be hunted. Pheasants were imported for sport hunting from Asia into Britain and much of Europe at the end of the Middle Ages. When European mariners explored the Caribbean and other islands during the early modern period, they would regularly release pigs, which they might hunt for food on their return. In the late nineteenth and early twentieth centuries, Eurasian wild boars have been repeatedly imported to hunting preserves in the United States, after which they escaped and became feral. Even when hunters have not deliberately transported game, they have often deliberately managed their habitats to increase game, as organizations such as Ducks Unlimited do for water birds in the United States.

Perhaps we need to rethink our traditional idea of domestication as a unique event happening within a specific era. Most domesticated animals – including dogs, pigs, honeybees and chickens – have wild counterparts. Sometimes the pets or livestock may live alongside these corresponding varieties and occasionally interbreed with them. The degree and nature of human intervention in their lives can vary greatly from one era to the next. Pigs were often allowed to roam freely in villages of the Middle Ages and fed scraps from tables, only to be ceremoniously slaughtered on feast days. Horses in Europe would also sometimes be set loose to forage in woods or fields until their services were needed. Until about the 1950s, domestic dogs were often given similar freedom in the United States. Chickens have often been, and at times still are, kept in a semi-domestic state, where they forage for food, leaving people with little work beyond collecting their eggs, a traditional practice that has been revived and is known today as raising 'free range' poultry. Today, we often control nearly every detail of the lives of domestic animals, but for most of history they have been almost wild by current standards.

Harvesting and Gathering

Anthropologist Bertrand Hell distinguishes two basic models of deer hunting practised today in Continental Europe. In the first, which he calls 'hunting as harvesting', the hunter manages the deer by feeding them, protecting them and trying to maintain the maximum possible population density. The hunter may even try to improve them genetically by culling those with asymmetric horns according to the theory that irregular growth is a sign of poor reproductive capacity. The hunter will then move through the woods relying on stealth, in search of the animal that will make the best trophy, which he will shoot. This is the model that prevails in Germany, Austria, Poland, Hungary, Alsace and some additional parts of France.

The other model Hell calls 'hunting as gathering'. Hunters who use this method do not endeavour to manage game. The purpose is not to acquire trophies but, in addition to obtaining meat, to protect farms from foraging animals. Hunters go into the forest in groups and beat the vegetation in order to drive deer from their cover so they may be killed. The attitude of the hunters is pragmatic, and ceremony is kept to a minimum. This is the method that prevails in Greece, Italy and most of France.

Hunting as harvesting is an elite practice that requires control over a large parcel of land, as well as the funds and leisure to manage it. In consequence, it may only be practised by a very small part of the population. Hunting as gathering, by contrast, is an endeavour of the community in which there is relative equality. It is predicated on a sharp distinction between the human and wild realms, which goes back to the traditions associated with animal domestication.[8]

The two methods of hunting seem profoundly different, but, according to Hell, they are founded on the same underlying assumptions. In both approaches, hunting has the potential to lead to a frenzy, in which the participants themselves become like beasts. In German, this is known as *Jagdfieber*, 'hunting frenzy'. This state somewhat resembles several quasi-religious trances, such as the rapture of Dionysiac revellers, Viking berserkers, charismatic Christians, Sufi dervishes and so on. Like all of these, it is precariously poised between holiness and transgression. Is it a liberation from the blandness of daily life? Insanity? Supernatural possession?

In several medieval stories, this sort of reverie is a prelude to religious revelations. *The Golden Legend*, a popular collection of religious tales from the latter thirteenth century, tells how it led to the conversion of St Eustace. Originally named 'Placidus', he was the commander of the army of the Roman Emperor Trajan. One day he was hunting with his soldiers when they came upon a group of deer, including a stag that was especially large and beautiful. It ran into the depths of the forest, and Placidus followed it, leaving his companions behind. Finally, the stag climbed to a peak. Looking up, Placidus saw the stag had a crucifix between its horns. Christ spoke to him through the mouth of the stag, telling him to be baptized. Placidus obeyed, converted his wife and children, assumed the name of Eustace, and was eventually martyred and then canonized as a saint.[9]

Essentially the same story is told of St Hubert, a knight at the court of King Pepin, father of Charlemagne. He devoted his life entirely to the chase, and once when he was hunting on Good Friday, he also encountered a stag with a crucifix between its antlers. This time it was the figure on the crucifix that spoke, threatening him with damnation if he did not give up his frivolous ways. Hubert renounced hunting, gave away his possessions and entered the service of the Church, eventually becoming a bishop.[10] He did not entirely repudiate the hunt, but he set up ethical rules for conducting it, and Hubert is the patron saint of hunters to this day.

For men up until historically recent times, hunting frenzy seemed to be a sort of relentless drive, similar to sex in a Freudian perspective, which could only be held precariously in check by elaborate taboos and regulations. Rev. Gilbert White wrote in the late eighteenth century of his native village of Selborne:

> Though large herds of deer do much harm to the neighbourhood, yet the injury to the morals of the people is of more moment than the loss of their crops. The temptation is irresistible, for most men are sportsman by constitution, and there is such an inherent spirit for hunting in human nature as scarce any inhibitions can restrain.[11]

Ritualizing this compulsion and confining it to the nobility seemed to be one way of keeping it under at least some control.

People feared that, if a hunter went too far in engaging with wild beasts on their own terms, he might become one of them. This fear runs through all European hunting traditions, but they differ in how they regard the prospect. Is hunting frenzy something to be judiciously avoided, indulged in moderation or carried to the ultimate extreme? Both hunting as harvesting and as gathering are based on an organization of the world according to the dichotomy of savagery, represented by the woods and wild animals, and civilization, represented by towns and farms. Hunting mediates between the two, attempting to find an appropriate balance, but always involves some danger of transgressing the limits of civilized life. The conceptions of the hunt differ primarily in where they place the boundaries and how they protect them.

The culture of the Hebrews, as recorded in the book of Leviticus, had many extensive dietary restrictions, especially a provision against consuming meat with blood in it (Leviticus 17), which rendered eating food from the hunt almost impossible. Slaughter of food animals was confined to the more controlled conditions of a temple sacrifice. Few cultures have gone so far, but virtually all at least surround hunting with restraints and taboos. The danger of being too preoccupied with the hunt is expressed in medieval and early modern legends of the Wild Hunt, often by a spectral horde of hunters that ride across the sky on horses and with dogs during storms. The figures may be ghosts, fairies or the dead. Sometimes they are led by the god Odin. In some versions the hunter is a solitary figure. According to a German legend recorded by the Brothers Grimm, Count Eberhard von Württemberg once rode out into the forest to hunt. There was a great noise, and he saw a lone horseman riding through the sky. The count was very frightened, but the figure dismounted, stood in a tree and reassured Eberhard that he meant no harm. The spectre then confessed how he had once so loved the chase that he begged God to let him hunt until the Day of Judgement. The wish was granted, and so he had been pursuing the same stag for over five hundred years.[12]

In the folk culture of Europe, hunting frenzy is identified with 'black blood'. This legendary substance, a bit like testosterone, is allegedly concentrated in various animals and to various degrees; domesticated animals have the least, while deer and boar have a far larger share. It is concentrated in certain parts of the animal's body, with relatively little in the haunches and more in the entrails. Most significantly, it is found in different kinds of people, with non-hunters and women having little while poachers and woodsmen have the most.[13]

Peoples of the Mediterranean including the Greeks and Romans have since Neolithic times been relatively fastidious about transgressing what they perceived as the boundaries of civilized life. This has meant, with respect to alimentation, a preference for grain from cultivated fields, wine from vineyards, fruit from orchards and meat from domestic animals.[14] For the most part, the Greeks and Romans had little interest in hunting game, but, even among them, the frenzy of the hunt was not unknown. Some Roman emperors such as Trajan and Hadrian were obsessive hunters, though they generally preferred more dangerous animals such as boar and bear to deer.[15]

One Greco-Roman tale of hunting frenzy is the myth of Actaeon and Diana. Several versions of it have come down to us, but the one recorded by Ovid is best known. As it begins, Acteon and his companions have completed a successful day of hunting, and they begin to take up their nets. The goddess Diana and her nymphs, who have also been hunting, disrobe to bathe in a grotto. Actaeon, who is reluctant to retire, comes across them. The goddess reaches for her bow, but it is not there, so she splashes water at Actaeon. He feels his body changing and then looks into a pool to find out that he has been turned into a stag. He wants to call out but has lost the power of speech. His beloved hounds see him and, instead of obeying his commands, tear him to pieces.[16] In Greek versions, including one from *The Bacchae* by Euripides, Actaeon boasts to the goddess Artemis about his prowess as a hunter. Actaeon's transgression was probably originally hunting in a grove sacred to the goddess.[17] In all of the versions, Actaeon, through his excessive zeal for the chase, is punished by losing his humanity.

The Royal Preserve

Prior to the late Middle Ages, the extent of the forest in Central and Northern Europe seemed endless, and people understood the resources it contained as a gift from God. It was, in general, a shared domain known as the *silva communis*,[18] available not only to hermits in search of solitude or nobles in pursuit of game but to peasants in search of firewood, healers in search of herbs, cooks in search of edible roots or farmers who would leave their sheep or pigs there to forage. It was a bit like the sea or, in our own times, outer space. Though they were communal property, local people had many rules about how, and to what extent, these forests could be used for agriculture, hunting and foraging.

The Latin word for woods is *nemus*, which may come from *locus neminis*, meaning 'a place belonging to nobody'.[19] From ancient Rome to Colonial America, one way to claim land as property has been to cut down the trees that grew there. This perception of woods as communal is still with us in attenuated form today. In Scotland, Germany and much of Scandinavia, the owner of forested land cannot prevent people from walking through it. Even in the United States, where private property is perhaps more sacrosanct than anywhere else, the ownership of forest land appears less absolute than that of cleared fields or homes. In a protest against deforestation, Theodore Roosevelt wrote, 'Democracy, in its essence, means that a few people shall not be allowed, for their own selfish gratification, to destroy what ought to belong to the people as a whole.'[20]

A forest, as we will see, has always been defined far more by its mythic character than by its vegetation. It is contrasted with the city, which is governed by laws and customs. It is essentially a wilderness, a place of vast solitude with neither the amenities nor the corruptions that accompany civilization. It is where one may be tormented by demons but may also achieve communion with God. For this reason, opposed though they might seem to us, the deserts of biblical stories often came to be conflated with forests. The wilderness was often described or painted as a sort of indeterminate landscape, with rocks, caves, mountains and trees. This was the sort of landscape where, according to tradition, the exiled king Nebuchadnezzar went mad (Daniel 4:25–30) and John the Baptist received his religious calling (Isaiah 40:3; Matthew 3:3; Mark 1:2–3; Luke 3:3–6). It was where saints such as Anthony and Paul the Hermit withdrew from the world.[21]

But as the population grew and the limits on resources became apparent in the latter Middle Ages, the constant usage of the forest by peasants interfered with both the solitude of the monastic orders and hunting by the nobility. The French word *forêt*, which is the origin of the English word 'forest', was first used by the Merovingians, who ruled a Franco-Germanic kingdom, in the seventh century.[22] It comes from the Latin *foris*, meaning 'outside', and is related to our word 'foreign'. A 'forest' was originally an area apart from the rest, where unauthorized use was not permitted. The first known use is in a charter of 648 CE, which grants an abbot the right to build a monastery in the forest of Ardenne, where monks might live in solitude.[23] The word gradually came to refer primarily to large areas set aside as the domain of the king, used for hunting and protected from other sorts of exploitation.

The most comprehensive record of forest law is *A Treatise and Discourse of the Lawes of the Forrest* by John Manwood, a lawyer who had worked as a gamekeeper in Waltham Forest in England, first published in 1598. According to Manwood, 'A Forest is a certain Territory of woody Grounds and fruitful Pastures, privileged for wild Beasts and Fowls of Forest, Chase, and Warren, to rest and abide there in the safe Protection of the King, for his Delight and Pleasure.'[24] People other than the king might farm or even own land within the forest. In William I's *Doomsday Book*, the first census of Britain, the size of a forest, something that could not be easily surveyed, was measured by the number of foraging pigs it supported.[25] What distinguished the forest was less the landscape than a legal system that was separate from that which prevailed elsewhere. The forest had not only its own laws but courts, administrators and customs.

Kings also claimed the chase as a royal prerogative and protected the forest to that end. In the *Capitulary of Villis*, around the start of the ninth century, Charlemagne placed the hunt and the forest under protection of strict laws, prohibiting deforestation and most forms of exploitation. This was an expression of his power and prestige, not simply as a king or emperor but as the representative of God on earth. It meant that not only people but even trees and animals were subject to his power and secure in his protection.[26] He was extending the concept of property, and with it the realm of 'civilization'. In many ways, claiming the forest was an early form of colonization, which would eventually be extended to foreign lands. This did not immediately do away with communal rights to use the forest for such purposes as collecting wood and grazing livestock. These were well established by tradition, and the new laws were often hard to enforce. There were, in addition, many local variants in the way forests were traditionally administered. But the new laws did establish a trend, which was to continue for many centuries, towards increasingly centralized control of forest management.

The Carolingians also changed the nature of the hunt. Previously, the method had been to drive deer into nets, which was relatively efficient. This was replaced by the ceremonial *par force* hunt, where a deer would be chased by dogs and men on horseback until it finally collapsed from exhaustion. The procedures for the hunt were laid out in detail and ritualistically followed. According to *The Book of the Hunt* by Gaston Phoebus, first published in 1387, on the day before the hunt, the party would meet to banquet in open air. The noble or king would meet with the entire hunting party, from hunters and grooms to dogs, and assign each a role, and then he would set a meeting point for the hunt to begin the next morning. Scouts would select a stag, ascertain its location and use some of its droppings to familiarize the dogs with the scent. The start of the

Illumination from Gaston Phoebus, *Livre de chasse* (Book of the Hunt), 15th century. Note that the peasants on foot, even though they are in the foreground, are much smaller than the nobles on horseback or, for that matter, the stag. The medieval hunt affirmed a hierarchal, feudal order in which common people were accorded a lower status than the hunted animal.

hunt would be announced with horns. The leader of the hunt would make sure the party remained on the trail, even if the stag ran across streams. Finally, when the stag could run no further, he would kill it with his sword.[27]

The most highly ritualized part of the hunt was the division of the stag, in which each participant in the hunt received a part commensurate with his or her role, thus affirming and reenforcing the social order. The esoteric knowledge of exactly how to divide the stag was the mark of a cultivated gentleman. The genitals, liver and some other parts are placed on a forked stick. The torso is carefully divided. The entrails are placed on the skin of the stag and given to the dogs. Finally, the head of the stag is placed on a branch and given to the king or highest ranking noble in a pageant, announced by blowing horns. According to Klingender, this trophy represents the ruler's own head, and signifies a sort of resurrection after the symbolic regicide of the hunt.[28] There were, of course, local and individual variants of the ritual. When James 1 of England killed a stag, he would cut its throat and then personally daub the faces of courtiers with the blood, which they were forbidden to wash away. Women generally did not participate in the high hunt, but there were many exceptions, and they would sometimes wash their hands in the blood of the stag in the belief that this would whiten their skin.[29]

The high hunt of medieval times carried the mystique of hunting to an extreme of complexity. An elaborate etiquette and vocabulary grew up around it, and mastery of the rules became the mark of a true noble. Even mistakes in pronunciation could be grounds for punishment.[30] Like contemporary hunting as gathering, it was an endeavour of the entire community, but, like hunting as harvesting, it affirmed a strictly hierarchal order.[31] For royalty and nobility in the Middle Ages, hunting

The Unicorn Crosses a Stream (from the Unicorn Tapestries), South Netherlands, 1495–1505, wool, silk and silver. The hunters go about their tasks in a way that seems ritualistic, acting out a drama of sin and redemption.

often became a consuming obsession. When William I conquered England in 1066, he almost immediately set aside several huge tracts of land, including the New Forest, as hunting preserves. After the conquest of England, he and his three immediate successors over about the next century almost seemed to live for the hunt. By the early twelfth century, about a quarter of England was under forest law.[32]

Rather like the mass, the high hunt was a ritualistic enactment of the Crucifixion of Christ, with the deer in the role of Christ and the hunters as his persecutors. This was encouraged by the way deer would at times turn and face their pursuers, in effect sacrificing themselves like Christ. The division and distribution of the game, which was its culmination, resembled the Eucharist. That might seem a bit paradoxical, but Christians relate to God primarily as sinners. The goal of believers was never to refrain completely from transgressions. Christians held that human beings were conceived in sin. The goal was to be reborn into a sort of primal innocence, which was symbolized by the forest and the deer.

This religious dimension is apparent in the Unicorn Tapestries from late fifteenth-century Flanders, now in the Cloisters of the Metropolitan Museum of Art in New York. Ladies, nobles and their servants go about a hunt of the unicorn in a manner that, while their expressions at times suggest cruelty, is pervaded by a solemn stillness. After the hunt, the same people mournfully carry off the body of the slain unicorn. In one tapestry, the unicorn, purifying a stream by dipping his horn into it, rests across from a stag,[33] perhaps representing respectively the church and state.

In Thomas Malory's *Morte d'Arthur*, the adventures that will lead to the quest for the Grail begin at the wedding of Arthur and Guinevere, when a white stag runs through the hall chased by a pack of dogs. Sir Gawain and his brother, Sir Gaheris, ride off in pursuit of the stag, but the quest only leads to pointless carnage as knights challenge them along the way. The stag takes refuge in another castle, where it is killed by the dogs.

Near the end of the epic, the initial scene is repeated but with knights who are wiser and less impetuous. Sir Bors, Sir Percival and Sir Galahad see a white hart chased by four dogs. They follow the hart to the dwelling of a holy hermit, who is singing mass. The hart becomes Jesus Christ, while the dogs become the symbols of the four Evangelists – a man, ox, eagle and lion. The five all take their places at an altar and, when the hermit finishes, leave through the glass window without breaking it. A voice proclaims that in such a form the son of God entered the womb of Mary. Finally, the hermit explains that the stag was Jesus Christ, 'for oftentimes . . . Our Lord showed Him unto good men and good knights in likeness of an hart'.[34] Many traditions, including those of Celts, Greeks, Romans, Chinese and Mesopotamians, have attributed some sort of divine status to the stag. In pre-Mycenean art, for example, it was often harnessed to the chariot of the sun. A tradition that may be Zoroastrian in origin but developed in medieval Europe makes the stag, representing Christ, the enemy of the snake, representing Satan.[35]

Lord of the Forest

In terms of pragmatic goals, the high hunt was absurdly inefficient. It took an entire party much of the day to kill one stag, when a single bowman could have done it in minutes. The hunt also did nothing to keep down the population of deer, which might still nibble crops or prevent the regeneration of forests. But such considerations, if they were taken into account at all, were strictly subordinate to the ceremony.

The tradition of hunting as gathering, by contrast, was practised by peasants during the latter Middle Ages. They were allowed to hunt only the animals that were considered less noble, particularly when these were considered harmful to more exalted game such as the deer and boar. These included the fox, badger, hare and squirrel, and sometimes also the rabbit and wolf. Peasants were not permitted to possess any weapons other than clubs and pikes, but they could use traps and nets.[36]

The divine right of kings was a religious, even mystical, idea, and the Carolingians extended this numinous power to what had previously been communal forests. But, as is so often the case, mystical values were intimately tied to economic ones. This is not because the economic ones are prior, as Marxists have generally believed. It is simply that religious and economic trends both respond and contribute to the same complex of cultural and environmental conditions that we call 'society'. The monarch may be an important symbolic figure, but he cannot continually live, much less govern, on that level. The various goods associated with forests such as firewood, edible roots and herbs as well as privileges such as pasturing were becoming commodities, which could be disaggregated. The king could then grant, sell, forbid, rent, exchange or lend these privileges to others in ways that were strictly regulated.[37] That economic consequence was reenacted in the elaborate ceremony of dividing up the stag. The emerging capitalist order was not, and has never been, self-evident. Like other social institutions, it needed to be modelled and sacralized through ceremony.

The religious aspect of the hunt, as well as respect for the prey, declined as the Middle Ages drew to a close. The painting *The Stag Hunt*, executed by Lucas Cranach the Younger in 1544, shows a hunt in Saxony, in which a large herd of deer is chased along a carefully appointed path through the forest until the animals have no choice but to take refuge in a lake. As the deer swim, the most noble of the party shoot them with crossbows, since guns were still considered unchivalrous. The shooters include John Frederick, the Elector of Saxony, Sybille, the Electress, and Charles v, Holy Roman Emperor. They are all concealed from the deer by bushes but elaborately dressed, and the scene is basically a pageant.

This hunt never actually took place, but the painting depicted fellowship between the Elector and emperor in hope of inspiring a reconciliation between them.[38] Far from enacting a grand drama of sin and redemption,

Lucas Cranach the Younger, *Stag Hunt of John Frederick I, Elector of Saxony*, 1544, oil on canvas. The stags are killed on an almost industrial scale with crossbows reserved for high-ranking lords and ladies. The hunt remains largely ritualistic, and firearms, which were still considered unchivalrous, are not used.

the deer were being killed in an almost industrial manner, but the hunt remained associated with the upper class and had become a vehicle for diplomacy. Perhaps the military precision with which the deer were driven to water was a hint at how effective the Elector and emperor might be as allies in war.

The Medieval Forest

Already in the ancient world, southern Greece had been reduced to semi-desert through heavy grazing and excessive cultivation. By the time of the Roman conquests, Italy was dotted with villages and the land was largely given over to agriculture. There were few old-growth forests, most of which were sparsely wooded and used as pastures.[39] Nevertheless, the Romans and Greeks set aside hundreds of sacred groves that might serve as the abode of the gods. Among the oldest such groves was that of Dodona in northwestern Greece, which is mentioned by Homer, where the Greeks considered the rustling of oak leaves a medium of prophecies. These groves varied considerably with the local practices. Some sacred groves, though not all, were surrounded by walls. Cutting, foraging and access might be restricted or forbidden.[40]

The creation of royal and noble forests in the Middle Ages took place within a Christian context, but it was not entirely different from the Greco-Roman ones. In both cases, the forests were generally inhabited by divine figures that stood a little apart from the religious hierarchies. In Rome and Greece, these included dryads, fauns and satyrs. In medieval Europe, they included elves and dwarves. In both cases, the forests were places where deities remained relatively immanent, when they were elsewhere beginning to appear distant and abstract. But the Romans and Greeks considered their deities to be immortal, while Christians worshipped a god that had died and been resurrected. As we have already seen, one major embodiment of that deity was the stag.

In the late Middle Ages, the forest took on royal charisma, which was partly a substitute for the beauty and grandeur that the forests had steadily been losing. Large predators such as wolves, lynxes and bears had become rare. Biodiversity had been steadily diminishing. As Christianity was universally adopted, people no longer thought of the forests as the home of deities. But, with medieval forest law, they were reconsecrated.

Medieval European forest law viewed poaching the king's deer as a symbolic regicide. According to a Carolingian law from the tenth century, 'The vassal loses his fief when he strikes his lord, bears arms against him, fishes in his ponds without authorization or hunts in his *garenne* (hunting preserve).'[41] This would deprive the vassal of both his income and social standing. The punishment for poaching by a free man would later be amended to a hefty fine, but a serf who committed that crime would forfeit his life.[42] In England, under the forest laws of William the Conqueror, any peasant who poached a deer in the royal forest could be blinded, castrated or sewn into the skin of the stag and then killed by dogs.[43]

Although forest law was notoriously harsh and bitterly resented, it did not give the monarch unlimited power. It did make them the centre about which all procedures and rules revolved. She or he was the owner of the wild animals in the forest, especially the deer. She or he also owned the trees and vegetation. In summary, the monarch was master of everything 'wild'. Nobles might have forest preserves as well, and their role was analogous, though on a smaller scale. Zooarcheologist Naomi Sykes writes with reference to Norman England, 'By restricting hunting rights to the elite, the "wild" became associated with high social status whereas "domestic" equated to the lower classes.' Forest law associated game animals with royalty and aristocracy, placing these in a more exalted category than peasants and farm animals.[44] It is true that deer, unlike the peasants, were ritualistically sacrificed, but they were also identified with 'Christ the king'.

The forest has long been deeply influenced by human institutions, especially the monarchy, clergy and nobility, and so it is odd that we should understand it as a primeval condition that prevailed before humankind. Perhaps part of the reason is that as the West gradually moved toward constitutional government, the king himself began to seem like part of a romantic past. The forest became a sort of theme park, a kingdom within the kingdom, which contrasted with the emerging capitalist order. The forest was where the monarch could still rule 'like a king' and not a bureaucrat. Queen Elizabeth I of England, a hunter herself, would sometimes assert her authority, as well as magnanimity, by sparing a stag and prohibiting others from pursuing it.[45] Following a stag into the forest and being separated from the rest of a hunting party is a trope that begins many medieval romances.[46]

Most of the action in Malory's *Morte d'Arthur* takes place in the forest, yet the forest is so full of knights, ladies, castles, monsters and wonders as to seem anything but primeval or even natural. There is, by contrast, very little mention of trees or woodland animals apart from deer. The author understood the forest as a dreamlike landscape where almost anything is possible, not so much a place of nature as of adventures. It is, in other words, an area that is set apart from the domestic realm, where the usual expectations no longer apply.

The legendary Robin Hood and his merry men, in tales from late medieval ballads to Victorian books for young people, live in the forest by poaching the 'king's deer', but poaching is never the centre of their tales and is mentioned only in passing.[47] Like many other romantic rebels, Robin takes on the mystique that he appears to rebel against. Robin becomes, in other words, a sort of forest king. Like an order of knights, the merry men prove themselves by deeds of courage and martial valour. They then entertain themselves, much like knights, with contests in martial skills such as marksmanship with an arrow or fighting with a quarter staff. Although many of the merry men have professions such as a miller, tanner or friar, they never seem to practise these but, apart from their adventures, lead a life of leisure. Like the king of England, Robin is engaged in a battle against modernity, trying to preserve his domain against the incursions of urban civilization.

But the stories of Robin Hood largely reverse many formulas of chivalric romances, where knights live in castles and ride into the forest in search of adventure. Robin and his men live in the forest, but almost all their adventures take place in towns or at least along roads. Unlike the knights, they never have to contend with dragons, sorcerers or even wild beasts. This reflects the reality of late medieval and Renaissance hunting preserves, which could be managed almost like gardens. Grazing by cattle reduced the understorey, enabling people to pass through easily even on horseback. Otherwise, the high hunt would have been impossible. Basically, the stories of Robin and the merry men are a knightly idyll that has been secularized and partially democratized. As for the deer, they were deprived of their numinous qualities and simply became food. Perhaps the most fundamental difference between the merry men and a knightly order is that Robin and his crew practised hunting as gathering, something that might have seemed blasphemous to the nobility.

Over the centuries, the severe prohibitions of traditional forest law were gradually replaced by complex regulation. The hunt of deer retained much of its mystique as an expression of manhood and gained additional appeal as a rebellion against the feudal order. During an economic downturn in England during the early eighteenth century, rural people of the

Sir Edwin Landseer, *The Monarch of the Glen*, c. 1851, oil on canvas.
The twelve points on the horns of a deer were considered a mark of royalty.

lower class began conducting extensive poaching raids on the deer of country estates. Since they endeavoured to camouflage themselves by blacking their faces, they were called Blacks. In response, the government passed a law known as the Black Act of 1723, which reinstated the death penalty for poaching deer under certain conditions.

Gilbert White complained, 'towards the beginning of this century all this country was wild about deer-stealing. Unless he was a hunter, as they affected to call themselves, no young person was allowed to be possessed of manhood and gallantry.' He described how former Blacks would tell their stories over ale in a tavern, and they were full of gratuitous cruelty. One watched a pregnant deer until her fawn was born and then immediately seized the baby deer and slit its feet with a knife, so, when fat enough to be profitably killed, it would be unable to run away.[48] The basic model followed by Blacks was, of course, hunting as gathering, but the combination of pressure from the authorities and hunting frenzy conspired, in the view of White, to overcome all restraints. There was an element of sport for them, but it consisted less in outwitting the prey than the authorities.

The Black Act was mostly repealed in 1823. As commoners became occupied with hunting deer, the aristocracy shifted its attention to the fox, which nobles pursued in a ritualized *par force* hunt on horseback and with dogs, much as they had previously done with deer. But if the practices were similar, the symbolism was not. The fox hunt was not a ritualistic regicide designed to release tension and prevent a real one from taking place. The fox represented the upwardly mobile peasantry and middle class, just as it had in the Reynard the Fox tales of the European Middle Ages. The nobles were ritualistically pursuing their rivals for wealth and power. Since foxes had become nearly extinct throughout Britain, they had, ironically, to be imported from Continental Europe. The fox hunt was even less pragmatic than the stag hunt had been, for the tiny portion of meat it provided was far from beloved. Nevertheless, expensive

F. A. Lydon, illustration to the poem 'Address to a Wild Deer' by Wilson, especially the opening lines: 'Hail, king of the wild, whom nature hath borne/ O'er a hundred hill tops since the mists of the morn'. From *Gems from the Poets* (1859–60).

accessories such as handbags or stoles for ladies were sometimes made from the skins of foxes with the heads and tails still attached.

Wilhelm Heinrich Riehl, the major theorist of conservatism in nineteenth-century Europe, especially Germany, saw national identity as an organic whole which encompasses land as well as human beings. It was also, like the body of an animal, hierarchically organized, with all parts working in harmony. The forest, where aristocrats could hunt and peasants forage, corresponded to the feudal order, while the field was the realm of the middle classes. The extent of communal forests was a measure of ascendancy in the conflict between the old ruling class and the new one. The division of the communal forest into privatized fields was an evil of the modern era. Nevertheless, the forest remained the source of spiritual vitality; the future would belong to heavily forested countries such as Germany and Russia.[49] This was a fantasy based on nostalgia for the woods as a communal possession in some indeterminate era of the past.

Aristocrats continued to hunt deer on their estates, but increasingly by stealth using firearms rather than in full pursuit. In Victorian times, the deer retained its association with royalty, and, though she lost power, the monarch retained and even increased her symbolic significance. Royal ceremonies became more frequent and elaborate, and she was even given new titles such as 'Empress of India'. Artists often depicted a stag on a hill surrounded by other deer gazing out over a rugged land-scape. Perhaps the best known such painting is by Edmund Landseer, painted in 1851 and entitled appropriately *Monarch of the Glen*. It was initially commissioned to adorn the House of Lords, but the House of Commons, perhaps sensing the symbolic veneration of the upper class, refused to pay for it, so the painting was sold to a patron instead. Kenneth Clark writes that the painting 'epitomizes the self-satisfaction of the Victorian ruling class – masterful, courageous, aggressively masculine, dominating the whole environment'.[50]

The stag has the sort of horns that have for many centuries been an obsession with trophy hunters, who value them for their symmetry, their number of points and, above all, their size. These are often erroneously said to be an indication of genetic fitness, but the real reason is that they suggest a crown. Since large horns are constantly sought by sportsman, their possession puts the stag in jeopardy. The ostentatious display of the horns in the picture by Landseer would certainly have come across as a challenge to hunters. For the nobility, the danger to the stag from poachers may simply have added a touch of tragic grandeur. Perhaps the smugness that Clark saw reflected in the painting was only part of the story. Many in the aristocracy, who realized it was in a slow but inexorable decline, may have felt like hunted deer.

The Deer in America

The word 'forest' still meant a royal domain at the time of the early colonization of the Americas. In that sense, there were no 'forests' in the New World, but the meaning of the word was expanded to cover other vast areas covered in trees. They were viewed more as an extension of the hunting preserves than of the urban areas and farming communities, which helps to explain many of the resentments that colonists would eventually feel. The king may not have hunted in Massachusetts or Virginia, but he still took it upon himself to protect and exploit the colonies. He could rule on matters such as which trees might be felled or preserved. A notorious example starting in the late seventeenth century was the marking of trunks of large white pines with 'the king's broad arrow', three strokes of an axe, to indicate that they should not be cut, since they were intended to become masts for ships of the Royal Navy. This prohibition caused wide popular resentment and proved impossible to enforce.

As we have seen, hunting deer in England and much of Continental Europe was closely tied not only to the institution of kingship but matters of wealth and class as well. The English Game Act of 1605 had set stringent qualifications of property and income for the privilege of hunting, so a yeoman farmer might not even be able to hunt on his own land.[51] For early settlers in English colonies, hunting was a form of recreation for gentlemen and ladies of leisure, and they had trouble comprehending how it might be a matter of subsistence. The Native Americans, who might spend their days hunting, impressed them as idle.[52] It even suggested that the native peoples themselves were close to being beasts. Getting meat from domesticated animals seemed to be a more civilized and virtuous alternative.

Deer hunting, however, was often necessary to colonists in the Americas for their survival, especially on the frontier. It eventually took on a meaning almost opposite of the European one, as the activity of people with modest means. Nevertheless, the association with wild nature could suggest a spiritual sort of aristocracy. The hunt was romanticized in figures such as Daniel Boone and Annie Oakley. The archetypal hunter was Natty Bumpo, the central character of James Fenimore

Henry Sumner Watson, *Modern Invasion of the Woods*, 1910, oil on illustration board. The artist expresses a fear that modern conveniences, in this case a telephone, are feminizing the woods and taking them away from rugged males.

Cooper's Leatherstocking novels, whose many nicknames included 'Deerslayer'.[53] For Natty Bumpo, the hunt would be quick, humane, efficient and not accompanied by any rituals. Nevertheless, the underlying significance of the killing may not be so different from that of the late medieval hunt.

Well into the twentieth century, the American emphasis on survival in a dangerous wilderness, with the violence that entailed, served to make forests into a male preserve, a place where men might go to escape feminine demands, expectations and complaints. It was an area where men endeavoured to 'get away from civilization' by 'roughing it' on fishing or hunting trips. In the 1980s there was a vogue for 'wild man weekends' in the woods, where men would sit around a campfire and talk about their problems.

A Life in the Woods

Hunters have always tried to assume the point of view of the prey in order to anticipate how it was likely to behave. The intense identification of predator and prey, which is very probably also found in the animal kingdom, is the paradox of the hunt. Felix Salten made it the foundation of his novella *Bambi: A Life in the Woods*, first published in 1923, which tells a coming-of-age story about a young stag. Salten himself was from a Hungarian Jewish background. His family had moved to Vienna when he was a child, and he had gradually attained a distinguished position as a man of letters. He had been an avid hunter for all of his adult life, and he eventually even purchased a forested plot for that purpose.

Another related paradox is that of adapting the perspective of the stag, at least as a narrative convention, to enable him to tell the story from an utterly anthropocentric point of view. The animals regard humankind, which they conceive of as a single man, with a combination of terror and veneration that is inspired by that felt towards Yahweh of the Old Testament, other deities of the ancient world and, in medieval times, kings. This is still more emphasized in the translation by Whittaker Chambers published only five years after the original. Chambers capitalizes every pronoun that refers to 'Man', much as one did with references to the deity.

In many ways, the book is written from the perspective of Social Darwinism, which was very popular at the time. The woods are utterly filled with terror as animals perpetually chase, catch and devour one another. The difference between man and the other animals is not so much one of motivation or behaviour, it is simply that man is better at killing than the rest. One stag named Gobo is temporarily captured, kept in a sort of petting zoo and then released back into the wild. He tells the animals that man is really kind and good, but, because he has lost his natural wariness, is soon shot by hunters.

Placing extreme anthropocentrism in the mouths of animals rather than people may make it seem more plausible, but it nevertheless remains entirely a human fantasy. For the most part, animals in the woods are not obsessed with humankind; in fact most have no awareness of us whatsoever. The story questions man's benign nature only to emphatically reaffirm his importance. But, towards the end of the story, there is a partial explanation. The wise old stag, a mentor and perhaps the father of Bambi, takes him to a place in the wood to show him the body of a poacher who is lying face upwards in the snow, killed by a wound to the chest. He could have been killed by the antlers of the old stag, though may also have been shot by a game warden. At any rate, the book continues:

> 'Do you see, Bambi,' the old stag went on, 'do you see how He's lying there dead like one of us? Listen Bambi. He isn't all powerful as they say. Everything that lives and grows doesn't come from Him. He isn't above us. He's just the same as we are. He has the same fears, the same needs and suffers in the same way. He can be killed like us, and then He lies helpless on the ground like all the rest of us, as you see Him now.'

At first, Bambi looks on in apparent incomprehension, but the old stag urges him to speak. Then Bambi says, 'There is Another who is over us all, over us and over Him.' The old stag, his final mission accomplished, goes off to die alone.[54]

The stag and the hunt have been both greatly, though not completely, secularized. The animal remains a sort of monarch of the woods, ceremonially yet never permanently deposed by human beings. But who is this 'Another', over the poacher and all others, to which Bambi refers? Perhaps it is a form of the Judeo-Christian God. Salten may have added that sentence to keep the story, which was already very harsh, from appearing completely nihilistic.

But there is another possibility. Salten was, as already mentioned, an avid hunter, and John Galsworthy, in his preface to the first English edition, says of the book, 'I particularly recommend it to sportsmen.'[55] This book is not against those hunters that Salten considers legitimate, who not only abide by the laws but by many largely unspoken rules of the hunt that are established by custom. It is against the poacher, who kills indiscriminately in all seasons. And whom does Bambi refer to as above the poacher? It might be the forces of order that regulate hunting and preserve the forest. Using the old stag as a spokesman, the author seems to be looking down on the poacher as a pretender, with a combination of pity and contempt. This attitude is reminiscent of medieval forest law, where the penalty for poaching deer might be death.

In 1942 Disney Studios released an animated film based on the novella entitled *Bambi*. While the book obsessively emphasized predation and death in nature, the movie eliminated that entirely. It showed owls cavorting with cute little birds and rabbits, which they would in reality be trying to devour. The movie manages to preserve much of the book's sombre poetry, but it does so by attributing all destruction in the woods, including a forest fire, to 'man'. It makes no distinction between the legitimate hunter and the poacher. The scene with the dead poacher, which places at least some limits on both human power and villainy, is left out. The movie preserves and even accentuates the extreme anthropocentrism of the original by attributing to humankind virtually limitless power. Man was more a deity than ever, even if not a benign one. The film was also a remarkably effective attack on the institution of hunting. Bambi's mother is killed by a hunter and, even though that happens offscreen, the event shocked viewers when the film was first released.

Most Americans would have been incapable of making or even understanding Salten's fundamental distinction between the legitimate hunter and the poacher. The old forest laws, where hunting deer was confined to the king and the nobility, seemed to represent everything in the Old World that colonists had endeavoured to escape through emigration.[56] In consequence, there were hardly any restrictions placed on hunting in America for a very long time.

Disney, in placing the story of Bambi in the United States, had made the deer into mule deer, found only in parts of the Midwest. This may have been intended to avoid the even greater controversy that would have come from featuring the white-tailed deer, which has a larger range

White-tailed deer on the author's property in New York state.

Two hunters carrying dead deer over their shoulders,
early 20th century, photograph.

Deer hunters posing with their victims strung up by the feet
in the Adirondack Mountains, beginning of the 20th century, postcard.

Certificate of membership in the Foresters of America, January 1898. The brotherhood of foresters had become a benevolent association. Along with the bald eagle, its symbol was the heraldic stag in the centre, whose horns repeat the curves of the surrounding branches. Among the many symbols of forests here, a gun is noticeably absent. By this time, American deer had been hunted to near extinction, and the foresters wanted to signal that they were interested in preservation rather than conquest.

and is a more iconic part of the American landscape. These deer are known for their beauty and grace, and they are named for their white tails that appear to sway, sort of like a flag, as they run. They were very common when the first settlers arrived from Europe. By 1900 uncontrolled hunting had extirpated them in most of the Northeast, and there were only an estimated 350,000 scattered in less heavily populated parts of the United States.[57]

Numerous photographs taken of hunters with their slain deer in the late nineteenth and early twentieth centuries show just how unceremonious, unrestrained and even vicious the hunt of deer had become. Hunters were often shown posing with their guns before large numbers of killed stags that were dangling by their hind legs, which were fastened together, from rafters or trees. Deer were being killed on a scale beyond what could probably be used for food and with an ease that casts doubt on any claim to sport. Deer still represented royalty and nobility, which made them into enemies of American democracy, and so, even in death, they were not accorded any dignity.

To prevent their complete extinction, limits were finally set on the numbers that could be hunted. The deer population gradually began to recover, but at least until about the mid-1960s they remained rare. When one occasionally came across one in the woods, it seemed a miracle. This not only reflected their rarity but a changing attitude toward royalty, as Americans increasingly thought of royalty as a romantic fairy tale and Elizabeth II became perhaps more popular in the United States than in Britain.

By the 1970s deer were far more visible, and people began to complain about them vociferously. The deer had lost their fear of humankind and started to be regularly sighted in suburbs, at times even making forays into large cities such as New York. They nibbled at gardens and were often involved in car accidents. They spread ticks, which carry Lyme disease, to human beings. Finally, they prevent rejuvenation of woods by nibbling at shoots that would otherwise become trees. Instead of as a natural wonder, many people started to regard them as 'rats with hooves'.

The hunting restrictions had enabled their success, but they were not the only reason for it. Deer thrive best not in the depths of forests but at the forest edges, which is precisely the sort of environment favoured by human beings. The extensive but fragmented forests of the northeastern United States are not well suited to many species, especially those of birds, but they are an environment in which deer can thrive. It provided them not only with pasture but also, when necessary, cover as well. Human beings had greatly reduced the number of their natural predators such as wolves and bears. The Native Americans, who had once regularly hunted them, had been largely driven from the eastern states in the early nineteenth century. By the 1990s the number of white-tailed deer in the United States had risen to an estimated 25 to 40 million,[58] possibly more than there were when Columbus first landed.

This increase in deer raises complex practical and ethical questions, which involve more than balancing the interests of humans and deer. Policies must also consider the interests of trees, birds and other living things that make up the forest community. The consensus of foresters is that neither recreational hunting nor birth control is remotely enough to keep the deer population in check.[59] Predators of the deer such as bears and coyotes are also increasing in the American Northeast, but there are not nearly enough of them to impact the deer populations. In the past, the deer population has been partly controlled by climate, as deer would regularly starve in winter and die of dehydration in summer, but enough would always survive to continue the population. That pattern is likely to be accentuated by climate change, but, while that seasonal fluctuation in population is natural, allowing it does not seem humane. The same may arguably apply to diseases, which often reduce dense populations of animals and plants in the wild.

Who is the true ruler of the forest? The simplest and best answer is that there is none. It was never the bear, wolf or tiger. For all the anthropocentrism in the story of Bambi, as told in both the book and the movie, it is also not humankind. But perhaps deer deserve the title for their resilience, having managed to thrive despite almost every imaginable natural or human threat.

Caspar David Friedrich, *Chasseur in the Forest*, c. 1814, oil on canvas.

6

The Forest and Death

It's so dark now I cannot see myself. But the song continues,
and the air around us is full of invisible wings.

Helen Macdonald, *Vesper Flights*

Caspar David Friedrich's 1814 painting *Chasseur in the Forest* shows the small figure of a cavalryman from behind. He is on foot, lost among the enormous trees of Germany. On a stump behind him perches a croaking raven. Winter has begun. He is about to die. This is punishment for the Napoleonic invasions. The attack is defeated by the force of nature, represented by the primeval German woods.

That is at least how the painting has usually been understood, but only the use of a Gallic word in the title and the date, shortly after Napoleon's disastrous 1812 campaign in Russia and the battle of Leipzig, tell us that the man in the picture is French. You cannot tell much from his uniform. Cavalrymen in the Napoleonic *grande armée* had many different uniforms depending on their regiment and rank. He could just as well be Prussian. For that matter, you cannot even see for certain the colour of the cloak, which comes across to us as a greenish brown that may reflect the pines. We see that he is on foot, but that does not necessarily mean that his horse is lost. Perhaps it is just behind the trees. There seems to be a path veering off to the right of the viewer, so he may not even be far from what we call civilization.

The clearing suggests that the cavalryman may indeed have been part of a regiment that passed through recently in an invasion and is now in retreat. The detail supports, but does not conclusively prove, the idea that the soldier was part of Napoleon's invasion of Russia. But the woods of Russia are mixed and deciduous with a large number of birches, not a monoculture of conifers. Could it be that part of the army strayed into Prussia?

Or perhaps the picture represents not an event in the past but a plan for the future. Not long before the painting was executed, Friedrich

Ludwig Jahn, who bitterly resented the French, had proposed that forests filled with wild animals be planted on borders of Prussia for protection, since the French, like the Roman invaders long ago, would not know how to negotiate them.[1] But Friedrich was never a painter of military or political propaganda. To understand the painting, we must think of it in a much larger context than simply events of the day.

One might suspect the artist of teasing the viewer with confusing suggestions, but that was not Friedrich's style. He was not a jokester. His work was always earnest, though without being preachy. Friedrich did not illustrate ideas in his paintings; he created them. Very few if any of his paintings lend themselves to allegorical interpretation, whether political or religious. Nevertheless, all of the objects in his paintings seem charged with symbolic significance. Friedrich's imagination was visual rather than verbal, and it may be that he had not even thought of the alternatives under discussion here. He was, in effect, thinking with a paintbrush.

For now at least, the time has come to leave the cavalryman to his fate. To better understand how he came to this place in the woods, or how the woods grew up around him, we must go far back in history.

Germany in Roman Times

In the second half of the first century CE, the Roman encyclopedist Pliny the Elder wrote that in Germany the 'northern region is the huge expanse of the Hercynian Oak Forest, which, impervious to the passage of time, is coeval with the world and exceeds all marvels with its almost limitless age'.[2] This referred to the Black Forest and the area beyond it, which Pliny imagined extending back almost without limit. It was a bit like the frontiers of space today, always beckoning yet unconquerable. Pliny often uncritically reported things he had heard, but he had been stationed in Germany as a soldier and knew something of the territory first hand. It is likely that he may have seen stands of enormous trees, perhaps almost comparable to those of sequoias and redwoods that still stand in California or the white pines that once stood in parts of the northeastern United States and Canada. Pliny was particularly impressed by the oaks, which were sacred to the Roman god Jupiter.

In *Germania*, first published in 98 CE, the Roman historian Tacitus characterizes Germany as 'covered either by bristling forests or by foul swamps'.[3] He goes on to describe the customs of the Germans in considerable detail. They are portrayed as generous, fierce, impulsive, cruel and childlike, yet without affectation. At times, he uses them to shame the decadence of his fellow Romans, for example, when he writes, 'No one in Germany finds vice amusing or calls it "up-to-date" to seduce and be seduced.' He also believed that the Germans were a pure race, implicitly contrasting them with the many peoples that blended in the Roman Empire.[4] According to Tacitus, the Germans, like the Romans, conciliated their gods with animal sacrifices, but they did not consider it right to place their deities within the walls of a temple. He writes, 'Their holy places are woods and groves, and they apply the names of the deities to that hidden presence, which is seen only by the eye of reverence.'[5]

In the year 9 CE, the Roman general Publius Quinctilius Varus, who had been made governor of Germany, was massacred together with three legions at the Battle of Teutoburg Forest. There are several accounts of the battle by Roman authors, but they are sketchy, and the battle belongs perhaps as much to myth as to history. The major account of it is by Tacitus in his *Annals of the Roman Republic*, published in the late first or early second century CE, according to which Varus, after being wounded in battle, committed suicide with his own sword. Tacitus tells how the Romans, under General Germanicus, later revisited the scene of the battle and were horrified to see piles of decaying bodies of men and horses as well as human heads nailed to trunks of trees. Nearby were altars to Germanic gods, where Roman tribunes and centurions had been offered to deities as human sacrifices.[6]

Tacitus' description of the battlefield sounds sensationalized. We have the forest of terror, possibly for the first time in literature. The 'barbarian' deities and even the Germans themselves resemble the witches, ogres, devils, giants and similar figures so often encountered by the hero in the fairy tales of Grimm and others. By the time of Tacitus, Rome had grown to dimensions far beyond any other city, and it had over a million inhabitants. Tacitus himself was a confirmed urban dweller who, unlike Pliny, had no interest whatsoever in the woods except as a setting for human adventures. The vagueness of his descriptions of the woods makes it easy for the reader to project fears and fantasies onto them. It is tempting to call the horror of the woods here Gothic, and the term has an amusing and almost excessive sort of appropriateness. It comes, of course, from 'Goth', which is more or less a term for the early Germanic peoples, the alleged perpetrators of these horrors.

The German and Roman Forests

In reading Tacitus' accounts of Germany and its people, one has the strange impression that except for the absence of firearms, this could just as well be an English account set in North America during the seventeenth or eighteenth century, in which the Romans are colonists and Germans are Native Americans. That is because Tacitus was relying on stereotypes of 'barbaric' lands and peoples that had already been established before him and would continue with amazingly little change for the next two millennia or so. In the era of colonization, the European view of Native Americans was not very different from the Roman perspective on Celts, Scythians and Germans.[7] Tacitus often refers to the Germans collectively not by their tribe or ethnicity but by the general term 'barbarians' (essentially the same in Latin as in English – *barbarus*). At one point he writes, 'For with barbarians, the more eager a man's daring, the more does he inspire confidence, and the more highly is he esteemed in times of revolution.'[8]

In *Annals of Imperial Rome*, Tacitus depicts Arminius, the Germanic chieftain who defeated the Romans at the Battle of Teutoburg Forest, as something like a Homeric hero – fierce, brave, patriotic, imperious and cruel.[9] This was not very different from the way in which, almost two millennia later, Americans would think of the Native American rebel Geronimo. In one elegiac passage, Tacitus calls Arminius 'the deliverer of Germany', adding that he defied Rome not at the beginning of its history but at the height of its power and, after many indecisive battles, remained unconquered.[10]

Tacitus hints strongly at an analogy between Rome closer to the time of its foundation and Germany. Just about all Roman writers believed that the site of their city had originally been heavily forested.[11] The Romans celebrated an arboreal heritage by maintaining many sacred groves and by giving minor forest deities such as satyrs, fauns and dryads a major role in their legends and iconography. Tacitus furthermore reports that Arminius eventually tried to claim the kingship of his tribe, offending the egalitarian sympathies of his people, and was assassinated. This establishes a parallel between Arminius and Julius Caesar, perhaps suggesting that Germany and Rome might simply be at different stages of the same trajectory.[12] The Romans thought of Germany as resembling their own imagined past, which explains the combination of scorn and nostalgia. In a similar way, European settlers in the Americas identified the allegedly 'primitive' natives with figures of antiquity such as the lost tribes of Israel in societies that had remained unchanged. Landscape historians consider that at the time of Tacitus, Germany was largely forested, but not nearly as densely or uniformly as he described it. The land also contained settlement, heath, moor and farmland.[13] Tacitus stereotyped the land, as well as the people, as barbarous.

There were several subsequent Roman incursions into Germany after their defeat at Teutoburg Forest, but the Romans soon accepted the Rhine as the eastern boundary of their empire and built a wall known as the 'Limes' along it. The reason why the Romans did not persist in attempts to conquer Germany was in part because it had relatively little to offer them, far less because it was forested than because, east of the Rhine, Germany did not possess sufficient waterways for communication and trade, so it could not easily be integrated into the Roman Empire.[14] The Rhine provided a natural boundary for the Roman Empire, which was far more easily defensible than any settlement further to the east would have been. The German forests may even have provided a buffer against the horsemen of the steppes, who would become a perpetual threat in the late Roman Empire. For those who might not have appreciated such strategic considerations, the terrors of the forest provided a simple explanation, and even an excuse, for refraining from further incursions into Germany.

A reason why Tacitus could express even a qualified, patronizing admiration of the Germans was that, though unconquered, they did not pose any imminent threat to the Romans. Pliny could admire the German forests for similar reasons. With their vast mining operations and their huge orchards of grafted trees, the Romans had sufficiently subdued the natural world to be able to safely admire its power. Roman gardens, which had previously been laid out according to ostentatiously unnatural geometric patterns, began to incorporate wild areas in the late Roman Republic.[15] Because of the lack of commercial and intellectual contact, Germany seemed exotic to the Romans, a place where they could easily project their fears, daydreams and other fantasies. In other words, the Romans 'Orientalized' Germany.

In the late Roman Empire and early Middle Ages the boundary between city and woods became more permeable. The decline of Roman authority led to the Migration Period, in which peoples such as Huns, Slavs and Goths swept across Europe. Without a central authority to protect them and with trade routes disrupted, urban centres declined. But the reasons were not solely a matter of administration, for climate

Johann Knolle, after Correggio, *Mary Magdalene Reading in the Wilderness*, 19th century, engraving. The figure is in a sort of indeterminate landscape between forest and desert, where she is completely safe and secure.

also played a role. In the late Roman Empire, the weather became colder, wetter and less stable. Severe storms ensued and the forested area increased.[16]

Far from being the boundary of civilization, the forest became a refuge from both human and meteorological volatility. Hermits and, later, entire monasteries withdrew into the forest, which became a place for communion with God. As the trade networks of the Roman Empire were increasingly disrupted, people within it could no longer rely on its vast orchards and enormous hen houses for food. They had to increase local production, and that meant returning to the forests. To an extent, they reverted to patterns of life that had prevailed before Roman civilization.

Gauls and Germans would make temporary clearings near the edges of the forest or even some distance within it, raise crops until the soil began to be exhausted, and then move on to other areas. Small groups of people formed hamlets within forests, where they lived by farming. Forests were also increasingly used for a variety of purposes such as pasturing pigs or cattle, collecting leaves to use as fodder, collecting firewood, taking wood for building and so on. The forest became a refuge, provider and protector, meanings that it has retained up to the present.

The Dark Wood

The motif of the dark, terrifying woods disappeared from the literature and art of the Middle Ages to reemerge at the beginning of the Renaissance in Dante's *Divine Comedy*. Tacitus' *Germania* had passed into obscurity during late Antiquity and the Middle Ages, so it is likely that Dante had not read it. He had read, and thought highly of, Pliny the Elder,[17] who could possibly be a source of the motif. It may also be that Dante did not take the motif from other authors but rather absorbed it as part of the Renaissance world-view. This was a perspective that saw light as divine and darkness, such as that of the forest, as diabolic. It also emphasized order, symmetry and geometric proportions, qualities found in the meticulously laid-out gardens of the period. Dante's own cosmology is so orderly that readers have no trouble mapping out the various parts of hell, purgatory and heaven in detail. A natural forest, with its unpredictable mix of vegetation, would have come across as the epitome of disarray.

Dante's *Inferno* begins as the protagonist suddenly finds himself lost in a dark wood. He does not know how he entered the forest, or where it begins and ends, and he is petrified by fear if he even tries to describe it. The poet Virgil appears to mentor him, and, with the guidance of Beatrice, his muse, they move together through nine levels of hell to finally encounter Satan himself. He is like an enormous tree, which Dante climbs to finally reach the surface of the earth and glimpse the stars.

The dark wood seems to encompass all of the terrifying places in hell, but it especially resembles the Wood of Suicides in canto seven. Dante and Virgil enter a dense wood where the branches of trees are all gnarled and twisted. Around them, they hear laments, yet no person is to be seen. At Virgil's suggestion, Dante plucks off the branch of a tree. Dark blood issues from the fissure, and words come as it flows. The tree identifies itself as the spirit of Pietro della Vigna, who tells how he was a loyal counsellor to Emperor Frederick II of Sicily. He was slandered by enemies, blinded and thrown in prison, where he committed suicide by beating his head against the wall. Pietro explains that all of the trees are suicides. Minos, Lord of the Dead, takes the souls of those who have killed themselves and throws them into the wood, where they fall at random and grow into trees. Harpies fly through the Wood of Suicides, rending the trees with their claws, causing blood to flow and lamentations to be heard. When the Judgement Day finally comes, all other souls will be returned to their bodies, but the suicides will retain their present form, with their bodies hung on branches as a reminder of what they discarded.[18]

Earlier, in the first circle of hell, Francesca told Dante the story of her love affair with Piero, and how the lovers were doomed to drift together, buffeted by strong winds throughout eternity. Overwhelmed with emotion, Dante had fainted.[19] He does not lose consciousness on hearing the pathetic story of Piero, since he has learned to accept the judgement of God. Readers of generations that were yet to come would celebrate Piero and Francesca as great lovers. Even their fate did not seem like a punishment, for they would be together for eternity. Dante

Harpies in the Forest of Suicides, illustration by Gustave Doré for Dante's *Inferno* (1887).

did not have the conceptual tools to articulate his ambivalence. Such concepts would be developed over the next few centuries, for example, that of inspired melancholy. Despair could become a source of creativity, transforming Dante's dark wood into a place of wonderful adventures.

Modern readers also have no compunction about feeling sympathy for Piero, and the Wood of Suicides, a place of horror for Dante, anticipated the romantic aesthetic, in which the things that seemed hideous to Dante would appear beautiful. Dante preferred trees with straight trunks and branches, perhaps following an aesthetic of utility. These are the trees suited for building and for making tools. But, in the centuries to come, the romantic aesthetic of painters such as Friedrich would most prize precisely the sort of trees that Dante found hideous – ancient, unplanted trees with gnarled, knotted and twisted limbs, rather like those in the Wood of Suicides. For those who did not share his religious and social beliefs, the terror of Dante's *Inferno* would become a sort of Gothic horror, a combination of terror and romance that conveys a twinge of pleasure.

In a way, Dante is our Virgil. The Roman poet takes Dante to the threshold of Purgatory yet can go with him no further. Dante takes us almost to the portals of Romanticism, but we must then take leave of him. Particularly in *Inferno*, he gives us images and concepts that would appeal intensely to the romantic imagination of generations to come, yet his religious convictions compel him to reject them. Softened by time, his conceptions would retain their poetic power yet take on a significance very different from what Dante had intended.

The New Germany

Tacitus' *Germania* had been largely forgotten in the late Roman Empire and Middle Ages. It was rediscovered in the Italian Renaissance, where Italian scholars at first read it as showing the 'barbarian' lack of culture and refinement. The book was republished in Germany by the Humanist Conrad Celtis in about 1500. Germany, at the time, was divided into numerous petty kingdoms, each with its own local dialect. They were held together only as parts of a loose confederation known as the Holy Roman Empire. Even the German language would not be standardized until a few decades later, when Luther would publish his translation of the Bible in instalments during the first half of the sixteenth century. But *Germania* suggested that these diverse peoples had a common heritage.[20] It contained the idea of a German nation, which would be passed on primarily in the works of poets before it finally became a reality in the latter nineteenth century.

Celtis was an antiquarian, who wrote only in Latin yet became the poet laureate of the German city of Nuremberg. He was passionate by temperament, and he read Tacitus' *Germania* almost as though it were contemporary. His German nationalism was not a matter of politics, language or even 'culture', as we would understand the term today. It was more a matter of territory. With the Holy Roman Empire, the centre of civilization had passed from Rome to Germany. He saw the Germans as Tacitus did, as undeveloped yet possessing a sort of primeval vitality. He wanted the Germans to study the literature of Rome, much as the Romans had studied that of Greece, until they finally equalled or surpassed it.[21] Paradoxically perhaps, an indigenous perspective on the forests was superimposed on a Roman one, making the deep woods simultaneously a place of refuge and of terror. As the art historian Christopher Wood has put it, 'The glamour of the forest lay in its precarious double nature: awe could easily collapse back into fear, mystery into obfuscation, heroism into barbarism.'[22] Tacitus' attitude towards Germany resembled that of later European settlers in early America toward the New World. Colonists would take pride in their territory being unspoiled and even primeval, while at the same time making every effort to destroy it by promoting a European way of life.

This perspective enabled proponents of an emerging nationalism to simultaneously claim a status for Germany as the peak of civilization and the possessor of primeval vigour. It left, however, an implicit question. What if the Germans, like the Romans before them, were to succumb to decadence? What if they already had? The perspective of early nationalists such as Celtis suggested a cyclical theory of history, with alternating periods of decadence and civilization. But how could you tell where Germany, or any nation, was positioned in this cycle? The idea created contradictory expectations which run through not only German but all European culture of the modern period.

Celtis believed, with Tacitus, that all of Germany had been covered with 'unmeasurably large groves filled with ancient oaks, which by longstanding custom and religion were venerated as holy'. In an act of homage, he attempted to walk what he believed were the sites mentioned by Pliny and Tacitus.[23] In a poem, he wrote, 'it is the woods that the Muses love – poets hate the city with its distracted crowds.'[24] The idea that the Germans were a single people was starting to reemerge,

Little Red Riding Hood and the wolf, illustration by Arpád Schmidhammer, Munich,
c. 1904. The Germans often misleadingly stylized their forests to make them appear
at once ancient and young. It is not likely that a forest filled with trees this huge would
have such a rich ground cover and understorey.

Albrecht Altdorfer, *Landscape with a Double Spruce*, *c.* 1521–2, etching. Altdorfer
is often considered the first landscape artist in Western tradition. In this etching,
vegetation dominates the scene and makes the human structures seem insignificant
by comparison. The trees he favours are contorted, irregular and practically the
opposite of those that were usually preferred in the Renaissance.

especially in the work of poets. *Germania* became an important document of German identity. Arminius would often be celebrated as a hero, even as the founder of Germany. The terror of the woods softened into a gentle melancholy.

As Celtis wrote about the German forests, his contemporary Albrecht Altdorfer was painting them. To an extent, the paintings were an extension of stylized, luxuriant foliage that filled the Gothic churches of his era. Like Celtis, Altdorfer gloried in the darkness and danger of the woods.[25] His trees are anthropomorphized in that the branches and leaves often seem to be gesturing or reaching out like limbs of a human body,[26] a technique that would later be used by Friedrich. In some paintings, such as *St George and the Dragon* (1510),[27] the forest background dominates the ostensible subject.[28]

Death in the Forest

The association of the forest with death, especially by suicide, was a note that Tacitus added to the literature of forests and Dante revived. It would be taken up by many poets and writers, especially among the Romantics, but not with the horror that we find in the story of Pietro. It is a longing for annihilation, thought of as a rest from worldly care. Only enough of the old terror remains to generate a touch of excitement.

One English example is the ballad 'Babes in the Wood', which dates to the sixteenth century and is known in many versions. Two children, brother and sister, survive kidnapping but wander in the woods until they die. In the best-known version, the ballad ends:

> Thus wandered these two prettye babes,
> Till death did end their grief;
> In one another's armes they dyed,
> As babes wanting relief.
>
> No burial these prettye babes
> Of any man receives,
> Till Robin-redbreast painfully
> Did cover them with leaves.[29]

We are not told what the children died from, only that they fell asleep in one another's arms and did not wake up. The time and manner of their deaths is so perfectly appointed that it does not seem like death at all. In a few versions, they do not die but are taken straight into heaven. The illustration by Ralph Caldicott shows foxes, hares, geese and other animals as mourners at their funeral.

The same basic conception appears in 'Ode to a Nightingale' by the English Romantic poet John Keats, written in 1819. The poet listens to an unseen nightingale, which he calls 'light-winged dryad of the trees'. He imagines it in a grove 'Of beechen green, and shadows numberless'. The song leads him into a reverie, in which:

> Darkling I listen; and, for many a time
>   I have been half in love with easeful Death,
> Call'd him soft names in many a mused rhyme,
> To take into the air my quiet breath;
> Now more than ever seems it rich to die,
>   To cease upon the midnight with no pain,
> While thou art pouring forth thy soul abroad
>   In such an ecstasy![30]

In all of these poems, the author first evokes, at times very subtly, the terror of the forest and then softens it. The beauty of the woods is a means of seduction, and untimely death is the likely fate of whoever succumbs.

Forests also have an uncanny ability to absorb human artifice and render it, or at least make it appear to many people, almost entirely natural. The monocultures of spruce that were planted to replace many indigenous German forests inspired at least one of the most celebrated lyrics in the German language, 'Wandrers Nachtlied II' (Wanderer's Night Song II) by Johann Wolfgang von Goethe:

> Über allen Gipfeln
> Ist Ruh,
> In allen Wipfeln
> Spürest du
> Kaum einen Hauch;
> Die Vögelein schweigen im Walde.
> Warte nur, balde
> Ruhest du auch.[31]

On mountain peaks,
All is calm.
In summits of trees,
You can sense
Hardly even a breath:
The little birds hush in the woods.
Just wait, for soon
You too will rest.

In 1780 Goethe carved the poem on the wall of a cabin on Kickelhahn Mountain in Thuringia, now a state in central Germany. The mountain was, and still largely is, covered by a spruce monoculture, as may be seen in pictures of it going back to at least the nineteenth century.[32] Like most

Goethe's cabin on Kickelhahn Mountain, where he wrote his
most famous lyric poem, drawing from *Die Gartenlaube*, no. 40 (1872).
The forest is a monoculture of conifers.

monocultures, the area probably had few birds or other wildlife to begin with. It may be that Goethe mistook the absence of birds for their silence. Except for the noisy raven, Friedrich's painting *Chasseur in the Wood* could easily be taken for an illustration of the poem.

Nature and Humankind

Perhaps the figure in Friedrich's *Chasseur in the Wood* is not quite so alone as he seems. The setting in the painting owes at least as much to commerce as to nature. The trees in the background of the painting are all the same size and evenly spaced, indicating that they had been planted together. There are no stones on the ground, which is an indication that the area had once been used for agriculture. A few trees have been recently cut, but they are growing back quickly. Unlike the ones looming behind them, they are of varying sizes, indicating their predecessors were cut not very long ago.

From the perspective of forestry, the most puzzling feature in the painting is one of the three stumps in the foreground, which is leaning to the viewer's left and half-uprooted. Trees may be knocked over during storms, but stumps generally stay in place as they decay. How did the stump come to be raised and balanced so precariously without falling? The best explanation that I can come up with is that it started to fall before being cut and then ended up leaning on other trees for support. Perhaps partial deforestation opened a corridor for wind to blow it over. But the trees to the left of it are still only mid-sized and would not have provided much of a cushion. Besides, their branches are not broken or bent, as they probably would be from holding up another tree. The odd position makes the stump appear animated, and the root, like a ghostly hand, is pointing towards a sapling to the viewer's right.

In fact, the entire forest seems animated. One branch of a fir, to the viewer's right, seems to point directly to the cavalryman's head. All of them seem to be gesturing expressively. The woods might perhaps represent, as they often have, the unconscious mind. The man, by contrast, seems to be losing his humanity as he blends into the woods around him. He has the form of a spruce tree. His legs are placed together like a stem. He wears a green-brown cloak that is wide at the bottom and tapers towards his helmet, which culminates in a point like the top of a spruce tree. Taking only a quick glance at the painting, it would not be hard to mistake him for one.

If an invading army is guilty of hubris, aren't the creators of the forest monoculture far guiltier still? The cultivation of an entire forest represents one of the comparatively few instances prior to the twentieth century that human beings would claim power on such a vast scale, which had previously been a domain of the elements such as wind, fire and rain. So perhaps the painting is less about French invaders and German landscapes than about humankind. Are we to be destroyed by our creations? Or perhaps, in working on such a scale, we surrender our identity as individuals and even as human beings, to become one with the natural world.

The *chasseur* is what is known in German as a *Rückenfigur*, a figure seen from behind. Such images are used in many, possibly most, of Friedrich's paintings. The figure is never an adversary. It is both a projection of the artist and a stand-in for the viewer.[33] We see the landscape though the eyes of another person, whose back is turned to us. The effect is usually to frame the scene, to prevent it from moving out into the endless distance. But the *Rückenfigur* is generally rather apart from the scene and not the centre of our attention. The image is a bit like a first-person narrator in a novel who, partially but not completely, represents the author. If the figure in the painting is indeed a French invader, the artist was identifying rather intimately with an enemy.

To make the man the subject of the painting, Friedrich has used a technique that, so far I know, is unique to this painting. There are two such figures, one in front of the other. The second *Rückenfigur* is the raven. The painter's use of these two surrogates makes the forest into a story within a story, subject to a wide range of interpretations. Whether the man is facing death or merely taking a stroll, he does not seem more significant than, or even much different from, the woods around him. The raven is more a part of nature than the cultivated fir trees. The bird calls out, something that the *man* can certainly hear. Is it a cry of welcome or doom? The French word *chasseur* can be used to refer to a cavalryman, but it more frequently means 'hunter'. If the latter meaning is intended here, which is the hunter – the man or the raven?

In a deliberately planted monoculture, intended to be harvested, the boundary between life and death becomes clear. Every tree is destined in time for the axe or saw, and its majestic height will only make that more poignant. Its demise will be abrupt and complete. The tree will be replaced not by sprouts from its own seeds but by others brought in from outside.

7

Lord of the Forest

Death used to be an executioner, but the resurrection of Christ makes him nothing but a gardener. When he tries to bury you, he's really planting you, and you're going to come up better than before.

GEORGE HERBERT

As late as 1658, Rev. Edward Topsell could still accuse those who questioned the existence of the unicorn or the powers of its horn of impiety.[1] The more fantastic a tale, the more it proved the power of God. Medieval storytellers competed with one another to make their narratives ever more amazing, and so, perhaps a bit more discreetly, did adventurers and churchmen. To mistrust a fantastic tale was to cast doubt on divine majesty, and just about anything might be believed with proper provenance.[2]

The advent of modernity brought a feeling of disenchantment, and people looked for places that might preserve a sense of endless possibility. Perhaps the first was the margins of medieval manuscripts, which were filled with the most uninhibited fantasy, at times juxtaposed with scientifically accurate illustrations of familiar flora and fauna. Another was accounts of travel in exotic lands, which were filled with giants, phoenixes, dragons and countless other amazing creatures. Then there was the discipline of alchemy, which also became a theatre for grand dreams.

The enchanted forest is originally a literary device to facilitate suspension of disbelief. It is a motif that developed mostly in the late Renaissance and early modern era. Unable to either eliminate magic or live with it, people attempted to find a place for it. They constructed, or conjured, the enchanted forest as a sort of preserve where it could be cultivated. It was a realm, at least somewhat apart from normal life, that retained a sense of enhanced possibility. The forest became a second home for creatures of the imagination. Then, as the forests were increasingly domesticated and cut down, that role was taken by the newly articulated concept of the unconscious mind.

According to Bruno Bettelheim, the forest represents the 'dark, hidden, near-impenetrable world of our unconscious'. We enter it if we are psychologically unable to confront a crisis, and 'when we succeed in finding our way out, we shall emerge with a much more highly developed humanity.'[3] We allow, in other words, the self to fragment into isolated images, preferences, impulses and so on, so that it may be reconstituted on a firmer basis.

For Freud and his school, the unconscious was tied to repression, especially of sexual material. It was the place for all things that we were afraid to contemplate and had blocked from our minds. For Jung and his followers, it was a vast repository of images and associations that had simply not yet come to conscious awareness. For Freudians, the conscious mind was prior, for it had consigned unconscious materials to their place. For Jung, the unconscious was prior since it contained a vast array of archaic materials. Consciousness was only a relatively modern innovation that came with civilization. In practice, the term 'unconscious' was used loosely, and the difference between the two positions was not always clear.

However one makes the distinction, it is dependent on the conception of the individual self. As the division between the objective, or 'external', and subjective, or 'internal', worlds became more pronounced on the threshold of the modern era, it became possible to think of the inner realm as autonomous and nearly all-inclusive. The self, which had once seemed to be a fairly simple thing, expanded to include entire kingdoms to be discovered, mapped and explored. What had hitherto been the unknown became the unconscious.

The very concept of the unconscious mind, which is unseen yet somehow thought of as dark, is basically an intellectualized version of the folkloric woods, displaced from a geographic frontier to that of the human mind. The idea of the forest as the unconscious was the foundation of Stephen Sondheim's hugely popular and critically acclaimed musical *Into the Woods* (1986), in which popular fairy tales are re-enacted as psychological dramas. It has by now become a commonplace in both popular and academic culture.

The Soul of the Forest

In folklore, fairy tales, psychology and alchemy, the forest is a point of convergence for mind and matter, life and death, dream and reality, time and eternity, the natural and spirit worlds. It is a primeval, relatively undifferentiated state. But, to dialog with the forest, we must personify it as a single being, a sort of soul. Only then can we follow its commandments, quarrel with it, destroy it or seek its wisdom. I will call this figure the Lord or Lady of the Forest.

Matilde Battistini writes, 'The heart of the woods, usually represented as a clearing, stands for the sacred enclosure within which the protagonist makes contact with the divine.'[4] This is where Gilgamesh encounters Humbaba, Dante encounters Virgil, St Hubert encounters Christ, Vasilisa the Beautiful encounters Baba Yaga and Isaac McCaslin encounters Old Ben. It need only be added that the divinity of the figure deep in the woods is not always apparent at first. It may take frightening forms but generally leads the protagonist to good fortune in the end.

The *Epic of Gilgamesh* is the first known instance of this mythic structure, with Humbaba as Lord of the Forest, which is still found in tales of the forest for millennia after it was written. A hero, driven by either hardship or pursuit of glory, makes a journey into the depths of a forest and encounters the guardian of the woods. If she or he kills the spirit of the forest, the woods lose their terror, wildness and vitality. If she or he reaches an understanding with the spirit, it will be possible to live alongside the woods in relative harmony. The Lord or Lady of the Forest is especially ubiquitous in fairy tales; in fact the motif of the enchanted forest seldom appears without such a figure.

But how can you personify the forest? In the late Middle Ages through at least the nineteenth century, it was common to personify abstract qualities as allegorical figures of women, intended to represent Beauty, Nature, Truth, Justice, Freedom and so on. The forest is less abstract and therefore harder to idealize. The soul of the forest could not be fixed in a single, standardized image because forests and our experiences of them are so diverse. To relate to the forest as a whole, people of a region had to give it a familiar, tangible and partially humanized appearance. In European folk literature, the Lord or Lady of the Forest is usually a combination of the human form and vegetal qualities such as the colour green, the organic curves of vegetation, a garment of leaves, possession of mysterious powers and an ability to heal easily from cuts. This figure may initially be either frightening or benign but is almost always at least somewhat ambivalent. She or he cannot easily be standardized but, like foliage, must be forever recreated.

The Lord or Lady of the Forest lives in the deepest part of the woods. If the figure is human, it is generally in a hut, a castle or even a cavern.

In the knightly epic *Parzival* by Wolfram von Eschenbach, written in Middle-High German in the early thirteenth century, the Lord of the Forest is Anfortas. His home is the castle of Munsalvaesche, the Castle of the Grail, which can never be found by searching but only by providence. It is full of splendours, yet no tree has been cut within 30 miles.[5] Especially before the compass became widespread, finding your way in the woods was at most a matter of intuition. In folktales, the hero generally comes across the mysterious structure in the woods by chance and almost never by following explicit directions, still less by means of maps. This is how Sir Gawain, in the anonymous late fourteenth century Middle English poem *Sir Gawain and the Green Knight,* will find the Green Chapel.

The Green Knight

The poem begins at the court of Arthur, where the Knights of the Round Table have been celebrating the Christmas holidays. Suddenly, the large figure of a strange knight, whose skin and clothing are green, walks in, holding aloft a holly sprig in one hand and an axe in the other. After taunting the knights of Arthur for their lack of valour, he challenges all the revellers to a game. One knight must take his axe and behead the Green Knight, but the volunteer must then seek him out at the same time next year and be decapitated in turn. When there are no immediate takers, King Arthur himself agrees to be the one. Then the young Gawain volunteers to take his place. Gawain severs the intruder's head. It rolls on the floor until the body of the Green Knight, which can still move, retrieves it. The body holds the still-severed head up high. Then it speaks, telling Gawain to seek him out at the Green Chapel in one year's time.

After a year has elapsed, Gawain sets out on his horse, wearing armour and fabric that is so elaborately bejewelled and decorated that it seemed more appropriate to a ceremony than an arduous journey. His shield and garments are decorated with the pentacle, an occult symbol of perfection. He has no directions but asks anyone he encounters for the way to the Green Chapel. None have heard of it. He passes through dark, desolate landscapes, where he contends with wild men, wolves, bears, serpents, boars and giants. There are groves of huge oaks, hazels and hawthorns overgrown with moss. This is the forest primeval of the medieval imagination.

Illumination showing Sir Gawain and the Green Knight from the original manuscript, *c.* 1450. Although the figures are not finely drawn, the expressions on their faces effectively convey the combination of fear, amazement and consternation that the appearance of the Green Knight evokes.

Finally, on Christmas Eve, Gawain finds himself before a castle in the woods a few days before the appointed time. There he is welcomed and celebrated for his deeds by people who know of him and anticipated his arrival. The Lord of the Castle is Sir Bertilak, whose bushy beard was brown as a beaver's fur. With him is his lovely wife and a crone who is not initially named but is treated with great respect. Lord Bertilak tells Gawain that the path from the castle to the Green Chapel is short, and Gawain agrees to rest as a guest in the castle until the final day, while Bertilak goes hunting. At the end of each day, each will give whatever he has attained to the other.

On the first night, Bertilak's wife goes to Gawain's bed and gently endeavors to seduce him. Gawain refuses her advances with both firmness and courtesy, allowing her only to give him a single kiss. Bertilak returns and gives Gawain a deer that he had killed; Gawain gives Bertilak the kiss but does not reveal its source. On the second day, the wife tries again to seduce him, this time more aggressively, but Gawain only lets her kiss him twice on the cheek. This time Bertilak gives him a ferocious wild boar that he has killed, and Gawain gives him two kisses in return. On the third night, after seeing that Gawain will not be swayed by either flattery or taunts, Bertilak's wife offers him a green sash that, she says, will protect him from all wounds. Gawain accepts it, hoping to escape the axe, and she gives him three kisses. Bertilak returns having killed only a mangy fox, which he gives to Gawain. The young knight gives Bertilak the three kisses but says nothing about the sash, which he wears in secret.

On New Year's Day, Gawain sets out for the Green Chapel, which turns out to be a mound in the earth. The Green Knight is waiting for him. Gawain bows his head to be decapitated, but then he flinches, and the Green Knight checks his blow. After taunting Gawain for cowardice, the Green Knight prepares another blow. This time Gawain does not flinch, but the Green Knight once again stops short, saying he had only been testing Gawain's nerve. Gawain tells his tormentor to strike and be done with it. The Green Knight raises the axe a third time, but the blow only nicks Gawain's neck. With his obligation fulfilled, Gawain draws his sword to defend himself. The Green Knight then explains that he is Sir Bertilak. The whole event was staged by the elderly woman, who is the sorceress Morgan le Fay, and he and his wife had acted in concert to test their guest. Gawain has earned his reprieve by refusing her advances, but the slight wound on the neck is for accepting the sash. Gawain is ashamed of his bad faith and wants to return the sash, but the Green Knight tells him to keep it. Gawain agrees to wear it as a reminder of his shame, but, on his return to Camelot, the knights at the court of Arthur decide to all wear such a garment as a reminder of Gawain's adventure.[6]

Life in the Middle Ages was pervaded by a sense of the miraculous, but there were still practical limits to what one might accept, and late medieval storytellers such as the Gawain Poet might play with them ironically. The initial entry of the Green Knight into Arthur's court blends terror with a touch of comedy. His sudden appearance and his challenge are so outlandish that perhaps the knights may be initially too stunned to respond. Especially since the Green Knight poses no threat, common sense would be to decline the challenge.

The Green Knight appears in literature almost as mysteriously as he does at King Arthur's court in the story, with no clear model or precedent. He has some resemblance to many other figures of medieval lore, including Jack in the Green, wild men and Robin Hood, but he cannot be unequivocally identified with any of these. The author of *Sir Gawain and the Green Knight* must certainly have seen many images in English

Illustration showing Al-Khadr from Mughal India, *c.* 1760.
He is traditionally depicted riding on a fish to show his intimacy
with water, which is a foundation of life.

churches of Green Men emerging from the sculpted foliage, dressed in leaves and with more leaves growing from their mouths. They could have influenced his conception of the Green Knight, even though such foliage is absent from that figure. The connection of the Green Knight with vegetation lies only in his colour and his regenerative powers.

One theory is that the ultimate model for the Green Knight could be Al-Khadr, an ancient figure from Arab culture, probably a vegetation deity that was incorporated into Islamic folklore. He may go back to Utnapishtim, also the original of the biblical figure of Noah, in the *Epic of Gilgamesh*, who survived a great flood with his family and then was granted immortality. Al-Khadr wears green robes and is sometimes green himself. According to one legend, he drank from the Spring of Life, and so grass springs up wherever he treads. He is traditionally identified with an unnamed sage who accompanies Moses in the Quran, and he often functions as an emissary of supernatural powers.[7]

Fairy Tales

Sir Gawain and the Green Knight is a blend of many traditional genres. In many ways, it seems closer to a fairy tale than a knightly epic. Knightly epics generally have more linear plots in which every event is distinct and leads directly to the next. Fairy tales are often structured around repetitions, especially in groups of three – three tasks, three trials or three nights.[8] In the case of Gawain, he must resist the advances of his hostess three times. Meanwhile, the lord of the castle goes hunting three times and, at the end of the day, each must give the other what he has received. Lady Bertilak gives Gawain three kisses, which he passes on to her husband. Later, the Green Knight aims three strikes with his axe at Gawain's neck, checking his blow each time.

In spite of massive scholarship, fairy tales remain a mystery. They started being recorded in increasing frequency in the early modern period, and they first became an object of serious study with *Tales for the Hearth and Home*, edited and collected by Jacob and Wilhelm Grimm. The first edition was published in 1812–15. The book was later revised and expanded by Wilhelm alone, who devoted increasingly more attention to adapting the tales for children and less to preserving them as artefacts of formal study. The book went through seven editions, the last of which was published in 1856–7. Wilhelm Grimm theorized that the tales went back to very remote times, but until recently the consensus of most scholars was that they were relatively modern. Recent research by Jashmid Tehrani and Sara da Silva, however, confirms that many are thousands of years old.[9] But the fairy-tale world of castles, dragons and witches is far more late medieval to early modern than ancient. The enchanted forest is, together with kings and princesses, part of a rhetoric of fairy tales that is especially characteristic of the Grimm Brothers but also found in the work of other collectors from the nineteenth century from Franz Schönwerth in Bavaria to Alexandr Afans'ev in Russia.

Sir Gawain and the Green Knight also differs from knightly epics in the way it deemphasizes martial skills and virtues. There is no combat involving Gawain, the Green Knight or anyone else in the poem. Possible conflicts are vaguely and humorously suggested in Gawain's journey to find the Green Chapel, but none are specified. In knightly epics, the protagonists are constantly fighting, sometimes against monsters and always against other knights. Gawain here, unlike most knights, does not devote himself to any lady other than Mary. He does not prove himself by winning a lady but rather by refusing the advances of one. Resisting Lady Bertilak does come across a bit like fighting a monster but only in a humorous sort of way. After resisting her temptations twice, Gawain succumbs, though only a little bit, by accepting the sash that he hopes may make him invulnerable.

In the poem, Gawain himself does not excel at martial skills. He does demonstrate physical courage, though not in battle. He does it by faithfully keeping his word. He turns out to be flawed, but his failing does not become an epic battle of sin and redemption. It is only a relatively minor failure of nerve. The author had doubtless grown a bit tired of macho posturing, which is a special fault of Gawain in many other knightly epics, and he was making gentle fun of it. His Gawain is much like the heroes of fairy tales, who are distinguished not so much by special abilities as by goodness of heart.[10] The status of Gawain as a knight seems almost incidental to the poem. Setting it in Arthur's court was a way of saying, 'Once upon a time'. It placed everything in an indefinite, romantic past, a time so magical and remote that it seemed the beginning of the world. The basic trajectory of Gawain's story is much like that of fairy tales, in which the protagonist leaves home as a youngster to prove him- or herself and return home as a mature adult. The major theme of most European fairy tales is coming of age.

Alchemy

In the Renaissance and early modern periods, alchemy was about transformations, especially that of common metals into gold. Closely aligned with that quest was the search for the Philosopher's Stone, which was said to have many mystical properties, and for the Elixir of Life, which could grant immortality. These pursuits were, however, not simply a matter of hunting for treasure or mixing chemicals, since the alchemists believed the goals could only be reached by somebody who had attained spiritual purity. They expressed physical and mental processes in terms of elaborate symbols and allegories, as fantastic as the late medieval marginalia yet less quirky and more mystical.

With regard to both content and style, there are many similarities between fairy tales and alchemical writings.[11] Alchemy, like storytelling, was a refined activity that cut across social divisions. Many artists from Pieter Bruegel the Elder to Jan Steen depicted alchemists from the lower, as well as the elevated, social strata. Their world resembled that of fairy

Philips Galle, after Pieter Bruegel the Elder, *The Alchemist*, after 1558, engraving. This alchemist works in a very crowded, squalid peasant domain, yet he refuses to heed the distractions and focuses on his work. Like many artists, he may come across as either heroic in his dedication or irresponsible.

tales, in which a simple villager might indeed marry, or at least dream of marrying, a prince or princess. Furthermore, alchemists tended to be very secretive and spoke of their discoveries using highly abstract symbols, rather like the fantastic images in fairy tales. Both alchemy and fairy tales generally view the cosmos as animistic. The alchemists believed that elements must suffer on the path to perfection; fairy tales are full of talking animals and even plants. Finally, alchemists shared a rare optimism with the tellers of fairy tales, which so often end with the protagonist living 'happily ever after'. They believed that all things were naturally on a journey towards perfection, just as base metals were destined to be transformed into gold. The alchemical processes paralleled the transformations of an individual soul as he or she approached ever nearer to God.

In yet another parallel between alchemy and fairy tales, beheading is often a means of disenchantment in folk literature, which allows the true self to emerge. This is the case, for example, in the Scottish tale 'The Well of the World's End', which is the oldest known version of Grimm's famous tale of 'The Frog King' (or Prince). At the enchanted frog's request, a young lady decapitates him, and he regains his human form.[12] The beheading game in the story of Sir Gawain could have been originally based on such a transformation, where a blow from the axe turns a bewitched knight into Sir Bertilak. The poet made the Green Knight, instead, into a shapeshifter whose true form, if he has any, remains unknown.[13]

Psychologist Joseph L. Henderson uses imagery of alchemy, intentionally or not, to describe the process of initiation into adulthood. For the subject, 'his identity is temporarily *dismembered* or *dissolved* in the collective unconscious. From this state he is then ceremonially rescued by the rite of the *new birth*' (my italics).[14] This seems to describe Gawain well; after the three strikes with the Green Knight's axe, he rises with renewed vigour. The process is not confined to young people coming of age. It may happen in a relatively dramatic way when one confronts a personal crisis, and takes place on a more modest scale when one simply walks through the woods. The self that one shows to 'the world' – that is, to other people – is placed in abeyance. Things like status and social position lose their meaning. Attention becomes divided among many strange and beautiful forms of life. The old self is reconstituted, perhaps a bit differently, as soon as one walks back to town.

The beheading game of *Sir Gawain and the Green Knight* first appears in the Old Irish tale of *Bricriu's Feast*, in which the celebration is held by the heroes of Ulster. Cú Chulainn has approximately the role of Gawain and Cú Raoi that of the Green Knight.[15] Cú Chulainn is the son of the sun. As late as 1485, probably over a hundred years after *Sir Gawain and the Green Knight*, Malory's *Morte d'Arthur* shows that the figure of Gawain still retained strong traces of that solar origin. We learn that Gawain's strength and belligerence, like the power of the sun, increased in the morning, remained at its height for three hours and began to wane at noon. At one point, when Arthur and Lancelot are at war, Gawain, who has sided with Arthur, challenges Lancelot to single combat. Lancelot accepts and then fights defensively until midday, at which point he attacks and gives Gawain several severe wounds, including one to the head. Gawain quickly recovers and then challenges Lancelot a second time, but with the same result. On recovery, he is about to issue a third challenge, but Arthur decides to retreat.[16] Gawain shows not only remarkable strength but recuperative powers, like those of the sun through the cycles of night and day as well as winter and summer.

The pentacle that decorates Gawain's shield in *Sir Gawain and the Green Knight* represents purity, gold and, by association, the sun. Decapitation, such as Gawain initially performs on the Green Knight, is a common symbol of the initial stage of purification in alchemy known as *Negredo*.[17] Both Gawain's decapitation of the Green Knight and the reciprocation after a year has passed take place approximately at the winter solstice, the time of the year when the sun is weakest and the nights are longest. It represents the death and rebirth of the sun in a new year.

The Green Chapel, which turns out to be the interior of an earthen mound, is a bit like an alchemical furnace. The three nights that Gawain spends in the castle suggest a repeated process in alchemy, probably three stages of purification of metals. The entire story recalls the symbol of the Green Lion, sometimes a Green Dragon, devouring the sun, which was an allegorical symbol of purification constantly used by alchemists.[18] The sun is the metal gold, while the green lion or dragon is sulphuric acid corroding its impurities. It also suggests the process we know as photosynthesis. This had not been scientifically identified, but it has always been easily apparent that plants crave sunlight, turn towards the sun and die if it is not available. The sun nourishes vegetation, and its blessing is never exhausted. According to Jonathan Hughes, 'the Green Knight is another manifestation of the *uroboros* or dragon, the spirit of sulfur or nature and a principle of the endless capacity of nature to renew itself.' The nick delivered to Gawain by the Green Knight could represent the removal of contaminations.[19]

The Green Lion devouring the Sun, from an alchemical and
rosicrucian compendium, *c.* 1760.

The ancient forest where the Green Knight lives represents the dark, primordial matter at the beginning of alchemical transformations. The holly sprig he holds in one hand and the axe he holds in the other as he first enters Arthur's court represent life and death respectively, yet both are ambivalent. The holly is a Christian symbol, in which the leaves are Christ's crown of thorns, while the berries are his blood. The axe, as any woodsman knows, not only brings down trees but stimulates new growth by creating openings for the sun. The Green Knight will initiate Gawain into the secrets of birth, death and resurrection.

Arthur Rackham, illustration of Hansel and Gretel encountering the wicked witch, 1909. Here, the hag seems not unlike the Russian Baba Yaga.

8

Lady of the Forest

Go out in the woods, go out. If you don't go out in the woods
nothing will ever happen and your life will never begin.
CLARISSA PINKOLA ESTÉS, *Women Who Run with the Wolves*

A stream of blood trickles from Gawain's neck. He jumps up, ready to fight, but the Green Knight serenely enlightens, praises and gently scolds Gawain. In a few lines, the Green Knight has gone from diabolical to almost godly, but he renounces any credit or blame. It was, the Knight explains, not he but the sorceress Morgan le Fay that orchestrated Gawain's adventure. She had sent him to Arthur's court in order to scare Guinevere, her adversary, to death, as well as to humble the Knights of the Round Table. The Green Knight calls Morgan a goddess, which Christians could take as blasphemous.

Gawain, it turns out, has had his life determined by the conflicts among powerful women who for the most part are less interested in him than in one another: Morgan, Guinevere, Lady Bertilak and his divine patron, Mary. Together with other women in the Arthurian cycle, they make up a feminine world. Collectively they are at least as powerful as their male counterparts, but their world only intersects with that of men occasionally, mostly through marriages and affairs. The power of the men is mostly worldly, exercised through force of arms. The power of the women is exercised though magic and intrigue.

The Arthurian epics constitute a literary rather than an oral tradition. The stories have been retold in epic poems countless times in English, French, German and other European languages. Nevertheless, they are full of figures that are reminiscent of folklore. In addition to al-Khadr in Islamic and the Green Men in Christian art, the Green Knight is reminiscent of the Wild Huntsman. His Hautdesert Castle where he stays resembles folkloric descriptions of fairyland, for it is a place of constant feasting and merry making yet pervaded by a sense of immense danger.

Nature usually, though by no means always, has been thought of as feminine, so perhaps the Arthurian women collectively represent the natural world. In European folklore and mythology, forest spirits connected with vegetation or with water are predominantly female. In Greco-Roman mythology, feminine woodland spirits include dryads, who live within trees but can leave them, and hamadryads, who perish if a tree is felled. The Ladies of the Lake in Arthurian tales resemble woodland spirits. They are roughly comparable to Greco-Roman water nymphs, Slavic rusalki, Serbian vilas, German nixies, the French Melusine and the mermaids of maritime culture. These are also powerful female spirits connected with bodies of water, which are dangerous yet often helpful to their favourites. In knightly epics of the High Middle Ages, the authors increasingly conflated the Fates, water nymphs, nixies, otherworldly lovers and other supernatural, feminine figures under the designation of 'fairies'.[1] In psychology, the forest is often interpreted as a symbol of 'unexplored femininity'.[2]

The figure of Morgan le Fay partakes of these myriad roles in literary works belonging to the Arthurian cycle. She is at times a Lady of the Lake, at times a shapeshifter. She can be a benign healer or a malign witch. She can be either Arthur's protectress or his adversary. The only constants in her character across the multitude of stories are her femininity and her enormous power. She is all things feminine, good or bad. Most of the time, she appears in the form of a youthful woman, but in *Sir Gawain and the Green Knight* she is a crone.

A similar figure associated with Gawain is the Loathly Lady in the story told by the Wife of Bath in Chaucer's *Canterbury Tales*, a shapeshifter who can be old and ugly or young and beautiful as it suits her purposes. Morgan also resembles the three Fates, who control the destiny of even the gods in Greco-Roman myth, or the Norns, their Norse equivalent. In Virgil's *Aeneid*, there is the Cumaean Sibyl, a wise, clairvoyant old woman who is destined to waste away until only her voice remains. Other crones with supernatural powers include the Norse Elli, who represents old age, and the Devil's Grandmother in Grimm's tale 'The three golden hairs of the Devil'. Benign variants include the Italian Befana, who brings gifts to children at Christmas, and the German Mother Holle, who is a guardian of young girls. Finally, there is the 'wicked witch' of Halloween who is usually shown smiling pleasantly and does not seem especially 'wicked' at all. The figure is feminine, as an embodiment of the natural world, and ancient, as befitting a primeval heritage. Why is Morgan depicted as an old woman in a story set near the beginning of Arthur's reign, a time when Gawain seems full of youthful promise and energy? The contrast dramatizes both the comparative innocence of Arthur's court and the primordial power of the enchantress.

Baba Yaga

One of the most elemental sorceresses in folklore is the Russian figure of Baba Yaga, described in detail in the story of 'Vasilisa the Beautiful', which was collected by Alexandr Afans'ev. Baba Yaga lives deep in the woods in a house propped up on chicken legs. Around it is a fence made of human bones, with skulls with gleaming eyes placed on spikes. The doors of her hut have human legs for posts and human hands for bolts. For a lock, she has a mouth with pointed teeth. She flies in a mortar, which she drives with a pestle, sweeping away the path behind her with a broom. She is old and hideous. She bakes people in her oven and eats them like chickens.[3] Though she has no husband or lover, Baba Yaga sometimes has daughters, which are much like herself. Some tales also make her the mother of toads, frogs, snakes, spiders, worms and other creepy crawlies.[4]

Terrifying as she may be, Baba Yaga will sometimes help those who come across her forest home. In his detailed study of the figure, Andreas Johns writes, 'Baba Yaga's manifold associations with nature have led many authors to interpret her as a metaphorical embodiment of natural forests, as a nature goddess or as a female totemic ancestor.' He adds that her fundamental ambivalence reflects our contradictory attitudes to the natural world.[5]

This is apparent in the darkly beautiful Russian story of 'Vasilisa the Beautiful'. Her dying mother has given Vasilisa a doll, telling her to keep it hidden, feed it and ask it for advice. A bit later, Vasilisa's father, a merchant, remarries. Her new stepmother brings two daughters from a former marriage, and all three are jealous of Vasilisa's beauty. They assign her to do all the household chores, but, unknown to them, these are taken care of by the doll.

One night when the merchant is away on business, according to a plan devised by the stepmother, a stepdaughter snuffs out the last candle in the house. The two stepdaughters then demand that Vasilisa go to Baba Yaga to get light. Reassured by her doll, Vasilisa goes deep into the forest until, one morning, she arrives at the hut of Baba Yaga. At that moment,

Ivan Bilibin, illustration of Baba Yaga for the tale
of 'Vasilisa the Beautiful', 1900.

the crone also arrives and announces that she can smell Russian flesh.
Vasilisa asks her for light, and Baba Yaga says that she can earn it by working at the house, but, should she refuse, Vasilisa will be eaten. Vasilisa
agrees, but the doll does most of the work. One day, Baba Yaga asked
Vasilisa how she gets so much done, and Vasilisa replies that it is through
the blessing of her mother. Baba Yaga says that she will have nobody that
is blessed in her house. She takes Vasilisa outside, gives her a skull with
bright eyes from one of the fence posts and sends her home.

Ivan Bilibin, illustration of Vasilisa holding a lighted skull
for the tale of 'Vasilisa the Beautiful', 1899.

When Vasilisa arrives, the house where she lived is completely dark. She learns from the stepmother that since her departure, no fire will stay kindled in the house. The stepmother takes the skull inside. The skull keeps the fire of its eyes focused on the stepmother and the two step-daughters. They try to hide, but the skull's eyes follow them until they are burned to death. Vasilisa buries the skull and goes to town in search of work the next day. An old woman gives her flax, and, with the help of her doll, Vasilisa spins it to create the finest linen. The old woman brings the fabric to the tzar, who is so impressed that he wants Vasilisa to make his shirts. Finally, Vasilisa marries the tzar and takes her father and the old woman to live with her in his palace. She keeps the doll with her for the rest of her life.[6]

Like many other fairy tales, this one not only has a heroine but takes place in a feminine realm. The active characters are all female: Vasilisa, her mother, her stepmother, her stepsisters, Baba Yaga and the old woman. The Russian word for doll, *kykla*, has a feminine gender, and the doll performs traditionally feminine tasks, so it is probably female as well. The father is entirely passive, and the tzar himself is only a trophy husband. This story illustrates how, in the realm of fairy tales, the forest represents the feminine domain.

As noted earlier, the origins of fairy tales remain elusive, in spite of massive scholarship. One theory, championed by the Russian folklorist Vladimir Propp, is that they go back to ritualistic initiation rituals, which became stories as they ceased to be practised.[7] According to Propp, the stories involve entrance to the world of the dead because initiation involves a symbolic death and rebirth. The rituals became stories when societies evolved from a foundation in hunting to one in agriculture.[8] This origin in an initiation would explain why so many fairy tales start with a young person who then leaves home, has adventures and finally returns to marry and take a place in the community. According to this theory, the forest represents both the land of the dead and the place of initiation.[9]

Propp maintained that fairy tales, or at least Afans'ev's collection of Russian fairy tales, can be reduced to a single story. It has seven character-roles and 31 episodes, which are always in the same order, though not every one of them may be found in a given tale.[10] But why would this tale be concealed in such a dazzling variety of ways? Why not simply tell the one story and be done with it? And if, as Propp believed, this initiatory structure goes back to remote times, why would it have remained constant millennia after the original meaning of the narrative had been lost?

But perhaps Propp was right about some tales, though not others. 'Vasilisa the Beautiful' certainly sounds like an initiation into feminine mysteries. This would explain why it, like many other fairy tales, seems to centre exclusively on female figures and why the father appears completely ignorant of what is going on.[11] The mother, the stepmother and old woman who helps Vasilisa seem to be different aspects of the same figure. Perhaps, as the mother, she gave Vasilisa a blessing and a doll but then ritualistically withdrew and, in the persona of a stepmother, had her daughter pushed out of the house to be initiated. On Vasilisa's return, she again helps her daughter, this time in the persona of an elderly friend. Finally, Vasilisa, together with her new husband, gives her mother, in the figure of the old woman, and father shelter in their old age.

Even more than in most fairy tales, the events in 'Vasilisa the Beautiful' seem stylized and theatrical. The scene where the candle is extinguished and Vasilisa is sent out into the woods, for example, sounds ritualistic. In this case, the story might even pertain to rituals that had not entirely ceased to be practised when it was written down. In the Rusalia festival, the Slavic day of the dead, as practised in Ukraine, the girls take straw dolls, probably like Vasilisa's, out into a field and then ceremonially defend them against their mothers in a series of dances.[12]

The bones around Baba Yaga's hut could refer to the many graves, even villages, that have been overgrown by the forest. The light that Vasilisa seeks could be the bioluminescence found in the forest, sometimes called foxfire or fairy fire. Many species of fungi give off their own light. The skull that Vasilisa brought home could even have been an illuminated mushroom.

Hansel and Gretel

The public has long regarded the tale of 'Hansel and Gretel' as a sort of paragon of the style of the Grimm Brothers. It features extremes of horror, particularly cannibalism and abandonment, but blends them with the paraphernalia of a fairly comfortable, middle-class life. It is set mostly in the forest, which is a place of terror, hope and enchantment. Of course, it has a happy ending.

At the beginning of the story, Hansel and Gretel are the children of a woodcutter. One night they overhear their father talking with their stepmother. She says that they are no longer able to feed the two children. She advises taking them into the woods and then abandoning them, after which they will starve or be eaten by wild animals. The husband resists the idea, but the wife insists until he finally agrees. When the adults have gone to sleep, Hansel steps outside and collects some glittering white stones.

The next morning, the parents lead the children out into the woods. Hansel keeps looking back at his home. He told his father that he is looking at his white kitten on the roof, but he is really dropping the pebbles on the ground. The woodcutter and his wife build a fire for the children, give them crusts of bread and then leave, but the children find their way back home by following the trail of pebbles.

A second time, the children overhear their parents at night, planning to take them even deeper into the woods and abandon them. Once again, Hansel tries to go out to collect pebbles, but he finds the door has been locked. As they leave, he scatters breadcrumbs instead. Once again, he turns to look back at his home and, when questioned by his father, says he is looking at his pet dove on the roof. Once more, the father and stepmother abandon their children, but this time, when the brother and sister try to find their way back home, they find that birds have eaten the trail of breadcrumbs.

The children follow a beautiful white bird, which leads them to a little house in the woods, which has walls of bread, a roof of cake and windows of sugar. They have begun to eat it when an old woman comes out. They start to run away, but she invites them in, gives them a fine meal and leads them to their beds.

But it turns out that the old woman is really a witch, and the house is a trap that she uses to lure children to cook and eat. The next day, she places Hansel in a pen. The witch makes Gretel into her servant, assigned to fatten Hansel up until he is ready to eat. She gives Hansel fine foods, while Gretel remains near starvation. Each day, the witch tells Hansel to stick out a finger so she can tell if he is fat enough to eat, but he holds out a chicken bone instead, and the witch, who cannot see well, decides to wait.

Finally, she loses her patience and decides to eat Hansel regardless of whether he has put on weight or not. She tells Gretel to light the oven and boil water in preparation and to crawl into the oven to see if it is hot enough. The witch is planning to bake and eat the girl as well as her brother, but Gretel says that she does not know how to check the oven. To demonstrate, the witch sticks her head into the oven, at which Gretel pushes her in completely and shuts the door. As the witch burns to death, Gretel releases Hansel. They take precious jewels and pearls from the witch's house and return home. Their stepmother has died, and, with their new wealth, the children and their father live happily.[13]

This fairy tale has been compared to that of 'Tom Thumb', where the protagonist enters the home of an ogre, kills him and takes his riches.[14] I am pretty certain, however, that 'Hansel and Gretel' is a version of 'Vasilisa the Beautiful'. The hero of the tale is Gretel, who takes the lead after the children are kidnapped and tricks the witch, while Hansel, who initially took the initiative by dropping stones on the path, becomes passive. Hansel has a subordinate role similar to that of Vasilisa's doll. In both tales, the father is completely passive. In both tales, the cannibalistic witch lives deep in the forest in a strangely built hut with an oven for baking people. The chicken bone that Hansel sticks out to show that he has not become fat may even be a remnant of Baba Yaga's association, and that of her victims, with chickens. Vasilisa involuntarily leaves home in search of light, while Gretel and Hansel are sent away for lack of food, but the tales are united by the theme of abandonment in a forest full of mystery, danger and opportunity.

Perhaps the strongest indication that the wicked witch was originally Baba Yaga is the way that Gretel tricks her. The same basic event takes place in the Russian tale 'Baba Yaga and the Brave Youth' in the collection by Afans'ev. In this story, Baba Yaga has a daughter, whom she has directed to cook a brave youth. The girl tells the youth to get in a pan. He does so but places one foot on the floor and the other on the ceiling, and so the pan cannot be moved. The daughter tells him that is not the right way, and he asks her to show him how. She then lies down in the pan and the brave youth shoves her into the oven. Baba Yaga returns a bit later and eats her daughter.[15] Analogous events occur in many other Baba Yaga tales.[16] But, unlike Baba Yaga in the tale of 'Vasilisa the Beautiful', the wicked witch in 'Hansel and Gretel' seems entirely evil.

The tale of Vasilisa is far more integrated into a body of folklore than that of the abandoned brother and sister, and it is probably older. 'Hansel and Gretel' has many suggestions of a comfortable middle-class life, which seem incongruous in the narrative of a starving labourer. Hansel has a pet cat and a dove, though keeping pets did not become widespread until the rise of the middle classes in the early modern and modern eras. The emphasis on feelings makes the style of Grimm's tale closer to that of a novella of the era of sensibility than to traditional folk literature.

The stories we have been looking at take place within, or at least on the periphery of, a feminine domain, with its own distinctive values, tales, skills, rivalries, expectations, rituals and even kinds of power. It is parallel to, and occasionally intersects with, the male domain. This is easily apparent in 'Vasilisa the Beautiful' but far less so in 'Hansel and Gretel'. One may understand this as progress, deterioration or simply change, but this feminine realm begins to disintegrate as we enter the modern era. What had been the male domain acquired a new universality, leaving women with an increasingly subordinate status. But a nostalgia for the feminine world remained, and it was felt by both women and men.

Woman of the Woods

The cognates for 'forest' in different languages have varying etymologies and associations, and they are not perfectly translatable. The Latin *silva*, which was commonly used in most of Europe until the early modern era, is feminine. So is the French *forêt*, but the German *Wald* and the Russian *les* are masculine. As to the figures that personify the forest, these may also be masculine, like Humbaba, or feminine, like Baba Yaga.

As Europeans became progressively more urban, the forest came to represent the Other, which for the masculine contingent meant the feminine. The forest was a sort of primeval womb out of which civilization emerged. From the viewpoint of toxic masculinity, that has meant the forest became something to be conquered or subdued, an attitude often taken by European settlers in recently discovered parts of the world. They were sometimes referred to as virgin, covertly suggesting that despoiling the forests was a bit like deflowering a girl or even rape.

But the forest was also a sort of graveyard in which villages and even entire civilizations would eventually be buried. It was a place of secrets, hauntings and feminine mysteries. A sorceress living in the remote depths of the forest became a common theme in romantic literature, especially in Germany. A major source is the late medieval legend of the knight Tannhäuser. In the version recorded by the Brothers Grimm, he rides through a remote area and visits a mountain that is the abode of the goddess Venus. After staying for a while, he feels guilty and homesick. Tannhäuser resolves to leave. Venus does all she can to persuade him to stay, even offering him one of her ladies for a wife, but Tannhäuser is unmoved. He goes to the pope to confess his sins and do penance, but the pontiff tells Tannhäuser that he will only be forgiven when papal staff sprouts green leaves. The knight leaves in dejection, but, three days later, the staff actually begins to blossom. Papal envoys search for Tannhäuser, but it is too late, for he has returned to the mountain.[17]

The story is about the conflict between chivalry, with its veneration of femininity, and the more severely patriarchal forms of Christianity. The sorceress is identified as a Greco-Roman deity, but the location in a remote forest and the motif of the dead staff sprouting suggest a more indigenous goddess of fertility, perhaps not unlike Morgan le Fay.[18] In legends and romantic works of literature, she may appear old or young. In 'Der Runenberg' (The Rune Mountain), a story by Ludwig Tieck, these two images shade into one another. She is an ancient maiden or youthful crone.

At the beginning of the story, a young man named Christian has become frustrated with domestic life in his native village and, instead of being a gardener like his father, has become a hunter. One day, he grows despondent and, almost without awareness, pulls up a mandrake root. He hears a piteous call, as though all of nature were lamenting, and starts to run away, but then he sees a stranger standing beside him. They talk pleasantly for a while, and the stranger directs him to a ruined castle on a mountain in the woods.

As Christian walks towards the castle, the path grows ever wilder and more perilous. Finally, he comes to a window. Looking through it, he sees a spacious hall adorned with crystals and minerals. Within it is a tall, powerful-looking woman with a severe, otherworldly sort of beauty. She sings, invoking archaic spirits, undresses and then strides about the hall, with her long hair flowing about her body. She takes a jewelled tablet and gazes at it for a while. Then she walks up to Christian, opens the window, hands him the tablet and says, 'Take this in remembrance of me.' Christian grasps it in a reverie and hurries away. At dawn, he finds himself on a distant hillside and the tablet has vanished.

He returns to his village, settles down, marries, has a child, farms and lives very happily for a time. One day, a figure approaches, who at first seems to be the stranger from the mountain, but, when she comes closer, he recognizes her as a hideous old crone. She asks a few questions about him in a terrifying voice and then reveals herself to be the Woman of the Woods. As she walks away, Christian sees the powerful limbs of the woman seen through the window at Runenberg Castle, for all three had been a single figure. Later, Christian feels irresistibly drawn to her, finds the Woman of the Woods by climbing down an abandoned mine shaft and leaves his family to do her bidding by collecting gems in the earth.

The statuesque beauty with skin like marble is clearly the Venus of the Tannhäuser legend, yet here she is more primeval than the deities of the Greeks and Romans. Christian is drawn to her by neither love nor lust but by a recognition of the vastness of nature, in which every stone or tree has a voice, and the smallness of human civilization. He cannot be a farmer or a gardener for, since pulling up the mandrake, he understands the laments of plants.

Serious literature, in fact art in general, often presents us with a vast perspective in which most of our everyday concerns, together with the vanities that accompany them, can easily be reduced to insignificance. They reveal that what we think of as 'common sense' is mostly an illusion. This entails many hazards. People might think the artist is arrogant, and they might be right. Even more seriously, this entails a sort of alienation, which can slide into callousness towards others or disorientation. Is Christian at the end of the story a shaman, a madman or a monster? That is left to the reader to decide.

Josef Freiherr von Eichendorff, a poet of the German woods, was able to maintain a delicate balance between the terror, calm and exhilaration that the forests inspired. In a poem entitled 'Waldgespräch' (Forest Conversation), Eichendorff tells of a figure much like the Woman of the Woods:

> Es ist schon spät, es wird schon kalt,
> Was reit'st du einsam durch den Wald?
> Der Wald ist lang, du bist allein,
> Du schöne Braut! Ich führ' dich heim!

> 'Groß ist der Männer Trug und List,
> Vor Schmerz mein Herz gebrochen ist,
> Wohl irrt das Waldhorn her und hin,
> O flieh! Du weißt nicht, wer ich bin.'

> So reich geschmückt ist Roß und Weib,
> So wunderschön der junge Leib,
> Jetzt kenn' ich dich – Gott steh' mir bei!
> Du bist die Hexe Lorelei.

> 'Du kennst mich wohl – von hohem Stein
> Schaut still mein Schloß tief in den Rhein.
> Es ist schon spät, es wird schon kalt,
> Kommst nimmermehr aus diesem Wald!'[19]

> It's getting late and growing cold.
> Why are you riding through the wood?
> The wood is vast; you are alone.
> Oh, pretty bride, I'll take you home.

'It broke my heart to learn how men
Will lie, deceive and cheat, and when
A hunting horn sounds through the trees
I think on that, and you should flee.'

A lovely woman on a horse
Bedecked with glittering gems. Of course.
God protect me! Now confess
You're Lorelei, the sorceress.

'Indeed I am. You've also seen
My castle high above the Rhein.
It's getting late and growing cold,
And you will never leave this wood.'

Lorelei was originally a *femme fatale* who led men to their doom, appearing in a poem Clemens Brentano wrote and then passed off as a folk ballad. Here she becomes a witch, as well as an embodiment of the forest with its dangers and seductive beauty. The rider, on encountering her, imagines that she is helpless and he is in control, but he quickly learns that she is vastly more powerful than he. Will she kill him? Will she imprison him? Can he escape? Is she a hallucination? We are left to guess. The melodrama is softened by the slightly prosaic title, 'Forest Conversation', which suggests that this is something heard in the rustling of leaves. The poem is a dialogue between humankind, with its hubris, and nature, which may seem utterly vulnerable but is much more powerful than people in the end.

The Mother Tree

Whether they see forests as places of danger or salvation, people have generally regarded the woods as female. This is implicit in the concept of the mother tree, developed by Suzanne Simard, a scientist who has done important work in showing how forest trees exchange nutrients and information through networks of mycorrhizal fungi. The term refers to an old tree that becomes the centre of a complex web of fungal species and nourishes the surrounding forest.[20] The mother tree, for her, is the oldest tree in the surrounding area, one that has survived times of adversity such as forest fires, infestations and drought.

This arboreal matriarch passes on wisdom to both her family and community.

But why a 'mother tree' rather than a 'father tree' or a 'parent tree'? Most of the trees she discusses have both male and female reproductive organs. In her autobiography, *Finding the Mother Tree*, Simard moves within a predominantly female world, working mostly with female colleagues and students as well as raising her two daughters. While her account never sounds hostile to men, all of them seem to hover on the fringes of a female community that they are either unwilling or unable to fully join. Simard constantly contrasts the old view of the male forestry establishment of trees engaged in competition with her own discoveries that trees nurture one another in families and even across lines of species. She upholds the mother tree not only as a discovery but as an ideal. For her, the forest is a matriarchy, a perspective that has ample foundation in tradition.

In his recent novel *The Overstory*, Richard Powers dramatizes the discoveries of Simard. It tells the interconnected stories of people and trees. The mother tree is a directionless college student, Olivia Vandergriff, who has been electrocuted, dies of heart failure and is then revived. Reborn, she is able to understand the voices of trees and becomes the leader of a band of eco-warriors. Together with an activist named Nick Hoel, she spends a year up in a redwood, preventing loggers from cutting it down. When finally forced to descend, she and her friends plan to destroy the logging equipment, but she is killed in an accidental explosion. The group burn her body and disperse, taking only their memories, like the seeds of a perished tree.[21] To me at least, Olivia and her group seem too slight, and the plot too contrived, to comfortably bear comparisons with ancient forests. But any Lady of the Forest will have a hard time living up to Baba Yaga or Morgan le Fay.

9

Classical, Rococo and Gothic Woods

Trees and plants always look like the people they live with, somehow.

ZORA NEALE HURSTON

The end of the Roman Empire could hardly have been more different from the apocalypse predicted in the Bible. There had been no grand battle between the armies of the Lord and the Devil. There had been no dragon knocking a third of the stars from the sky with its tail. There had been no Beast with seven heads emerging from the sea to blaspheme God. Rome had fallen gradually, in a way that seemed many centuries later to have been almost peaceful. Medieval painters had often suggested a tranquil transition to a new era by placing manger scenes in the ruins of a pagan temple. The apocalyptic expectations of early Christianity gave way to a more cyclic view of time, ruled by a rhythm of ascent and decline that seemed steady enough to soften the terrors of history – sometimes, at least.

In Europe, as in the entire world, the long-term trend has been towards gradual deforestation, but this has been far from unbroken. The extent of forests has constantly diminished or increased, depending on factors such as human population, technologies and patterns of settlement. Forests have spread in times of prolonged wars and famines, while they have decreased during those of relative prosperity. In Europe, they were initially increased by the fall of the Roman Empire and the Plague of Justinian, but, towards the end of the Middle Ages, there was a rapid increase in deforestation.[1] This was temporarily reversed as the bubonic plague killed over a third of the population of Europe in the mid-fourteenth century, but the forests declined again as the population recovered.[2] With industrialization, the exploitation of forests became linked to cycles of the economy, increasing in times of expansion and declining during recessions.[3] The European forests expanded, or at least stabilized, once more in the latter nineteenth through early twentieth

149

James Duffield Harding, *View of the Triumphal Arch of Augustus, Aosta*, 1850,
engraving. The pagan monument has been first transformed into a church
and later left to fall into ruin. The herders who work serenely in its shadow are,
in a sense, heirs to the Roman conquerors.

Eugène Lami, *The Grand Waterworks, Versailles*, 1844, engraving.
The palace of Versailles was intended as a demonstration of human mastery
of the elements, and a massive array of pumps even reversed the course of a stream.
By the mid-19th century, much of this aspiration remains, but the trees in the
background have been allowed to grow back with little control to a point where
they begin to ominously overshadow the artificial creations.

Peter Lely, *Elizabeth Wriothesley, Countess of Northumberland*, 1665–9, oil on canvas. The countess is probably pointing to her aristocratic manor. She stands in a dense forest, which is intended to dramatize the antiquity of her domain. Beside her is a ruin of a pillar, likely fake, that represents her storied lineage.

centuries for several reasons, including the migration of people to the New World, urbanization and the replacement of wood with coal for heating. The military and economic devastation of the two world wars led to another reduction in European forests,[4] which began to recover in the latter twentieth century.

At times the regeneration of forests was spontaneous, but often trees were planted to show the prestige of the owners or in commemoration of events. Kings and nobles would plant allées of trees leading up to the entrance of their residences, not only to shade the road but for dramatic emphasis. They would preserve especially large trees to dramatize the antiquity of their line of descent. These were stage scenery, designed to focus attention on the palace, where great events took place.

By the seventeenth century landscaping on a massive scale had become a preoccupation of royalty and aristocracy. From the Renaissance palaces of families such as the Medici to Versailles, these had dramatized human supremacy over the environment. Gardens were laid out in neatly symmetrical patterns and many of the trees were topiary, deliberately shaped to look as unnatural as possible. By the eighteenth century landscaping had become more subtle and discreet. Nature was no longer an adversary to be conquered but a potential ally. Forests seemed to embody the glamour and authority that came with great age, which could consecrate institutions from noble houses to republics. Rather than being openly proclaimed, messages about status and power were at least partially concealed, making them appear to be mandated by natural law. The forests were managed to reflect changing fashions, politics, artistic styles and philosophies.

As the power of royalty and aristocracy declined, the symbolism of forests was taken over by the growing middle class. The spectacle of forests reclaiming human structures had long become a familiar one. For Europeans, the images resonated with growing, if only half-articulated, fears that the innovations of the modern era might lead to an apocalyptic disaster.

The Forest and History

Giambattista Vico, the son of a Neapolitan bookseller, grew up in the eighteenth century surrounded by reminders of history. He thoroughly studied the Roman classics in their original Latin, the language in which he wrote his early works. He saw Roman ruins not as a tourist but almost every day, to a point where he might have noted their decay from year to year.

Vico articulated a cyclical theory of history, in which civilization first emerges out of the forests, succumbs to them and then emerges again. His book *The New Science*, first published in 1725, recounts a history of civilization. This begins after the expulsion of Adam and Eve from Eden as forests cover the earth, and the descendants of the first couple wander through them like wild beasts. They can hardly see in front of themselves, for the dense trees block their view, and so they can form no society. They are ruled by appetite and copulate indiscriminately. Since they are entirely orientated to the physical world, they become giants.

First comes the Age of Gods. The only direction in which the view of the giants is not obstructed by trees is upwards, and so they gaze at the sky. Like the arches of a Gothic cathedral, the trees direct the eye of the viewer upwards towards the abode of God. They see lightning bolts, which seem to be a manifestation of Jove. Utterly terrified, the giants take refuge in caves, and human society begins to form, with religion, marriage and burial of the dead. Then comes the Age of Heroes. People burn down the forests and plant fields. Warriors such as Hercules and Achilles have adventures, and bards such as Homer lay the poetic foundation for human culture. Last comes the Age of Men, when people settle in cities and try to order their society on the foundation of reason. Social bonds gradually decay until the society is destroyed by natural disasters, wars and decadence. Forests reclaim the land, and the cycle begins again. The major example used by Vico is the Flood. Of the sons of Noah, Japheth and Ham wandered the reforested earth and degenerated into a bestial state. Only some sons of Shem, the Hebrews, retained their civilization.[5]

The work of Vico remained little known for several decades but became influential in the Romantic era through the attention paid to it by Herder in Prussia, Coleridge in England and Michelet in France. Vico thought poetically, largely in images, which enabled his ideas to penetrate European culture unobtrusively yet so intimately that one can never tell where his influence begins and ends. There were loose copyright regulations in the eighteenth century, but mental images are usually passed on unconsciously. The dark forest of human origins; Jove in the form of lightning glimpsed through the trees; early people huddling in caves: such images from Vico would appear in art, science and literature, usually with no suggestion of their origin.

The idea that humanity originated from the forests is a modernization of Virgil's myth that the first human beings sprang from trees. The forest Vico speaks of, however, is itself a myth. People can easily see one another in forests, certainly enough to form social bonds, as the cultures of forest dwellers from Australia to Africa and the Americas demonstrate. Particularly in an old forest, the understorey is usually not very dense, and there is plenty of room between the trunks of trees. By contrast, it is the sky that may be hard to see through a dense canopy.

It is also not true that the forest is the primeval landscape to which abandoned land must necessarily revert. Growth of trees may be inhibited by climate, soil, herbivores, fires and so on. There are also taigas, grasslands, swamps, deserts and landscapes that elude easy classification. The forest of origin that Vico imagines is akin to that of Tacitus' *Germania* or Dante's dark wood. It is, briefly, an image of primeval chaos. Nevertheless, he envisioned the dark, primeval forest as a place of hope.

Vico articulated a mythic conception, already partly implicit in European culture, of the forest as a primal origin, a condition out of which civilization first arises and into which it finally decays. The stages he identified were not, however, consecutive but simultaneous, as the three stages of civilization might appear simultaneously in different parts of the world. The forest becomes an indicator of the status of a civilization. As Chateaubriand is reputed to have said, 'The forests precede human beings and the deserts follow them.'[6] As Vico was writing, different conceptions of the forest were starting to emerge in Europe. This was not primarily due to Vico's influence, which was always confined to a small part of the intelligentsia. It was also probably not a matter of conscious intent on Vico's part. But the Gothic forest in art and literature corresponded roughly to what he called the Age of Gods, the Classical forest to the Age of Heroes and the Rococo forest to the Age of Men.

The Classical Forest

By the seventeenth century sheep and cattle grazed peacefully in the overgrown ruins of the Colosseum, where gladiators had fought and animals had been slaughtered. The cities of Pompeii and the recently discovered Herculaneum, not far from Naples, had a more grandly apocalyptic end, destroyed by lava from an erupting volcano. Tourism, especially among artists, was growing in popularity, and Naples was second only to Rome as the favourite destination. The sights were not heavily commercialized, fenced off, restored or maintained. There were no tour guides to provide a running commentary and hurry groups along. The experience was leisurely and contemplative. Sites were simply left to ever so slowly decay as herders and other labourers went about their daily tasks in the ruins.

Claude Lorraine (often referred to in the English-speaking world as 'Claude'), a foremost landscape painter of Southern Europe, was born in France but spent most of his life in Rome, where he painted landscapes of Rome and Campagnia, the region where Naples is located, in the soft light of dusk or dawn. His landscapes featured ruins where Greco-Roman deities or idealized peasants went about their tasks. His painting *Landscape with Nymph and Satyr Dancing* (1641) may use figures from ancient myth, but the temple in the foreground is abandoned and overgrown with vegetation. Were these figures gods shown as peasants? Or peasants as gods? The paintings depict almost no historical events that might be dated, so they seem to be outside of time, as though the Roman Empire had not really fallen at all.

Neapolitan peasants, with their dances, colourful clothes, songs and folklore, were themselves becoming an object of endless fascination for the European intelligentsia. Campagnia was, and still is, notoriously poor. It was subject not only to volcanic eruptions but plagues, earthquakes

Claude Lorrain, *Landscape with Nymph and Satyr Dancing*, 1641, oil on canvas.

and severe storms. Nevertheless, artists who were passing through painted the peasants as youthful, healthy and carefree. They might be the heirs, even the direct descendants, of mighty Roman patricians or generals, yet seemed to wear that distinction lightly.

Most frequently, peasants were depicted herding sheep, an activity that had remained essentially unchanged since at least the time of Homer. This occupation established a continuity between the ancient and contemporary worlds. The peasants represented the force of nature reclaiming the abandoned temples, palaces and amphitheatres. The sights around Rome and Naples were as much a reminder of the transience of human accomplishments as of a glorious past. But the Neapolitan peasants also represented the future. These were 'primitive' people who had once built a great city and conquered much of the known world, and perhaps they might one day rise again. Rome, often called 'the eternal city', seemed to exist in mythic time, where the distinction between past and future could fade into insignificance.[7]

Claude's contemporary, the painter Salvator Rosa (known as Salvator), has often been considered his antithesis, yet they had a great

Claude Lorrain, *Dancers and Musicians before Village with Ruined Tower,*
c. 1630–60, pen and ink drawing.

deal in common. Salvator, who spent most of his life in Rome and Naples,
painted the same heavily wooded, rocky landscapes with ruins from
antiquity and diminutive human figures. But Claude showed them
against tranquil skies while Rosa often preferred threatening ones.
Rather than peasants, Rosa often painted bandits or soldiers. For critics
of the eighteenth and nineteenth centuries, Claude epitomized the
Classical landscape, Rosa the Romantic; Claude was a master of the
'beautiful', Salvator of the 'sublime'.[8] But these were simply sides, or
perhaps stages, of a single progression.

Pietro Fabris, *View of Mergellina and the Palazzo Donn'Anna Beyond, Naples*, 1777, oil on canvas. Depicted in the scene are fishermen drawing their catch, peasants grilling fish and other figures conversing.

Salvator Rosa, *Bandits on a Rocky Coast*, 1655–60, oil on canvas.

The Rococo Forest

An elegantly dressed young woman on a swing ascending towards the forest canopy kicks one leg, tossing her shoe far away. This is a deliberate act, not an accident. Her expression is one of careful concentration. Her eyes are fixed on the shoe, which she may even have carefully aimed. Below her a young man, also elaborately dressed, has been hiding, or pretending to hide, though she is clearly aware of his presence. By kicking upwards, she is giving him a fleeting glimpse of her leg. A bit higher, a statue of Cupid, which is so naturalistic that it appears alive, is enjoining silence with his fingers to his lips. Below her is a statue of two cherubs. In the distance is a shadowy figure of a man controlling the swing with ropes.

The lost shoe may be a perhaps slightly ironic motif taken from the story of 'Cinderella' as told by Charles Perrault, where the heroine loses a shoe as she leaves the ball, giving the prince a means to search for her. The shoe in the painting is an offering to the young man, who can now look for the shoe in the forest, find it and pursue her to give it back. Perhaps the reader has by now realized that this scene is from the picture entitled *Happy Hazards of the Swing* by Jean-Honoré Fragonard, painted in 1767.[9] Alongside Jean-Antoine Watteau and François Boucher, Fragonard was a major painter of the French Rococo.

The Rococo forest first appears in the fairy tales of Charles Perrault, *Histoires ou contes du temps passé* (Tales of Times Past), published in 1697. In 1663 he became employed by Jean-Baptiste Colbert, the powerful minister of finance to the French king Louis XIV, who, on purely economic grounds, expressed profound concern about the decline of the French forests. In part to emphasize their cultural importance as a royal and aristocratic heritage, Perrault set many of his tales in an enchanted forest,[10] most famously his versions of 'Sleeping Beauty' and 'Little Red Riding Hood'. He also established a Rococo ambience by adopting a playful, ironic tone. Like most of his protagonists, Cinderella seems to be from the nobility. While some of his characters become temporarily impoverished, none ever seems to have a profession or make a living by any means other than privileged status.

Following the directions of her fairy godmother, Cinderella finds the objects that will bestow glamour upon her not in a forest but in a garden, yet in context, there is little difference between the two. Both forest and garden are extensions of the royal or noble domain. The fairy godmother transforms her pumpkin into a coach, mice into carriage

Jean-Honoré Fragonard, *The Happy Hazards of the Swing*, c. 1767–8, oil on canvas.

Jacques Firmin Beauvarlet, after François Boucher, *Fishing* and *Hunting*,
18th century, engravings with watercolour. French artists of the Rococo made
activities in the forest into erotic games, even when the subjects were children.

horses, a rat into a coachman and lizards into footmen. At the ball, the
prince falls in love with Cinderella, but she must run away at midnight
when the magic will expire, leaving behind the shoe with which the
prince can find her.[11]

The Rococo style of painting was initially centred on the Gallic aristocracy during the reign of Louis xv in the early eighteenth century. The
French had been exhausted, emotionally and financially, by the incessant
wars and ambitious building projects of his predecessor, Louis xiv, and
aristocrats wanted to have a little fun. The Rococo adapted the practices
of Classical landscape painters such as Claude to an environment that
was more opulent and values that were less severe.

The peasants and deities of Classical landscapes were replaced by
young ladies and gentlemen of the high aristocracy. Instead of making
music or tending sheep, the subjects of French Rococo paintings would
be engaged in mildly erotic games. They might be swinging, playing blind
man's bluff or playing hide and seek. Often, they were picnicking or
simply flirting among the trees. They would not be dressed in Classical
simplicity but in the elaborate fashions of the court, which included
powdered wigs.

Instead of genuine ruins from antiquity, there would be expensive imitations of them in the background. These included many statues of pagan deities, especially of Venus and Cupid, cherubs and marble pillars that held nothing up. Far from appearing antique, the statues were often painted almost as human beings, observing and even discreetly participating in the scene. Activities such as fishing and hunting were used as metaphors for courtship or seduction.

The forests were elaborately landscaped estates next to sumptuous gardens. The mood was indeed playful, though with a sort of gaiety that can only come with great security. The content might also be rebellious but only mildly, for the erotic transgressions were at least as conventionalized as any elements of decorum. Love might be a sort of game, but it was one with many rules, some unspoken, which those not raised in the aristocracy would never hope to understand. The poses were theatrical, seemingly spontaneous yet obviously contrived. The compositions were based on organic curves, flowing lines which united human beings and vegetation. More than anything else, this was an eroticized vision of the woods. The setting among monumental trees helped make a code of etiquette that was so intricate that even aristocrats could feel stifled by it, seem natural.

Albert Henry Payne, after Daniel Chodowiecki, *Blind Man's Bluff*, 19th century, engraving.

Jean-Antoine Watteau, *The Shepherds*, c. 1717, oil on canvas. The couples dancing on the right and playing on a swing on the left are aristocrats, who appear very conspicuous on account of their elaborate dress and cultivated manners. They are playing at being shepherds and shepherdesses, but the other men and women are the genuine article. Watteau was by far the most subtle and perceptive of the French Rococo painters, and he is gently commenting on the futility of aristocratic games.

The Rococo style was very limited. The incessant playfulness could easily seem trivial. The image of eternal adolescence could be charming but also bleak. A touch of gravity is added by the forest itself. For all their artifice, the gardens were often overgrown, and the dark boughs could seem ominous, especially against a cloudy sky. For us, with the advantage of hindsight, they can even suggest a foreshading of the French Revolution, which put a final end to that world. There is just a hint in these paintings of the Gothic forest, the uncontrollable profusion of vegetation that is precariously held at bay. The sombre trees are a recognition, perhaps unconscious, that the rarefied atmosphere of the paintings cannot last.

The style spread to England, where artists such as Thomas Gainsborough and Joshua Reynolds muted the initial playfulness but painted portraits of aristocratic subjects against a background of wooded estates. The Rococo style went on to influence interior design throughout Europe and North America, particularly in the love of elaborate, whimsical and anthropomorphic decoration.

The Gothic Forest

The Gothic forest appears in literature slightly later than the Rococo, and its emergence corresponds roughly with the industrial revolution. 'Gothic' is originally, and most fundamentally, a style of the late Middle Ages in Northern and Central Europe. It culminated in the high arches of cathedrals, which are like trees forming a forest canopy. The term is used more broadly for art or literature where the mood is one of mystery, enchantment, passion, high drama and terror. The Gothic woods are dark, ancient and forbidding. They may at first seem uninhabited, but whoever wanders into them may find ruins or huts, often in the most desolate parts. They are inhabited by nymphs, witches, ghosts, giants, dwarves and other supernatural creatures, in addition to hermits and thieves. Such woods, as we have already seen, formed the settings of knightly epics. They are most closely identified with the fairy tales of the Brothers Grimm, who used forests as a setting somewhat in the manner of Charles Perrault but made them into a domain of the middle classes and the peasantry. Rather than Perrault's tone of playful irony, the Grimms told most of their stories with great earnestness, no matter how fantastical they were.

Gothic novels often begin where medieval European romances ended, after an interlude of many centuries, as the protagonists discover ruins hidden in the forest and learn dark secrets about the past. In the novel *Romance of the Forest* by Ann Radcliffe, first published in 1791, the hero, Pierre de la Motte, glimpses an edifice between the trees. Approaching, he 'perceived the Gothic remains of an Abbey: it stood on a kind of rude lawn, overshadowed by high and spreading trees, which seemed coeval with the building, and diffused a romantic gloom . . . The lofty battlements, thickly enwreathed with ivy, were half demolished, and become the residents of birds of prey.'[12]

In William Wordsworth's 1798 poem 'Lines Composed a Few Miles Above Tintern Abbey', the author looks out over seemingly unbroken woods hiding the ruins of the abbey, which he remembers but does not see. Lines of smoke rise from amid the trees, which he takes to be from the home of a hermit or a camp of vagrants. These are reminiscent of the victims, both religious and secular, of Henry VIII's destruction of the abbeys in 1532–3. He recalls the sensuous intensity of natural scenes in his boyhood, in a way that seems to recapitulate the early history of humankind:

Caspar David Friedrich, *Abbey in the Oak Forest*, 1809–10, oil on canvas.

Tintern Abbey, 1807, engraving with watercolour.

> For nature then
> (The coarser pleasures of my boyish days,
> And their glad animal movements all gone by)
> To me was all in all. – I cannot paint
> What then I was. The sounding cataract
> Haunted me like a passion.

He contrasts this with the more humanistic appreciation of his later years:

> I have learned
> To look on nature, not as in the hour
> Of thoughtless youth; but hearing often-times
> The still, sad music of humanity,
> Nor harsh nor grating, though of ample power
> To chasten and subdue.[13]

The abbey's fate is a reminder of human violence, yet nature has reclaimed it, making it once again a place of refuge and contemplation. This is a haunted ruin, and its Gothic character is concealed by a tone of serene detachment.

Northern painters in the Gothic style continued Claude's tradition of painting ruins, often with the dark forest as a backdrop, showing the ultimate destiny of structures abandoned by humankind. The ruins were no longer primarily those of temples and triumphal arches but of prehistoric standing stones, churches, castles, graves and monuments. They were often marked not only by natural processes but by the violence of history.

Caspar David Friedrich of Prussia painted twisted, crowded trees with gnarled trunks and branches, struggling to survive. He specialized in abandoned churches, which had not, unlike the temples of Claude, simply gone unused but could have been at least partially destroyed in the religious wars of the early modern era. As a devout Lutheran in an age of increasing religious scepticism, Friedrich must have seen, or at least felt, a relationship between the abandoned temples of his predecessors and the abandoned churches of his own age. The paintings of Christian ruins were a way to memorialize a religion that seemed to be in decline, while at the same time continuing, and even expanding, its legacy.

A Turn of the Wheel

The English critic John Ruskin saw Gothic art in a very different way. He loved the intricate ornamentation of Gothic architecture, which he saw as an art of freedom that contrasted with the more formulaic patterns of Neoclassical buildings. For Ruskin, Gothic art was unpredictable, often grotesque and close to the natural world. The first characteristic of Gothic art was that it was 'savage', a word that was usually an epithet of contempt but, in context, suggested a manual worker's intimacy with the elements. Gothic was an art distinguished not by fear but exuberance, where 'the cathedral front was at last lost in the tapestry of its traceries, like a rock among the thickets and herbage of spring.'[14]

What Ruskin described was not, however, what we usually think of as Gothic. It did not evoke terror and was at least as playful as it was awe-inspiring. He calls the paintings of Gainsborough 'supremely Gothic',[15] though they are usually thought of as English Rococo today. The two styles are bound together in a dialectical process, and something like Rococo art was reemerging in the writing of Ruskin.

The Classical forest is, as the name suggests, inspired mostly by Greco-Roman culture, but the Rococo and Gothic representation of forests is based on the biblical story of Adam and Eve in the Garden of Eden. The Rococo forests represent Eden before the Fall. Nature is benign, human dominion is effortless and sex is without shame or guilt. The Gothic forest, by contrast, portrays a fallen world after an angel with a fiery sword drives Adam and Eve from the garden. But the difference between the two styles is basically a matter of emphasis.

The Gothic and Rococo styles may seem like opposites, but they are both based largely on arboreal patterns. Both suggest a form of animism, since the vegetal forms often seem to have almost human moods and volition. The two approaches were complementary. As we have seen, Rococo painting usually contains a Gothic element in the overgrown gardens and, especially, the dark shapes of trees that often loom threateningly in the background. And Gothic cathedrals contained a sort of proto-Rococo element in the playful monsters and green men that adorned the facades and walls of cathedrals.

10

The Primeval Forest

*Yahweh God planted a garden in Eden, which is in the east, and there he put
the man he had fashioned. Yahweh God caused to spring up from the soil
every kind of tree, enticing to look at and good to eat, with the tree of life and
the tree of the knowledge of good and evil in the middle of the garden.*

Genesis 2:8–9 (Jerusalem translation)

We now know that the basic pattern of forest growth and decline in the Americas was not profoundly different from that in Europe. In Latin America, the abandoned cities of great civilizations such as the Maya and the Inca gave way to jungle. So did the city of Chaco Canyon in what is now New Mexico, which, however, was replaced by desert. Another was the city of Cahokia in Illinois, which once contained a population comparable to that of the largest European cities of the time but was abandoned to forests and grasslands by 1300 CE. The early European visitors to North America knew very little or nothing about these urban centres.

Europeans who first sailed to the shores of North America lacked the conceptual apparatus to accurately describe what they saw. In addition, they were generally too occupied with practical tasks to devote much effort to literary and scientific pursuits. As a result, they identified what they saw with episodes from European myth or history. Many explorers, including Christopher Columbus, John Smith and Samuel Purchas, a member of Henry Hudson's crew, reported seeing mermaids.[1] The rattlesnake was identified with the basilisk, a monster that could hypnotize its prey or, by some accounts, kill with a glance.[2]

American landscapes were identified with those of European mythology. Henry Wadsworth Longfellow begins his popular epic poem 'Evangeline: A Tale of Acadie' with these lines:

> This is the forest primeval. The murmuring of pines and
>   hemlocks,

> Bearded with moss, and in garments green, indistinct in the
>   twilight,
> Stands like the Druids of eld, with voices sad and prophetic ...

Acadie was a French colony encompassing what are now the Canadian provinces of Nova Scotia, New Brunswick and Prince Edward Island. But here the remote North American past becomes a 'Celtic twilight'. That, in turn, transforms into an agrarian ideal as Longfellow speaks of the 'thatch-roofed village, home of Acadian farmers'.[3]

William Cullen Bryant began his poem 'A Forest Hymn' with a reference to the claim of Tacitus that the early Germans worshipped not in temples but sacred groves:

> The groves were God's first temples. Ere man learned
> To hew the shaft, and lay the architrave,
> And spread the roof above them, – ere he framed
> The lofty vault, to gather and roll back
> The sound of anthems; in the darkling wood,
> Amidst the cool and silence, he knelt down,
> And offered to the Mightiest solemn thanks
> And supplication.[4]

There were many mythic conceptions of the newly discovered continent, but just about all of them identified it in some way with a European conception of the original conditions of the world, from the Garden of Eden to a desolate wilderness.

Equating the Americas with the European past involved minimizing the contribution of Native Americans to their environment, and they were viewed as belonging to the realm of nature rather than civilization. Colonists minimized the numbers of Indians and dismissed their cultures as 'savage' or 'primitive'. In many ways, the European view of Native Americans had been similar to their view of Claude's peasants or Salvator's bandits. All of these figures were regarded as possessing a primitive vitality. The difference was that, unlike bandits and peasants, Native Americans were excluded not only from positions of power but from the history of their land as well.

In fact, according to current estimates, there had been at least 43 to 65 million Native Americans in the Americas before the coming of Columbus, and some scholars believe the number was considerably higher.[5] Native Americans probably managed the landscape through controlled burnings of woodlands. Even the forests had an open, park-like appearance.[6] There were also extensive clearings, including grasslands. This look, together with the abundance of animal life, suggested the biblical Paradise, and the 'New World' also became known as the 'New Eden'. The resemblance to royal and aristocratic parks may also have contributed to the Puritan idea that the Native Americans lived a life of idleness.

Before the arrival of Europeans, just about all Native Americans of what is now the Northeastern United States lived in villages encircled by agricultural fields, where they grew corn and other crops. The Indigenous people in larger, more crowded settlements were most exposed to contagious diseases, so the communities became smaller and more remote, to a point where they appeared increasingly less 'civilized' to Europeans. As the Indigenous population was decimated by waves of disease, the Native Americans were no longer able to manage the forests.

W. H. Bartlett, *Wigwam in the Forest*, mid-19th century, engraving with watercolour. Disease greatly reduced the numbers of Native Americans and forced them to move from villages to tiny, isolated communities, which colonists later assumed was their traditional way of life.

In addition, pressure from colonists prevented them from starting or encouraging large fires. By the mid-eighteenth century the forests of North America had become denser, darker and, in some places, more extensive than they had been at any time in the previous millennium.[7] The destruction of Indigenous communities, especially in the Americas, and consequent reforestation may have contributed to the global cooling known as the Little Ice Age.[8]

The pre-Columbian fires in North America had been frequent but did little damage. They passed through quickly, sparing mature, healthy trees, consuming the underbrush and releasing nutrients. Some indigenous trees such as sequoias and jack pines even require fire to discharge their seeds. After European colonization, fires became less frequent but far more intense. They were fed by an accumulation of dead matter, frequently including the large quantities of wood discarded by loggers. The Europeans had made the woodlands into something like the terrifying, primeval forest that had long haunted their imaginations.

All of this happened so quickly that settlers were unaware of the sequence, and the opposing images of forests seemed to blend. A scene could be almost at once a paradise and a desolate wilderness, just as the Native Americans could be at once 'noble savages' and 'barbaric' ones. The negative images soon became dominant. In the early seventeenth century, John Winthrop, the first governor of the Massachusetts Bay Colony, famously called the New World 'a hideous and desolate wilderness, where there are nothing but wild beasts and beastlike men'.[9] To clear a plot of trees, fence it and dedicate it to crops was to advance civilization. The forests were the province of the Devil. Not only did early European colonists feel themselves surrounded by the forest, but they were haunted by the fear that they, in such an environment, could succumb to savagery themselves.

But terror was not an entirely negative emotion, particularly not for the Romantics. Edmund Burke had, in the mid-eighteenth century, theorized that terror was the foundation of the sublime.[10] The feeling was a tribute to the vast scale of the American landscapes, with their ancient trees, dramatic contrasts and expansive horizons. Softened with time and blended with other emotions, that terror became a foundation of American landscape painting. It was directed away from diabolic powers to become the grandeur of nature and even God himself. As Barbara Novak has put it, 'The older sublime was a gentleman's preserve, an aristocratic reflex of romantic thought.' It required considerable security and comfort to indulge vicariously in enjoyment of threatening storms, erupting volcanos and steep cliffs. She adds, 'The Christianized sublime, more accessible to everyone, was more democratic, even bourgeois.' [11]

European landscape painters of the seventeenth through nineteenth centuries such as Claude, Salvator and Friedrich were in most ways not terribly different from their counterparts in the United States such as the painters of the Hudson River School. They depicted approximately the same point in a pattern of civilization and becoming wild, but they did so from opposite trajectories. The Europeans showed the gradual encroachment of wilderness, while Americans depicted the subduing of wild landscapes. Both approached their task with a comparable ambivalence. Just as the ruined castle, temple or church had symbolized the mutability of European landscapes, the stump of a newly cut tree or a railroad track did the same for American ones. Europeans feared, yet often secretly longed for, a reversion to some primeval state. Americans feared the complete destruction of the forests and other landscapes that they had come to think of as their heritage.

John Muir wrote around the start of the twentieth century, 'The forests of America . . . must have been a great delight to God, for they were

John Gast, *American Progress*, 1872, oil on canvas. For the painter and almost all of his contemporaries, American expansion westward was synonymous with progress. In this scene, it brings agriculture, telegraph poles and railroads, while driving the Indians and buffalo away.

the best he ever planted. The whole continent was a garden, and from the beginning it seemed to be favored above all other wild parks and gardens of the globe.'[12] Poetic writers often compared the forests of America to either the original Eden or, like Longfellow and Bryant, to places of worship. The problem was that such metaphors elevated the forests above the mundane patterns of normal life, while giving no guidance for how one might live alongside them. If they were the Garden of Eden, did that mean that people should not need to work within them? If they were temples or cathedrals, did that mean one should only enter for the purpose of worshipful contemplation? In a country whose very identity was based on westward expansion, such comparisons could only be paralysing or sentimental.

The government was actively encouraging westward expansion, which could not be accomplished in many areas without very aggressive deforestation, but it wished to set aside areas of the original forest, almost like exhibitions in a museum, to preserve something of the original Eden. These were characteristically landscapes that stood out because of dramatic features such as high mountains, vast canyons and especially large trees. Even the pine woods of the Great Lakes region did not seem sufficiently astonishing. Furthermore, the landscapes were altered to look like preconceived ideas of a primeval wilderness. Setting aside areas to remain undeveloped was an important idea, but the selection of these

Niagara Falls was already recognized as a 'natural wonder' in early colonial times and began to draw large crowds of tourists. In this engraving with watercolour (after a daguerreotype by Langenheim), 1844, European contributions to the landscape are deemphasized, but later attempts would be made to hide them almost entirely.

Postcard of the giant conifers in California, *c.* 1950s. In 1890 American president Benjamin Harrison protected the sequoias and redwoods by signing legislation to establish the second national park. But, as this card shows, their status did not always preserve them from commercial exploitation.

places was based on a limited aesthetic that emphasized grandeur more than environmental significance or subtler kinds of beauty.

Since its discovery, Americans and Canadians had both regarded Niagara Falls as the greatest of their natural wonders, but by the 1860s it seemed to have lost much of its grandeur. There was less water, since much of it had been diverted to provide power for mills and factories. Buildings and other paraphernalia of urban civilization had been erected nearby, and some had fallen into disrepair. At the end of the 1870s a team led by landscape architects Frederick Law Olmsted and Calvert Vaux was commissioned by New York State to draw up a plan for restoring Niagara to its former glory.

Every detail of the falls' appearance was carefully managed. Structures around the falls were removed or else shielded from view. Unobtrusive paths for pedestrians and roads for carriages were designed to accommodate a large number of tourists without making the location seem more crowded than necessary. Companies were asked not to divert water during tourist season, and the flow of water was subtly managed to increase the spectacle.[13] To this day, the impression of wildness is retained only through elaborate artifice.

Yosemite Valley is America's first national park, placed under government protection in 1864. But to maintain the impression that this was a

Thomas Cole, *The Garden of Eden*, 1828, oil on canvas. Painters imagined the biblical
Paradise in terms of indigenous American landscapes.

primordial landscape, the government had to appropriate farms and raze
an entire village of early settlers, except for the church.[14] When Yellowstone
was made the first national park in 1872, the deception went much further.
To maintain the fiction that the territory was pristine, the government
not only had to ban Indigenous people who had lived there for thousands
of years but tried to eradicate any memory of their presence by telling
people that the geysers had frightened them away.[15]

Is a 'primordial' landscape one that prevailed before the arrival of
Europeans? Before the arrival of Amerindians? The end of the ice age? That
is hardly ever specified. In truth, such a landscape exists only in mythic time.
It is a secularization of the original landscape in the biblical account of
Creation. Adam and Eve were originally placed in the Garden of Eden, but,
because of their transgression, they were driven out into the wilderness.
The concept of a primordial landscape is at once Eden and wilderness. It
is fertile, nourishing and lovely to behold. It is dangerous and forbidding.
People visited with many contradictory expectations that might only be
resolved, and only temporarily, through art.

The Course of Empire

In the early to mid-nineteenth century American art and literature still had a reputation for provincialism by comparison with the great capitals of Europe. The leader of the painters now known as the Hudson River School, who were the first American artists to achieve international renown, was Thomas Cole. He had been born in England at the start of the nineteenth century and emigrated to the United States as a young man, taking odd jobs and eventually settling in Catskill, New York. He taught himself painting and specialized in landscapes showing the unique features of the Hudson Valley. Like other ambitious artists, Cole had embarked on a grand tour of Europe, which emphasized especially the antiquities of Naples and Rome. He knew well the work of artists such as Claude and Salvator, whose styles he had at times imitated. He had stayed in artist colonies and met contemporary masters such as J.M.W. Turner, John Constable and John Martin. Like most of his American contemporaries, Cole longed for the landscapes of Europe, where every stream or mountain had an associated legend. The compensation for this deficit was, in his view, the primeval wildness of American landscapes. He did not think to count the tales of the Native Americans, which might have given the Catskill Mountains associations as rich as those of Rome or Naples.

In his 'Essay on American Scenery', first published in 1841, which became a sort of manifesto for the Hudson River School, Cole compares the European, especially the Italian, landscapes with those of the United States. The view from a mountain on the edge of Rome inspires 'gigantic associations of the storied past'. He contrasts this with the scenes of America, which to him suggest no human past but only the future, adding that 'mighty deeds shall be done in the yet pathless wilderness; and poets yet unborn shall sanctify the soil.' That is the rhetoric of manifest destiny, the ecstatic expectation that the United States was destined to expand its territory from the Atlantic to the Pacific Oceans and found a great empire. But does Cole really believe that? He immediately adds a qualification so serious that it almost repudiates that idea entirely. He laments the passing of the American landscapes as forests are cut down, saying, 'the most notable scenes are often laid desolate by a wantonness and barbarism scarcely credible in people who call themselves civilized.'[16]

This sort of contradiction is just about universal in environmentally oriented American writers and artists of the nineteenth century. The most passionate preservationists among them would lament the destruction of the original landscapes and, almost at the same time, become lyrical about the settlements that would follow. Henry David Thoreau wrote in his essay 'Walking' that 'Nowadays, almost all man's improvements, so called, as the building of houses and the cutting down of the forest and of all large trees, simply deform the landscape and make it more tame and cheap.' He followed this a few pages later with a peon to westward expansion, quoting with approval the saying, 'Westward the star of empire makes its way.'[17]

Neither Cole nor Thoreau suggested even trying to slow the pace of westward expansion. Nobody attempted to delay or seriously regulate it. Somehow, they and their contemporaries were either unwilling or unable to fully acknowledge a necessary connection between massive deforestation and new settlements. In the case of Cole, we can look to his paintings to partially resolve the inconsistency. These are mostly elegiac. Cole was trying to record the splendour of the American woods before they vanished, perhaps forever. A painted stump seems far less a promise of a building than the absence of a tree.

The Course of Empire is widely recognized as his masterpiece. It presents a grand panorama of history that synthesizes American and European points of view. The series depicts a cyclical view that, in its broad outlines, is close to, though not identical with, that of Vico, a similarity that may be due to either direct influence or convergence. All five canvases show essentially the same location, but at different times of day, which correspond to the ages of man. Cole eclectically uses motifs from several civilizations, including those of Amerindians, ancient Britain, Greece and Rome.

The first of the pictures is set at dawn and is entitled *The Savage State*. The people appear to be Native Americans, whom Cole considered especially primitive. A man wearing a loincloth of fur and carrying a bow is chasing a stag, which is leaping over a stream. In the centre a larger hunting party, similarly dressed, is entering a dense thicket. On the far right is a circle of wigwams around a large fire. Sunlight illuminates half of the sky and of a mountain in the background, but the sky on the right is dark and gloomy.

The second painting is set at early morning and is entitled *The Arcadian or Pastoral State*. For the most part, the figures seem to be Greek or Roman, though there is a temple resembling Stonehenge just left of the centre of the painting. The forest has given way to a sort of park with

Thomas Cole, *The Course of Empire: The Savage State*, c. 1834, oil on canvas.

Thomas Cole, *The Course of Empire: The Arcadian or Pastoral State*, c. 1834, oil on canvas.

meadows and trees. Directly in the centre of the painting, a young boy is herding sheep. In the lower right, an elderly philosopher is drawing figures with a stick in the earth. On the right, a woman peacefully spins and looks after children. This is the Classical forest similar to those painted by Claude and corresponds roughly to what Vico called the Age of Gods.

The third painting is set at noon and entitled *The Consummation of Empire*. It is replete with symbols of power and prosperity. A ruler crosses a bridge in a chariot drawn by an elephant. Soon he will pass between two pedestals where gilded statues hold up a laurel wreath. He may be Andrew Jackson, the president at the time, whom Cole believed was ushering in an era of militarism and greed.[18] The forests are almost entirely gone, though remaining trees may be seen in the remote background, a slightly threatening reminder of the past. Otherwise, vegetation is confined to a few ornamental plants. Shielded by a wall from the militaristic pomp is a sort of Rococo scene in the foreground on the right, where children play beside a decorative fountain. The picture corresponds approximately to what Vico had called the Age of Heroes.

The fourth painting is set in the afternoon and entitled *Destruction*. The sun is hidden behind dark clouds. On the right, a fire is consuming a huge temple complex and the people are fleeing for their lives. The

Thomas Cole, *The Course of Empire: The Consummation*, 1835–6, oil on canvas.

Thomas Cole, *The Course of Empire: Destruction*, 1836, oil on canvas.

bridge in the left centre has collapsed. A few men, most of whom look like soldiers, are engaged in random acts of violence such as rape and arson, but one cannot distinguish opposing sides and the scene does not seem to represent an invasion. I believe that Cole was imagining the eruption of Mount Vesuvius or a similar volcano, and this represents the destruction of a town like Pompeii or Herculaneum. It is the culmination of something like what Vico had called the Age of Men.

The final painting is set at night and entitled *Desolation*, and most critics consider it the finest in the series. In the centre of the painting is a tranquil moon, and there is not a single human being in sight. Nature is reclaiming the city, which lies in ruins and is being covered with trees and vines. On a huge pillar in the left side of the picture, a stork has made her nest. This could almost have been painted by Claude, except that there are no diminutive figures of human beings. Perhaps the cycle will begin again, but no survivors are in view.[19] The painting shows a Gothic forest giving way to a primeval one. Perhaps it is a warning against the abuse of nature. But the scene of *Desolation* seems tranquil, to a point where we may wonder whether human absence could even be a good thing.

Paradoxically perhaps, the rejection of anthropocentrism in *Desolation* led Cole to a traditional form of Christianity. Prior to this Cole had seen divinity as immanent in the forests, mountains and streams of America

Thomas Cole, *The Course of Empire: Desolation*, 1836, oil on canvas.

to a point where religious expression rarely required symbolism or allegory. But the landscapes were being defaced or destroyed, while the idea of God's immanence was placed in the service of chauvinism and greed. The result was that after *The Course of Empire*, in the last years of his life, Cole went from being primarily a landscape painter to one who created visionary, religious art. His next major series of canvases was entitled *Allegory of Life*, and showed a man from childhood to old age, in a boat guided by an angel. When Cole died in 1848, he was working on a Christian sequel to *The Course of Empire* entitled *The Cross of the World*, which was based on the idea that the cycle of civilization and savagery could be transcended through faith.

The basic mission of the Hudson River School had been, in the words of painter and engraver Asher Durand, 'depicting nature as it might have been at the time of Creation'.[20] As the American Northeast became ever more extensively cultivated and settled, painters, much like loggers, moved on to 'wilder' lands. Albert Bierstadt moved westwards to paint the Rocky Mountains. Martin Johnson Heade travelled to Brazil, where he painted orchids and hummingbirds. Frederic Edwin Church, the unofficial successor to Cole as leader of the Hudson River School, retraced the itinerary of the famous explorer Alexander Humboldt and painted the rainforests of Ecuador.

11

The Forest of Dreams

I love Mickey Mouse more than any woman I have ever known.
WALT DISNEY

Nothing could be more urban than the Chicago of my childhood, with its factories, slaughterhouses, art galleries, skyscrapers, corrupt politicians and constant marches of protest. Nothing could be more rural than the rest of Illinois, filled with little towns, vast fields of corn and, beyond them, trees that seemed endless. City people thought of their country cousins with a blend of scorn and admiration. Country people were narrow-minded and unadventurous; country people were closer to the elemental experiences of community, love and death. As a boy, looking through the car window as my parents drove through that mysterious land we called downstate, I would imagine walking off through the forests and having adventures. The woods, I assumed, would provide.

What happens if you are in a forest with no path and no landmarks? To me, it seemed that one might end up anywhere. Even for adults, space and time seem different in the woods. Since the horizon is not visible, the only time of day we can know by the sun is when it is directly overhead at noon. The dials of a watch still count seconds, but these seem increasingly abstract, and you may wonder if they measure anything at all. Today, of course, we check mobile phones, but they only remind us of the chronology we left behind.

Space also seems altered in the woods. You cannot see far in any direction, and the ever-changing acoustics make it hard to know location by sound. Forests cannot be accurately surveyed by traditional methods, only by sophisticated technologies such as satellite photos or enhanced GPS. A small stand of trees can seem vast, while a vast one may appear small. The forest seems like a black hole, a discontinuity in time and space postulated by physicists, where one may enter at one point in space and time and then exit at a completely different location.

Sleeping Beauty

Few tales have so many suggestive parallels with myths throughout the world as 'Sleeping Beauty'. It resembles the Greek myth of Orpheus, who enters the underworld to retrieve his beloved Eurydice from death. P. L. Travers has written, 'The idea of a sleeper, of somebody hidden from mortal eye, waiting until time shall ripen has always been dear to the folky mind – Snow White asleep in her glass coffin, Brynhild behind her wall of fire, Charlemagne in the heart of France, King Arthur in the Isle of Avalon, Frederick Barbarossa under his mountain in Thuringia.' She continues with a long list of parallels from myth and folklore from Oisín in Ireland to Mother Holle in Germany.[1] The reason that the story has such a mythic resonance is that it follows a pattern often found in the natural world. Many animals from bears to turtles hibernate in winter. Most especially, the story seems to be inspired by caterpillars that spin a cocoon for protection, lie dormant, metamorphize and emerge as butterflies.

The act of spinning has always been closely associated with the passing of time. In Greek myth, the first of the three Fates, Themis, would spin out a thread for the life of every human being. In German, the verb for spinning also means telling stories, a major way of passing time at least until the invention of electronic media. In English as well, we speak of 'spinning a tale'. The turning of a hand spindle can symbolize the zodiac. In the Grimms' 'Briar Rose', the decision of the king to ban spinning expresses a wish to stop the passage of time. Written at a time when technological innovation was concentrated largely on textile production, that would have seemed a bit like banning use of the Internet today. But, as the heroine discovers when she finds an old woman spinning in a secret room, time continues covertly whether we choose to acknowledge it or not.

Spinning did much to drive the industrial revolution. At the end of the Middle Ages, the spinning wheel, invented in Asia, perhaps in India or China, was imported and largely replaced the hand spindle. The spinning jenny was patented by James Hargreaves in 1770, mechanizing spinning and leading to many further innovations in the textile industry. The pace of cultural and technological innovation became frightening, and it generated massive waves of nostalgia. Just about all of Western culture became subtly pervaded by a vague yet intense sense of longing for some usually unidentified era in the past. The story of 'Sleeping Beauty' or 'Briar Rose' expresses what was to become a tourist cliché, perhaps most associated with the American musical *Brigadoon*, first performed in 1947 and made into a movie in 1954. One would find some unchanged, unspoiled village deep within the woods and perhaps even fall in love, marry and stay.

The earliest known version of 'Sleeping Beauty' can be found in *Perceforest*, a massive epic written in French during the mid-fourteenth century, which provides a backstory for the Arthurian tales. The version tells how the knight Troylus journeyed to the island of Zeeland, where he and the princess Zellandine fell in love. After returning to his home in Scotland, Troylus learns that Zellandine had fallen into a deep sleep, from which she cannot be awakened. He returns to Zeeland and enters the temple of three goddesses – Venus, goddess of love, Lucina, goddess of childbirth, and Themis, goddess of destiny. He prays to Venus for guidance. After leaving the temple, he is magically transported to the chamber where Zellandine is sleeping naked. He asks permission to kiss her, but, of course, she does not reply. Venus appears and tells him that, if he makes love to her, Zellandine will be glad. When he does not immediately respond, Venus taunts him about his masculinity. Troylus finally does as Venus demands. He then exchanges his ring and Zellandine's as a sign that he has been there. Finally, he is lifted by an enormous bird and transported down from the tower.

Nine months later, Zellandine gives birth to a baby boy. He looks for her nipple but finds her finger instead. He sucks out a splinter, at which Zellandine immediately wakes up. Her aunt then explains that when Zellandine was born, her parents, according to the custom, had a feast in her honour at which they offered gifts to the goddesses. Themis, goddess of destiny, was not satisfied with the offerings given to her and laid a curse on the child that she would prick her finger when spinning and fall into a deep sleep from which she could not wake up until the splinter had been sucked out. Zellandine and Troylus are reunited and married, but their child, named Benuic, is carried off by a huge bird with a woman's face to have adventures of his own. His line of descent will lead eventually to Lancelot, the model of a Christian knight.[2]

Though the motif of the enchanted forest is elsewhere prominent in *Perceforest*, the castle where Zellandine sleeps is not surrounded by trees or by thorns. In the epic, Zeeland is an island near the coast of Brittany, where anachronistic practices continue. It remains thoroughly polytheistic, with mostly female deities, at a time when Brittany itself has adopted the monotheistic religion of the Sovereign God, a forerunner of Christianity.[3] Just as this version of the story of 'Sleeping Beauty' is about the transition from paganism to Christianity, so later ones will be about the passage from the Middle Ages to the modern era. The forest replaces the ocean as a barrier that isolates the castle from the larger world.

A version of the story recorded by Giambattista Basile in the early seventeenth century is set in the court of Naples. The father of the young girl, whose name is Talia, hears a prophesy that she will be endangered by a splinter of flax, so he forbids all flax within his kingdom. One day, however, she sees an old woman spinning, touches the spindle and then loses consciousness. Her father takes Talia for dead and abandons his palace, leaving her alone in a tower, which is then surrounded by forest. She is discovered by a king pursuing his lost falcon.[4] Unlike Troylus with Zellandine, the king unceremoniously rapes the girl and forgets her, but she has two children, one of which sucks the flax from her body and wakens her. She later is reunited with the king and becomes his mistress, setting off another chain of events that make up a different tale.

In the French version, written down by Charles Perrault and published in 1697, the forest is not just a setting but an essential part of the tale, as indicated in his title – 'The Sleeping Beauty in the Wood' ('La belle au bois dormant'). Here, the father invited many fairies to the christening of his newborn daughter, but one fairy who had not been invited shows up and angrily curses her, saying that the girl will prick her finger on a spindle and die. A good fairy, unable to undo the curse, softens it by saying that she will only fall into a sleep for a hundred years. The king forbids the use or even the possession of a spindle, which is to be punishable with death. But, when she has become a young woman, his daughter discovers a secret stairway that leads to a room in a tower where an old woman is spinning. The girl is fascinated by the spindle, which the old woman gives her, and she immediately pricks herself and loses consciousness. The good fairy appears and puts the girl and everyone else in the palace except for the king and queen to sleep.[5] The king forbids anyone to approach the palace, and a huge wall of trees interlaced with brambles and thorns grows around it. After a hundred years, a prince, who has heard tales of the beautiful princess, approaches the castle to find her, and the trees and thorns part on his approach. He finds the room of the princess, who immediately wakes up, and they soon get married.

'Briar Rose'

In the version that the Grimm Brothers published in the 1856 edition of their *Tales for the Hearth and Home*, the tale begins with a king and queen, long childless, who have just given birth to a baby daughter christened 'Briar Rose'. They celebrate at a feast where twelve wise women bestow blessings on the infant. A thirteenth wise woman, angry because she has not been invited, comes anyhow and interrupts the festivities with a curse. When the child turns fifteen, she will prick her finger with a spindle and die. Another wise woman, who has yet to bestow her gift, softens this fate, declaring that the girl will not die but sleep for a hundred years. Afterwards, hoping to avoid the malediction, the king orders that every spindle in the kingdom be burned. On her fifteenth birthday, the girl discovers a secret room in the castle, enters and finds an old woman spinning. She touches the spindle and, as was ordained, pricks her finger and falls into a profound sleep. Everyone else in the castle then falls asleep as well, from the king and queen to the cook and the kitchen boy. Even the wind stops, and a hedge of briars grows up, completely covering the castle. Years pass, and many young men try to cut or push their way through the hedge, but they become caught on the thorns and die. Finally, a young prince who has heard of the girl resolves to find his way to the castle. As in the version by Perrault, the hedge opens in front of him and closes behind. He finds his way to the chamber of the princess and kisses her, at which she and the rest of castle immediately wake up.[6]

Here, the forest enacts the desires of the sleeping girl. It appears when she needs it, as the rest of the castle goes to sleep. It stops the false suitors, lets in the chosen one and then leaves when its services are not required. Contemporary readers have criticized the heroine for being too passive, but Briar Rose merges with the forest, becoming a force of nature, until she is ready to take on a role as an adult.

The hedge of thorns suggests a castle wall, and, indeed, that may be the origin of the motif. Going back to ancient times, trees in Northern Europe have been deliberately pruned and trained to create nearly impenetrable barriers. In German, this was known as a *Wehrwald*, literally a 'protective forest'. As described by Julius Caesar, this mode of defence was practised by the tribe of the Nervi in what is now France. Young trees were coppiced or pollarded (cut off below the crown) so that many lateral branches would spread out, while bushes with thorns were planted below them, creating an impenetrable tangle. In the Rhineland and other

Anne Anderson, 'Aurora pricked her finger on the witch's spindle', illustration for *Briar Rose; or, The Sleeping Beauty* by the Brothers Grimm, *c.* 1930. The spinning wheel is a symbol of time. The tale is about attempts to stop time, as the pace of change during the Industrial Revolution renders it more frightening. To touch the wheel is to leave the timeless world of childhood and become aware of mortality.

parts of Germany, branches of trees were bent to the ground, where they would take root and grow into a thicket of exceptional density. One huge barrier constructed in such a manner protected medieval Silesia. Another existed around the city of Bonn. In late medieval Russia, a barrier against invaders included felled trees, ditches, pikes and piles of earth. Some of these defensive structures continued to be maintained in the seventeenth century, and so they could have been familiar to Perrault. They had the advantage of shielding settlements not only from attack but even from sight.[7] The buildings within would almost seem to disappear, except, as in the stories, for tall towers. Such protective woods probably contributed to the stylization of Gothic forests as dark, dense and filled with mysterious figures.

The story of Briar Rose follows an archetypal pattern that may be found in many domains. Much like the heroine, forest trees such as beeches can remain dormant, surviving but not growing substantially for decades, perhaps as long as a century, while the forest canopy blocks the sun. Then, when an old tree or two falls, opening the canopy, they will shoot up quickly to fill the gap. For people in general, at least in Western culture, adolescence is a time of great dreams of love, adventure, glory and many other things. Until the fantasies have subsided a bit, the boy or girl may not be ready for the responsibilities of adulthood.

The Disney Forest

When his kingdom, allied with Austria, was on the losing side of a war with Prussia, King Ludwig II of Bavaria withdrew from affairs of state, became almost a recluse and devoted his energy to constructing palaces in the forest. These included Linderhof Castle, in the Rococo style and centred on the French court of Louis XV, and Herrenchiemsee, never finished but intended as a slightly larger replica of Versailles. The most famous castle is Neuschwanstein, a neo-Gothic palace consecrated largely to illustrating the operas of Richard Wagner, scenes of which were depicted on the walls. Ludwig was declared insane by his ministers in 1886 and drowned shortly afterwards under mysterious circumstances, which may have been due to murder, suicide or an accident.

Few buildings blend so completely into their surroundings as Neuschwanstein. Its stone facade blends with the rocky cliff where it is perched. Unlike most palaces, it is completely asymmetrical, and there is something organic about the way it mixes together Gothic, Romanesque and Rococo styles. Renaissance and neo-Classical palaces were generally based on horizontal lines. Neuschwanstein is based on vertical ones, and the eye of the beholder wanders among the many towers capped by turrets. These towers, in turn, repeat the forms of the spruce trees in the surrounding woods and the mountains far away. The lack of symmetry makes each tower seem especially unique, inspiring the curiosity of the viewer. Among the turrets is one that is far higher than all the rest, suggesting the exalted status of the monarch.

But the forest itself is not very natural. It is a monoculture of spruce, planted to replace a mixed forest, which had been overexploited from the late Middle Ages onwards for the sake of wood. The location appealed to romantic ideas of the Gothic forest that were very current in Germany at the time yet had little to do with the reality of the original German woodlands. This forestry reflected values of the Enlightenment such as symmetry, uniformity and predictability. But, for those unfamiliar with their history, these woods could appear to be a primeval heritage.[8] The castle was built for Ludwig's sole enjoyment, but, immediately after his death, it was opened to the public as a theme park.

Neuschwanstein later became the model for the Castle of Sleeping Beauty in Disneyland, which opened in 1955 in Anaheim, California.[9] Disney Studios would go on to open similar theme parks in Orlando, Paris, Tokyo, Hong Kong and Shanghai, each centred on a castle inspired by Neuschwanstein, all asymmetrical with a multiplicity of turrets. In every Disney castle, as in Neuschwanstein, one turret towers above the

Neuschwanstein Castle, Bavaria.

Sleeping Beauty Castle, Disneyland, Anaheim, California.

rest. At Anaheim that is the room not of Sleeping Beauty but of Rapunzel, yet Disney princesses are in many ways interchangeable. Like the forests that always surround them, the princesses are both commodities, reflecting traditions of the Enlightenment, and embodiments of nature, reflecting those of Romanticism.

One thing that Disney shared with Ludwig was an obsession with royalty and, more broadly, an idealized feudal order. Ludwig was not only a genuine king but heir to the house of Wittelsbach, a royal line that went back at least to the twelfth century. However, he was not greatly interested in his ancestors. He was far more obsessed with Louis XIV of France, who was the model of an absolute monarch. Ludwig did not seem to care about the considerable power that remained to him as a constitutional monarch. He loved the glamour and pageantry of the Middle Ages endlessly but only as an elaborate fantasy, one with which no reality could ever compete.

As for Disney, most of the protagonists of his most famous films were princesses. They lived, when not abducted, in courts. They were supported by kings, queens and princes, and they were waited on by servants. He even made the Little Mermaid in his film of Andersen's famous tale into a princess, daughter of Triton, the king of the sea. The main attractions at his theme parks were, as already noted, the fairytale castles. Royalty would never abuse their authority, and only villains would challenge it.

One might expect that this obsession with royalty would not go over well in America, a country that was founded on the rejection of monarchy and aristocracy, but Disney tapped into an American nostalgia for royal glamour and pageantry. His trick was to democratize the ideal of monarchy. In America, every girl could be a princess. Love could make any couple into a king and queen. Disney also exploited a sort of solipsism that was implicit in the way Ludwig built giant palaces simply for himself. Louis XIV had reportedly said, 'I am the state,' but it was Ludwig who really acted out the part, and this resonated with a narcissistic element in American culture.

And Rococo, the predominant design in all these palaces, was, more than any other, the style of royalty. No other artistic movement in the West had ever been centred on a court the way Rococo was on that of Louis XV. This was an environment in which the royal and noble prerogative seems so utterly secure that it does not need to be aggressively asserted. Like the castles of Ludwig and Disney, it had mostly been a fantasy world ruled by a spirit of play.

What I have just written makes both Disney and Ludwig sound like irredeemable eccentrics. In their partial defence, I would say that both were, in many ways, authentic artists. Those who worked at Disney Studios had studied the old masters of graphic art, architecture and interior design. The people employed by Disney included such outstanding illustrators as Kay Nielsen and Mary Blair. The beauty of the animation in Disney films is still very widely admired, even by people who have serious reservations about some of their messages. As for Ludwig, his creations continue to fascinate people long after the Gothic follies commissioned by industrialists of his time, some of whom were far richer even than Ludwig, have been forgotten.

Reality and Dreams

Did Briar Rose sleep dreamlessly? Or did she have a century of dreams? Walt Disney seems to have thought the latter, as he placed her castle in the realm known as Fantasyland, located at the centre of his original theme park in Anaheim. Perhaps that is the connection Disney sensed between the fairytale princess and Ludwig. The Bavarian king was not only a great dreamer but an eternal child. He constructed a Moorish kiosk where he could act as sultan and a Chinese pavilion where he could play at being an Asian emperor. Like a little boy, he was egocentric, prone to tantrums and obsessed with play.

Like Ludwig, Disney created dreams, but unlike Ludwig, he marketed them as well. Just as Ludwig had constructed rooms with furnishings and murals depicting scenes from operas of Wagner, Disney filled his palace with dioramas showing scenes from the story of Sleeping Beauty and other fairy tales. For Disney, the forest was not part of the American heritage. In Disney World, the United States was represented by the deserts and prairies of Frontierland, another part of his theme park that was filled with settings taken straight out of movies of the time, such as saloons. In Disney cartoons, forests were European, and Europe itself was a sort of fantasyland, a giant forest filled with knights, maidens and dragons. Much as early European explorers and colonists had seen their remote past in the forests of America, Americans saw theirs in forests of Europe.

Disney took an eclectic view of the forest, blending neo-Rococo and neo-Gothic images while detaching both from any cultural and historical context. It is Rococo in its emphasis on ornament, play and gentle eroticism.[10] It is Gothic in its preference for huge, contorted trees. In the near view, it is mostly Rococo; it shows animals, even those that would normally be predator and prey, frolicking together in grassy meadows between the trees. When shown from a distance, it is mostly Gothic, with its high trees visible over rocky outcrops that often seem almost impenetrable. Such figures are in almost all of Disney's animated films, including *Bambi*, *Snow White and the Seven Dwarfs*, *Sleeping Beauty*, *Beauty and the Beast* and *Frozen*. The Disney forest is Gothic during storms and becomes Rococo when the sun comes out. As in the story of 'Sleeping Beauty', particularly the version by Grimm, the forest in Disney cartoons seems to become an extension of the heroine, expressing her feelings from playfulness to fear.

Disney made the animated movie *Sleeping Beauty*, loosely based on the tale by Perrault, a few years after the theme park in Anaheim opened. The castle in the movie was much like the one in the theme park yet even more flamboyantly Gothic, with yet more towers and turrets. Probably so that visitors to the crowded streets of the theme park would not expect a sleeping princess, Disney made a few changes in the plot. To hide her from the evil fairy, here named Maleficent, the three benevolent fairies take the girl, here named Aurora, into the forest, while the castle is put to sleep (though not for a hundred years) to await her. In her forest home, she is renamed Briar Rose by her fairy guardians. She sings the song called 'Once Upon a Dream' in a clearing in the woods. A prince, named Phillip after the consort to Elizabeth II of England, follows her voice and finds her. They fall in love. When Maleficent, trying to capture Aurora, turns into a dragon, the prince kills her with his sword and the kingdom immediately wakes up. The forest is the place of dreams, and dreams come true.

But where did I, a child who had probably never heard of Freud or Jung and was not a big fan of Disney, get the idea that I might wander off into the woods and live, with no means of sustenance, forever? What would have happened had I tried?

12

Law of the Jungle

Where nudes, bears, lions, sows with women's heads,
Mounted and murdered and ate each other raw.

w. h. auden, 'Woods'

In the late 1880s France appointed Captain Paul Voulet to explore the area between Niger and Lake Chad and bring it under national control. He had been selected partly for his lack of scruples, and his methods involved rape, torture, mutilation and mass murder. Voulet had entire villages burned. He strung up the bodies of young girls on trees. He collected the severed hands of his victims and placed their heads on pikes. Eventually, the flamboyant cruelty became too much for his superiors, and Voulet was relieved of his command. He told his troops, 'I am no longer French; I am a black emperor, greater than Napoleon.' A short time later, he was assassinated. Voulet may have been the model for Kurtz in Joseph Conrad's novel *Heart of Darkness*.[1] This is an extreme, but otherwise not atypical, example of the sort of events that might take place only on a frontier, in this case that of European colonization of Africa.

According to Frederick Jackson Turner's seminal essay of 1893, 'The Significance of the Frontier in American History', the existence of a frontier of westward expansion was the defining feature of American culture, responsible for its disrespect for established authorities, its democratic nature, its individualism and its boisterous energy. He called the American frontier 'the meeting point between savagery and civilization', and argued that it enabled America to maintain a sort of rude vitality. In his words, 'This perennial rebirth, this fluidity of American life, this expansion westward with its new opportunities, its continuous touch with the simplicity of primitive society, furnish the forces dominating American character.'[2]

Turner exaggerated the uniqueness of the American frontier, which in many ways resembled the Roman frontier in Northern Europe, the Amazonian frontier in Brazil and the Russian frontier in Central Asia.

193

For that matter, it was also not so very different from the frontiers of countries like Spain, Portugal, Britain and France in their colonial possessions. In all of these, there was lawlessness and violence, and they were wild in other ways as well. The idea that a frontier could be a source of primordial vitality that would revitalize the decadent arts of civilization was not unique to America but also runs through European culture of the time. Frontiers fostered fantasies of power, saintliness, wealth, eroticism, divine election and so on. They are places where new myths might be created and old, anachronistic ones might be preserved. They gave adventurers the opportunity to indulge in ritual, grandeur and absolutism that was becoming anachronistic at home. Frontiers indeed generated disruptive energy, but that could usually be channelled to support the interests of those in power.

Turner's idea of the American national character was itself in many ways a fantasy, a bit of wishful thinking. Americans were not so profoundly scornful of authority or democratic. He was writing in the era now known as 'the Gilded Age' (about 1870 to 1900), in which income inequality in America greatly increased and industrialists such as Vanderbilt, Carnegie, Rockefeller and Morgan assumed all the trappings

Emanuel Leutze, *Westward the Course of Empire Takes Its Way*, 1862, stereochrome. This huge mural (6.1 × 9.1 m), originally displayed in the U.S. House of Representatives, glorifies the American frontier.

of a traditional aristocracy, with their huge mansions, art collections and exclusive clubs.

The wealthy nations of Western Europe and North America identified their territories with their past. Western countries might have been more comfortable, more secure, more democratic and even, arguably, internally more just, but they also seemed increasingly bland. Colonialism offered the possibility of an escape from the technocratic monotony of modern life. Other European monarchs also looked to their colonies as places where they might still act out the pageantry, power and grandeur of bygone times. Ludwig II of Bavaria sought in vain to obtain an unspoiled territory where he might set up a new kingdom and rule with true majesty as a sort of Grail King.[3]

Victoria had the largest domain in history, but she had been given only the relatively modest title of queen. It didn't seem fair, and so, in 1877, she assumed the title of 'Empress of India'. But why couldn't she simply have been 'Empress of Britain' instead? Such a title would have sounded anachronistic in the modern West, which was gradually moving towards greater democracy. For her European and North American contemporaries, the new title had a ring that was pleasantly exotic but not threatening. This was the sort of anachronistic display of pomp and ceremony that a colonial frontier made possible.

During the period of their industrialization, Europe and North America may have been more obsessed with the past than any other culture before or since. They were constantly painting, investigating, reimagining, conjuring, deploring, romanticizing and imitating the past in an almost endless variety of ways. Oddly, perhaps, they also saw themselves as rendering the past irrelevant through progress. But their visions of the future, whether utopian or dystopian, were vague and not remotely as interesting as those of years gone by. And even these were, or at least were based on, idealized constructions of times that had allegedly existed in the past, from a putative medieval 'age of faith' to an imagined community before the advent of private property.

As Europeans modernized and endeavored to banish archaic myths, they projected them on to distant parts of the world. They and Euro-Americans regarded both the noble and brutal 'savages' as 'primitive', anachronisms belonging fundamentally to an earlier era of human development. In many respects, this distorted their perception of newly discovered territories, such as when they mistook apes for the satyrs of Greco-Roman mythology or Native Americans for the ten lost tribes of Israel. The colonies were places where staid officials could indulge in the splendour, pageantry, heroism, grandeur, debauchery and even flamboyant bloodspilling that would otherwise have seemed anachronistic. An ordinary Englishman could be Caesar or at least one of his lieutenants. He could be Alexander subduing the Persians or Joshua slaughtering the Canaanites. Europeans and Euro-Americans identified the various peoples of the world with eras in their past. In general, the Chinese and other East Asians were associated with medieval times, while Indigenous Americans were identified with the Greeks, Hebrews and Romans of antiquity. To go to these places meant essentially to visit the past and no longer be bound so strictly by bourgeois morality.

Africa seemed more archaic still, a land of wonders at the primeval beginnings of civilization. European colonialism of the modern era was driven by greed for wealth and power, by boredom and by longing for adventure. In Europe from the seventeenth until the nineteenth centuries, it was common to allegorize the four continents as female figures. The woman representing Europe would be dressed in a classical robe and be accompanied by a horse, a domesticated animal that symbolized the power of civilization. She was an image of dignity and decorum. The one

American advertisement for Texaco Oil, April 1943, depicting American soldiers of the Second World War fighting their way through the jungle. It recalls many earlier images of American pioneers on the frontier of westward expansion.

Adriaen Collaert, after Maerten de Vos, *Allegory of Africa*, 1580–1600, engraving.

representing Africa, by contrast, would be almost naked with a bare chest and accompanied by wild animals such as a crocodile, lion or snake. She might be wearing an exotic headdress and jewellery, and she might hold a cornucopia. The figure served to entice adventurers with the promise of sexual escapades and riches.[4]

Colonists were also searching for some sort of primeval innocence and vitality. Europeans of the modern era sensed a void in their culture, something that they tried to efface with ideologies from Catholicism to Communism, usually with no great success. Everything, even cultural accomplishments, seemed to be touched by nihilism. For their philosophers and poets, this was a pervasive malaise of the *fin-de-siècle*. It was the behaviour of Europeans and Euro-Americans as slave traders and colonists that revealed this nihilism in its most tangible, and terrifying, forms.

The Land of Wonders

In the early nineteenth century, most of the geography of sub-Saharan Africa remained completely unknown to Europeans. There were several settlements by Arabs, Portuguese and others along the coasts, which were used for trading, but there were not even many anecdotal accounts

John Thompson, map of Africa, 1813. An enormous area in the centre of the continent
is empty except for the words 'unknown parts'.

of the continent's interior. On a map published in 1813 by John Thompson, that area, nearly half the continent, is left entirely blank and labelled 'unknown parts'.[5] On a map by John Rankin published in 1860, the coastal areas have filled out but there is still a huge empty space in the centre making up about one-fifth of the continent, in which no settlements and almost no geographical landmarks are indicated.[6] Central Africa was as much of a mystery in Europe as Germany had been to the Romans in the time of Augustus Caesar. It was a void into which people could project all sorts of fears and fantasies.

A book of history and geography for young people by the highly popular Peter Parley, published in 1854, contains this description of an area approximately contiguous with what we call Central Africa:

In the four kingdoms of lower Guinea, Loango, Congo, Angola, and Benguela, the soil is generally rich and fertile. The natives are an inferior and degraded tribe; living in regions which nature has adorned with every luxuriance and beauty. Groves of tulips,

Fierce Snakes of the Jungle, 1889. Chromolithograph depicting snakes killing a white bird, which here is a symbol of innocence. The African is paralysed with fear, but the white colonist shoots at the snakes indiscriminately.

white lilies, roses, and hyacinths perfume the air with their fragrance and enchant the eye with their colors. On the other hand, animals of the fiercest nature, wander among these fairy scenes. Crocodiles haunt the rivers; boas of monstrous size wind round the trees, ready to spring on their prey and crush them in their folds. The woods are bright with the plumage of the parrot, the peacock and the pheasant.[7]

Apart from the blatant racism, what first stands out in this passage is its extreme inaccuracy. Tulips, lilies, roses, hyacinths, boas, peacocks and pheasants are not indigenous to Africa. Beyond that, the passage is a fantasy of Europeans and North Americans about a part of the world that was still completely mysterious to them. Essentially, it is a sort of daydream of the enchanted forests, where crocodiles take the place of dragons and natives take the place of woodland spirits. It was just waiting for a knight errant.

Towards the end of the eighteenth century, a new word emerged for the forest in the tropical zones – 'jungle'. Like 'forest', it was defined more by associations than by any scientific differentiation. In the jungle, vegetation was dense to the point of making passage nearly impossible. It was full of dangers from predatory beasts. The concept was probably influenced by the 'dark wood' of Dante's *Inferno*, especially in the way Dante finds his way forward blocked by a leopard, a lion and a ravenous she-wolf. It was not a realistic description of the tropical rainforest, where, as in other old-growth forests, the vegetation on the forest floor is not thick enough to block passage.

The word 'jungle' originated in Sanskrit and designated a desert, a place that seemed to be one of utter desolation. It evolved into the Hindi word *jangal*, which means a wasteland or an area overgrown with scrub. Gradually, that meaning was almost reversed, as 'jungle' was used to refer to an area overgrown with disorderly vegetation.[8] Inhabitants of such an area were referred to a *djangli*, meaning 'people of the jungle' or 'savages'.[9] 'Wilderness', which once had a similar meaning, became applied almost exclusively to landscapes of the northern hemisphere. It eventually acquired associations with the biblical Eden and came to mean an area of pristine nature, characterized by beauty and innocence. 'Jungle' entered English through the British Empire and was applied to landscapes of the southern hemisphere. It became the preferred word for forests in India, Latin America, Indonesia and Africa. The word suggested a place of primordial violence and disorder, which was only good for testing one's manhood and making one's fortune.[10]

The Heart of Europe

Just as Europeans called the centuries after the fall of Rome the dark ages, they also called Africa the dark continent. In both cases, the word 'dark' suggested people who were unenlightened, violent and crude. But in his novella *Heart of Darkness* (first published 1899), novelist and mariner Joseph Conrad viewed 'darkness' as a feature of Western civilization. The book is ultimately far more about Europe than it is about Africa and more about an internal journey than a geographic exploration. In ways, it is like Dante's *Inferno*. The hero ventures, like Dante, to the centre of hell, the jungle, and returns, though he does not pass on through purgatory to heaven. A sailor named Charles Marlow is piloting a steamboat up a river to a remote part of Central Africa, where he encounters the former Colonel Kurtz, a representative of the Belgian Congo, who has obtained vast amounts of ivory for trade. Kurtz lives in a hut surrounded by the severed heads of Indigenous people displayed on pikes.

Marlow, who is generally Conrad's mouthpiece, is very explicit about how the journey along the Congo River is also a voyage through time. In his words, 'Going up that river was like traveling back to the earliest beginnings of the world, when vegetation rioted on the earth and the big trees were kings. An empty stream, a great silence, an impenetrable forest.'[11] At another point, he compares his journey to that of an ancient Roman mariner who must pilot a boat through Gaul and Britain. He adds, 'The conquest of the earth, which mostly means taking it away from those who have a different complexion or slightly flatter noses than ourselves, is not a pretty thing when you look at it too much,' a sentiment that may sound platitudinous today but was almost daring when he wrote it.[12]

Kurtz is a man of great eloquence, but he has amassed his wealth through unrestrained brutality toward Indigenous peoples. He is the author of a treatise for an organization called 'International Society for the Suppression of Savage Customs'. Kurtz has written that whites 'must necessarily appear to them (savages) in the nature of supernatural beings – we approach them with the might as of a deity'. He goes on to say how this power enables white people to do 'good practically unbounded'. Many colonial adventurers from Hernán Cortés to James Cook have reportedly been worshipped by native people as gods. But perhaps Kurtz's hopes have been disappointed, for he later scrawled in the margin, 'Exterminate all the brutes.'[13]

When Marlow finds him, Kurtz is ill, and, not long after being taken aboard the boat for transport home, he dies. His last words are, 'The horror! The horror!'[14] Marlow not only recognizes the appalling brutality of Kurtz's deeds but the profound hypocrisy of European colonialism. He concludes that there is not much difference between Europeans and the so-called 'savages' in the end. Beneath all the glittering phrases lie elaborately rationalized greed and bloodlust. If one probes still further, there is utter nihilism.

Having realized the extent of Kurtz's crimes against humanity, Marlow strangely continued to regard Kurtz with admiration and even awe. This is especially paradoxical since he found no trace in Kurtz of compassion or regret. Nevertheless, this is psychologically a familiar phenomenon. Even while acknowledging that they are responsible for the needless deaths of vast numbers of men, women and children, people continue to admire the biblical Joshua, Alexander, Caesar, Charlemagne, Genghis Khan, Ivan the Terrible, Napoleon, Stalin and Hitler. In a paradoxical way, the vast scale of the destruction they caused and even recognition of their guilt can add to this admiration, since it seems to place them on a level apart from that of ordinary mortals. Great sin becomes the mark of a great man. This is a sort of admiration that can, and often does, exist alongside terror and even disgust. As Matthew White puts it near the end of his extensive survey of crimes against humanity through the ages, 'One of the most frightening things I discovered is that murdering huge numbers of people doesn't necessarily make you a bad person – at least, in the eyes of history.'[15]

Furthermore, only Kurtz stands between Marlow and total nihilism. To entirely repudiate Kurtz would be to throw into question the resonant ideals that had been placed in the service of colonialism, and Marlow was not intellectually or emotionally prepared for that. He could briefly acknowledge the rot near the core of European civilization, but he could not live with the constant awareness of it. Marlow is an alter ego not only of Kurtz but of Conrad himself, who also would only go so far in his condemnation of the colonization of Africa. He remained strictly loyal to Britain, his adopted country, despite her having by far the largest colonial empire of all.

Much later, Hannah Arendt was also trying to get away from this point of view when she articulated her famous thesis of the 'banality of evil' in *Eichmann in Jerusalem*,[16] though she remained far too imbued with the 'great man theory of history' to draw the consequences with any consistency. In Eichmann, she had found a man of great guilt but, in her opinion, little interest, something that seemed paradoxical to Arendt and her contemporaries. But she never called, say, Napoleon banal, even though he supported his wars of conquest only through platitudinous appeals to nationalism, enlightenment and glory. She was as evasive as Marlow, and I find it hard to blame either of them very much. As a humanitarian concern, the devastation of the Congo was least an intellectually simple matter. Conrad's story was important for helping to call public attention to it and impressing it on the collective memory. But, in a larger perspective, the devastation of Congo, much like the Holocaust, was a challenge to Western and world traditions so fundamental that there was, in my opinion, no way an isolated individual could do justice to it, and it could only be addressed collectively over generations.

For Conrad, the jungle is less a geographical location than an embodiment of nihilism. The forest had by then strong associations of wonder, chivalry and economic utility, but the jungle was, by its very nature, something to be conquered and transformed. In Conrad's words, put in the mouth of Marlow, 'The Great Wall of vegetation, an exuberant and tangled mass of trunks, branches, leaves, bows, festoons, motionless in the moonlight, was like a rioting invasion of soundless life, a rolling wave of plants, piled up, crested, ready to topple over the Creek, to sweep every little man of us out of his little existence.'[17] Conrad had himself been captain of a boat on the Congo river and was writing from experience, but the scene sounds less like a primeval wood than a jumble of severed tree limbs, stems and new growth shortly after a woodland has been cut. In some respects, the description could become a self-fulfilling prophesy. In Africa, the Americas, India and elsewhere, native populations were decimated by imported diseases, massacres and wholesale destruction of their environment. As Indigenous settlements were abandoned, the woods that the inhabitants had lived in, landscaped and farmed, became darker, denser and more forbidding, which Europeans then mistook for their original condition.

The Belgian Congo was granted to King Leopold II of Belgium not as a national possession but as a personal protectorate, and he attempted to enslave virtually the entire region in pursuit of profits from ivory and rubber, resulting in a death toll that scholars estimate at about 10 million people. That figure may be slightly high, as it contains, along with those deliberately murdered and/or killed by imported diseases, those not born because of a decline in the birth rate. On the other hand, it only includes those in Leopold's Congo, and the figure would be much larger if we add those killed in adjacent possessions of France and other colonial powers, where the same methods of exploitation were used.[18]

The idea that Africa represented the state of the world before civilization persisted, and was even amplified for a long time despite, or perhaps because of, the ravages caused by the trade in ivory and rubber. An American book for young people about Theodore Roosevelt's big game hunting, published in 1909, stated that, 'Africa alone is still in the dress it had when it emerged from the creator's hands – its natives are still savages, not far above the wild monsters that rove around in its forests looking for prey.'[19]

The Innocence of Animals

In early twentieth-century Western literature, especially that for children, the jungle becomes a place eternally at the beginning of time, where killing may be done with a Victorian sort of childhood innocence. This was also the reason for the huge popularity of big game hunting among the European and American elites in the late nineteenth and early twentieth centuries. They would go on safaris clutching guns and accompanied by vast entourages of native servants who carried their baggage. Their mission was to kill animals, not for meat but for science, trophies or, in many cases, simply to create a lengthy list of victims. The more, the better. The bigger, the better. In only three months, Theodore Roosevelt boasted of having killed 42 large animals in East Africa, including lions, hippopotamuses, giraffes, wildebeests, buffalo and an elephant.[20] For this, he was allegedly worshipped 'almost as a god' by the natives.[21]

The killing was an affirmation of manhood, but it had no practical or environmental goal. Indeed, the glory of killing seemed to lie in the very lack of a reason. It belongs to a world prior to technocratically governed society. After adoring descriptions of the vast quantities of game killed by Roosevelt, the book speaks in contemptuous terms of Africans who have killed two antelopes for a village feast: 'They will chew him up with their sharp teeth like the hyenas down to the marrow of the bones. Such a huge waterbuck not often falls prey to their gluttonous stomachs.'[22] The white hunter becomes a force of nature, exempt from the limits elsewhere imposed by either social or biological necessities. His relation to the Indigenous people, as described in the book, is much like that of the medieval lord of a hunting preserve to the peasants in his domain.

Such Europeans and Americans in Africa were, in effect, attempting to revisit the 'childhood of humanity'. In *The Jungle Book* by Rudyard Kipling (first published 1894), the hero, Mowgli, is raised by wolves in the jungle of India. In *Tarzan of the Apes* by Edgar Rice Burroughs (first published 1912), the hero, Tarzan, is raised by apes. Both are, at least until they return to civilization, beings between man and animal, and they have the advantages of both – the innocence of animals and the power of human beings. They dominate the other animals, taking what they want, favouring those animals they like and punishing any hint of insubordination with death. In the context of their stories, that is their right, and perhaps even their duty, as human beings. However, like a child that must finally grow up, both must eventually join, or rejoin, human society.

This is a fantasy of primal innocence that drove many an explorer into the jungle. *Tarzan of the Apes* expresses a daydream that, in ways, even resembles that of Kurtz. When a village of Black Africans moves into his domain, Tarzan, whose name means 'white skin' in the language of apes, constantly steals their weapons, food and decorative objects, not hesitating to kill the possessors. Written at a time when Blacks were being lynched in the American South, the book has Tarzan string up the son of a Black chief by the neck and then taunt the villagers by placing the young man's headdress on a skull in the village square. Like Kurtz, Tarzan is worshipped by the Africans as a forest god, and the villagers leave out offerings to placate him.[23] Tarzan's tactics are not very different from the ways European adventurers used native Africans to obtain rubber and ivory. But there is something cartoonish about the violence, and we learn that 'When Tarzan killed, he more often smiled than scowled, and smiles are the foundation of beauty.'[24]

Tarzan dominates an anarchic kingdom, but Mowgli's jungle is more like a military camp. It is a place of authority, rules and order, which contrasts with the perceived anarchy and decadence of human society. All animals except the lawless monkeys are bound by a code called 'the law of the jungle', which grants supremacy to humankind; killing humans or their cattle is forbidden. Bagheera, the panther, tells Mowgli, 'All the jungle is thine,' and then adds, 'and thou canst kill everything that thou art strong enough to kill; but, for the sake of the bull that bought thee, thou must never kill or eat any cattle young or old. That is the law of the jungle.'[25] When Mowgli's patron, the old wolf Akela, is deposed from a position of leadership in the pack, Mowgli obtains a torch, threatens the wolves with fire, asserts his superiority over them and finally leaves.[26] Later, by killing the tiger Shere Khan and taking his skin, Mowgli confirms his status at the apex of bestial society.[27]

Both *Tarzan of the Apes* and *The Jungle Book* contain virtually no description of the jungle itself, because, as mentioned earlier, that is far more of a concept than a place. For Tarzan, the jungle is usually too tangled to

Advertisement for Florida grapefruit juice, *c.* 1945. It depicts GIs with guns and native people in a strictly subordinate role, while advertising grapefruit as 'the commando fruit'.

Advertisement for Coca-Cola, 1945, depicting muscular American soldiers
almost as supermen and poking fun at 'superstitious' African tribesmen
who do not understand a walkie-talkie.

easily navigate on foot, and so he gets around mostly by swinging through the trees. Both books have variants of the myth of Edenic man alone in the garden before the creation of Eve, where he is lord of the animals. In the Abrahamic tradition, the animals and people are said to have been vegetarian before the Flood (Genesis 1:29). Here, they eat mostly meat, but killing is entirely without ambivalence. It offers a way for humans to affiliate with animals without sacrificing any of their dominance. The

Comic strip about Tarzan appearing in the *Syracuse Post-Standard*, 11 December 1938.

stories of Tarzan and Mowgli remained very popular for many decades and were constantly repackaged in sequels, radio programmes, television specials, movies, imitations and so on.

Almost all people from the colonial powers assumed that Africans were 'savage', sadistic and childish. The few who did not, like Joseph Conrad, generally remained silent on the subject. A good deal of ethnography had already been written on Native Americans by the late nineteenth century but hardly any on Africans. In the nineteenth century no written language was common among the peoples of Central Africa, who were fragmented into several distinct cultures. Their artefacts, with occasional exceptions, were made from perishable materials, so our knowledge of the Indigenous cultures prior to European colonization is still very limited.

Africa today – like Europe, the Americas and almost the entire world – is cut off from its past. The African continent is mostly, and increasingly, deforested. Large animals are now mostly confined to wildlife reserves, and yet African art and design remain largely zoomorphic. Animals of the rainforest are found everywhere: patterns on women's clothes, designs on pots, games for children, ceremonies and so forth.[28] And yet the vividness of wild animals in traditional African art, which has no Euro-American counterpart, shows that their forebears knew the creatures well, and contemporary ones show that much of the knowledge has been retained.

What's in a Name?

The concept of the jungle, like that of other kinds of woodlands, has always been defined more by emotional associations than by biological or environmental characteristics. It suggests a ruthless, Darwinian struggle for existence. Dangerous places in the city are referred to as the 'asphalt jungle'. The 'law of the jungle' no longer means, as it did in Kipling, an elaborate set of rules but rather domination by the strong. The saying 'It's a jungle out there,' means that people are always ready to take advantage of somebody who shows any weakness. Today, the word 'jungle' remains fairly popular, but it is hardly ever used in scientific or environmental publications. Many people find a hint of racism in the way it disparages environments – and, by implication, people – of the southern hemisphere.

The word 'jungle' has become anachronistic in other ways as well. Until at least the middle of the twentieth century, people saw life in the tropical forest as governed by ruthless competition. Trees, they believed, were continually struggling in the canopy for light and in the ground for nutrients, with the losers condemned to death. Today, the emphasis is much more on cooperation, with trees exchanging nutrients, often with other species, through networks of mycorrhizal fungi. In truth, it is almost impossible to tell competition from cooperation in the forest, since individual identity is so unclear, and even the distinction between life and death can be uncertain.

13

The Man with the Big Axe

The glass case was completely dark, but when you pressed the big red button, it would be lit up by a yellow lightbulb representing the sun. Then you would see a typical middle-class American family of the 1950s, consisting of the man, his wife, a daughter, a son and a dog. They were standing proudly in front of their house and car. All of them, including the dog, started to sing about how everything in their home was made of petrochemicals. When they finished, the boy said, 'But not the cat. The cat is one thing in our home that is not made of petrochemicals.' A deep voice came out of the sky, replied jovially, 'Well, not yet,' and laughed. Then the case went dark again.

That was a fairly typical exhibit in the Museum of Science and Industry in Chicago, which I visited many times as a child in the 1950s and '60s. It was really a museum of advertising, and the main purpose of the exhibits, as with all ads, was to get attention. At the time, science was surrounded by an aura of almost religious gravity, and the exhibits contained just enough science to convince visitors they were on a sort of pilgrimage. The exhibits also contained a huge model of the human heart that would beat as you walked through it. There was even a camera where you could see yourself on television, a privilege then confined to celebrities and politicians.

The biggest exhibit of all, right in the centre of the main hall, was devoted to the hardwood industry. You would enter a little log cabin and look out the window to see a gigantic model of the logger Paul Bunyan's face, which would move its lips and shift its eyes. Sometimes it did this in silence, but at other times there were pre-recorded stories about Paul's deeds in logging camps. At the time, the lore of Paul Bunyan was widely regarded as an American folk epic that might be placed alongside the stories of King Arthur or Hercules.[1] Poet Carl Sandburg wrote, 'Some of Paul is as old as the hills, young as the alphabet.'[2]

The popular stories of Paul Bunyan are all based on a single theme – grandeur of scale. Paul is a giant, sometimes seven feet tall, sometimes eight and sometimes larger still. He is accompanied by his mascot, a huge blue ox named Babe. Paul digs out the great lakes and drops shovels of dirt in the St Lawrence River to create the Thousand Islands. He moves rivers so they can carry his timber. He creates the Grand Canyon by dragging his axe. The pan used by the cook in Paul's logging company is so large that in order to grease it, men need to skate around the surface with steaks on their feet. Paul calls his lumbermen to dinner using the trunk of a hollow tree as a bullhorn.

These stories epitomize a particularly American folkloric genre known as 'the tall tale', stories based on exuberant exaggerations and never intended to be literally believed.[3] They express the exhilaration of the industrial revolution, when many things that had previously seemed almost unimaginable were becoming part of daily life: railroads, telegraphs, skyscrapers, electric lights, telephones and so on. At the same time, the tales' extravagant humour helped to allay uneasiness. The element of self-parody alleviated the impression of arrogance that might accompany celebrations of power.

In the industrial revolution, people had learned to reshape entire landscapes with a speed and reliability that had once seemed the exclusive province of nature. They accomplished this by such means as digging long canals, building huge dams, dynamiting rocks, redirecting rivers and, of course, massive clearcutting. The formula of tall tales was to take results achieved at least in part by industry and attribute them to old-fashioned human strength and ingenuity. The result was to at least partially humanize industry while making its accomplishments seem even more spectacular.

Paul may be a logger in the backwoods, by some accounts illiterate, but the tales of him are permeated by the ideology of capitalism and progress. So many inventions are attributed to Paul that Harold Felton's extensive *Legends of Paul Bunyan*, which did not distinguish between authentic folklore and popularizations or fabrications, devoted an entire section to them. Paul reportedly invented the doughnut and the grindstone, as well as numerous devices for cutting trees, drilling oil, harvesting crops and so on.[4] According to one relatively authentic legend, he built a shotgun that would hit geese so high up that their meat was spoiled by the time they fell to the ground. He then salted his buckshot to preserve them.[5]

Tall tales faded in the latter twentieth century. While the industrial revolution involved increasing the size of technological devices, the digital revolution miniaturized them. The smartphone is a scaled-down yet more powerful version of the sort of computer that would once take up an entire room. Furthermore, factors from nuclear bombs to environmental pollution made the dangers that accompany new technologies impossible to ignore.

Tall tales are entertaining and easy to make up. The Paul Bunyan stories are spirited and funny, but there is nothing profound, lyrical or tragic about them. Unlike most heroes of folklore, Paul never seriously fails. He is never even tested by an especially formidable adversary. He just goes on cutting lumber, in forests that themselves seem inexhaustible. The tales express the spirit of an era infatuated with the idea of bigness – big men, big plans, big deeds, big dreams and, above all, big business. But the stories were initially told by relatively powerless laborers, and perhaps all the bluster hides a sense of vulnerability.

And what about the big forests? They were indeed being cut down on a big – that is, industrial – scale. By some accounts, Paul and his crew cleared 100 million board feet of white pine in 40 acres.[6] Paul also logged some states so completely that he turned them into prairies, an accomplishment announced with admiration and approval.[7] One tale has him cutting trees not with an axe but with a giant scythe, essentially reaping them the way a farmer would cut stalks of wheat.[8] Paul was to American trees what big game hunters were to African wildlife.

But the era of Paul Bunyan was an extremely ephemeral historical moment, lasting only a few decades at most. Many of the loggers who told Paul Bunyan stories around the fire probably realized their way of life was passing and wanted to give it a bit of glamour before it disappeared. By around the middle of the nineteenth century, the old growth forests of the Northeastern United States had been, except for a few isolated stands in the most inaccessible areas, cut down. There were, of course, second, third and fourth growth forests, but they did not yield the same quantity or quality of wood. The demand for wood was increasing since – in addition to traditional uses such as building, heating and blacksmithing – there were also industrial ones such as providing ties for railroad

American classroom poster from the 1950s on the uses of wood. Forests,
while still romanticized, were heavily commercialized as well.

tracks, fuel for engines, firewood for blast furnaces and wood pulp to
manufacture paper.

Like settlements, the timber industry moved westward initially to
the states around the Great Lakes. From 1878 to 1883, white pine lumber
production in the region more than doubled. It then fluctuated a bit but
continued to increase until 1892, when it began a very sharp decline that
continued for decades until, by 1920, production was far below the level
that had prevailed when the boom began.[9] The forests of the Great Lake
States were exhausted, and the timber industry would move on to those
of the South and the Pacific Northwest, which would soon meet the
same fate.

The first documented tales of Paul Bunyan were told in 1885 in the
vicinity of Tomahawk, Wisconsin.[10] Over the next decades, they appeared
in local Wisconsin newspapers and were collected by a few folklorists.
The initial tales were a good deal rougher than later versions. The loggers
were itinerant laborers, though some were highly skilled. They were
crowded together in temporary bunkers and had to do dangerous work,
sometimes in freezing weather.

To fell a tree, they would cut notches on one side with an axe and
then saw on the other side until it collapsed toward the side that had

been scored. But, especially with very old trees, there was always the possibility that they might be at least partially hollow at some unknown location inside, causing them to fall unexpectedly and in the wrong direction, something that could cause serious accidents and even deaths.

Since logging took place in remote areas with no railroads and often no roads nearby, the logs needed to be transported by streams. Since the banks were highly irregular, this would often cause logjams, which needed to be broken up. Loggers would have to balance on logs and then push the jammed logs along with poles or else resort to dynamite. Falls or explosions could cause injuries, and the loggers had no accident insurance.

Not surprisingly, when the camps broke up in spring and the loggers went to town after months of hard work, they became notorious for brawling, heavy drinking and whoring. Many loggers had scars and other highly visible injuries from fist or knife fights. Towns, much as they regretted the violence, had large brothels and saloons to accommodate them. There were probably early tales about Paul Bunyan's prodigious appetite for drinking, fighting and sex, but the loggers did not like to tell them to outsiders. A few informants hinted at their existence, and there are even a few brief references to Paul's drinking binges, but no substantial tales of that sort have come down to us.[11]

The mass popularity of Paul Bunyan tales is due entirely to advertising. In 1914, William B. Laughead, who had once been a logger but worked in the advertising division of the Red River Lumber Company, wrote a pamphlet entitled *Introducing Paul Bunyan of Westwood, California*, which contained descriptions of the company's products introduced with anecdotes about Paul Bunyan. The flyer was sent to potential customers and followed by a new edition two years later, but it was not a big success. The company advertised 'Paul Bunyan Pine' and used a picture of Paul as its logo.[12]

In 1922 Laughead published a promotional pamphlet entitled *The Marvelous Exploits of Paul Bunyan*.[13] Apart from a few pages on the products of the Red River Lumber Company, it centred entirely on the lore of the legendary lumberjack but took considerable liberties. From fragmentary, unconnected tales, Laughead constructed a coherent cycle. He named Paul's ox 'Babe' and made up colorful, folksy nicknames for Paul's companions, who had previously been anonymous, such as 'Johnny Inkslinger' and 'Sourdough Sam'. Writing from a corporate perspective, Laughead made Paul into an ideal manager.[14] He also greatly inflated

Bunyan's already considerable size and powers, making him less human and more divine, while implicitly making fun of the credulous loggers.

The names and other details invented by Laughead quickly entered the Paul Bunyan canon and even the oral traditions. Once Laughead established a frame, it was easy for others to invent Paul Bunyan tales for literary and popular purposes, and the written tradition immediately overwhelmed the oral one. It became impossible to separate folklore from popular entertainment. In addition to popular books, mostly for children, the craze for Bunyan lore included toys, games, cartoons, tourist destinations, restaurants and far more. He began as a figure of folklore but was transformed into a sort of comic-book superhero, rather like Tarzan or Superman.

The commercialization infuriated folklorist Richard Dorson, who used Paul Bunyan as the major example of what he called 'fakelore'. He called Paul Bunyan 'the pseudo folk-hero of twentieth-century mass culture, a conveniently vague symbol pressed into service to exemplify "the American spirit"'. He went on to list the many and contradictory ways that Paul had been used to exemplify ideals from the mythic proletariat to the efficient corporation. Finally, Dorson concluded that 'there is no myth, just a vacuous giant and his vacuous ox.'[15]

Statues of Paul Bunyan and Babe the Blue Ox at the California Trees of Mystery site, Klamath.

Dorson was a purist, endeavouring to establish folklore as an academic speciality. For that reason, he tried to sharply separate it from literary and, most especially, popular media. In this, he was ultimately not very successful. If many previous writers had greatly exaggerated the foundations of Paul Bunyan stories in the oral tradition, Dorson was still wrong to disregard the few authentic folktales about him almost entirely. More generally, Dorson failed to appreciate how intertwined oral and written traditions are and probably have always been. We regard the Arthurian tales as folk literature, yet there is no way to tell whether they were ever told very often around a hearth. All we really know for sure is that they formed the basis for many medieval epics. For all his aspiration to place folklore on a scientific basis, I suspect Dorson may have secretly clung to a very romanticized view of it. He thought of folklore as embodying the wisdom of a people and did not fully appreciate that folktales need not be any more profound than individually composed tales or works of journalism.

When Dorson was writing in the mid-twentieth century, commercial culture was far more sedate than it is today, and members of the intelligentsia were in perpetual rebellion against what they saw as pressure toward blandness and conformity. This spirit of revolt took many forms, such as existentialism, beatnik poetry and even rock 'n' roll. In folklore studies it was expressed as a demand for authenticity. Dorson saw the roughness of tales about Davy Crockett and Mike Fink – which could be crass, cruel and racist – as indications of their authenticity, especially in comparison with the comparatively sanitized ones of Paul Bunyan.[16] Dorson did not realize that tales of the frontier, with their emphasis on exaggeration and hyperbole, reflected and contributed to the commercial culture of the United States. Advertisers were, after all, greater boasters than even Mike Fink. And mass culture, even in its apparently most insipid forms, can, when examined carefully, tell as much about a society as any other sort of story. Paul may represent big logging, while Babe may represent big agriculture, but they are not vacuous.

There is a much bigger problem with the Paul Bunyan stories that has nothing to do with their genre. Most folklore celebrates the natural world, and that is a large part of its appeal. There is virtually nothing in the Paul Bunyan stories – whether folkloric, popular or literary – that hints at any spiritual or aesthetic appeal of the forests. The trees are nothing but commodities, to be exploited in as rapid and efficient a way as

Statue of Paul Bunyan at a gas station in Elmsford, New York, probably from the 1950s. Paul Bunyan was a bonanza for advertisers, who found ingenious ways to exploit his story. In this case, the British Petroleum corporation realized that their initials were the same as those of the legendary logger, 'PB', though in reverse order, and so they used him to advertise their product. After many decades, the statue is still standing, though now missing an arm.

Thure de Thulstrup, 'Logging in Northern Wisconsin', engraving from *Harper's Weekly*, 28 February 1885.

possible. The same applies to the animals, which, in some of the tales, are hunted on a comparably prodigious scale.

This confirms the assessment of forestry in the United States at the time by Gifford Pinchot, who would eventually become the first director of the United States Forest Service, that 'the greatest, the swiftest, the most efficient and most appalling wave of forest destruction in human history was then swelling to its climax in the United States, and the American people were glad of it.' He went on to tell how, as a nation of pioneers, American had regarded the forests simply as an obstacle to progress.[17]

Government Land

In one very early tale of Paul Bunyan that, for obvious reasons, does not make it into most anthologies, the big man does not have enough money to pay his loggers. He runs into the camp shouting that the men have been cutting trees protected by the government and will all soon be jailed. The men grab whatever possessions they conveniently can and run off in many different directions without demanding their money.[18] As usual, Paul is clever, but this time devious and dishonest as well. Almost alone in the Paul Bunyan tales, this one acknowledges an awareness that some people would consider clearcutting of ancient forests wrong.

As Paul and his crews were destroying the old-growth forest of the Great Lakes region, a movement for forest protection was indeed starting to grow. In 1864 President Lincoln had signed the Yosemite Valley Grant Act, which set aside Yosemite and some adjacent land for public uses such as hiking and recreation. In 1872 President Grant had signed a bill making Yellowstone the first national park. I imagine the loggers may have vaguely heard of these events without entirely understanding them. In partial defence of the loggers, we can add that the rationale for these parks was often vague, inconsistent and not easy to understand. In the context of the folktale, the idea of protecting the forests of Wisconsin is assumed to be absurd yet not so far-fetched that the crazies in Washington might not do it.

Today, however, we may well wonder why the old-growth forests of Wisconsin and other areas of the Great Lakes and South were not at least partially protected by the government. They had many huge trees but none that compared in width with the sequoias in the far west. They also lacked spectacular features such as vast gorges or high mountains. They were every bit as natural as Yosemite and often even less settled, but they were not so spectacular.

It is likely that setting aside national parks and rendering their landscapes as almost sacred could have made unrestrained clearcutting of other American forests easier. It alleviated people's consciences about the destruction of the natural world. Another option would have been to allow farms already established at Yosemite to continue while protecting substantial parts of the old-growth forests near the Great Lakes. Unfortunately, the exalted rhetoric about the grandeur of nature left little or no middle ground between veneration and commodification.

Repeated over millennia, the global pattern of deforestation, settling down, exhausting resources and moving on has created a pervasive feeling of nostalgia, a longing for some unknown way of life in the remote past. From Greco-Roman temples to Gothic cathedrals and Chinese pagodas, houses of worship are built on the model of forests, which are often considered sacred. This can, however, lead not only to their preservation but to their destruction. Much of deforestation since the start of the modern era has been driven by an almost religious intensity for icon smashing. Forests have been reviled as savage or simply an obstacle to progress.[19] But, even as they have destroyed forests, people have constantly mourned them. And perhaps our very concept of nature is basically a sort of nostalgia, a longing for something about which we know only that it has been lost.

The Tree of LIBERTY, — with, the Devil tempting John Bull.

James Gillray, *The Tree of Liberty, with the Devil tempting John Bull*, 1798, hand-coloured etching. This cartoon contrasts a tree of liberty, such as those planted during the French Revolution, with a tree of British tradition in the background.

14

The Politics of Trees

When a Frenchman reads of the garden of Eden, I do not doubt but he
concludes it was something approaching to that of Versailles, with clipped
hedges, berceaus, and trellis work.

HORACE WALPOLE

The biggest paradox in forest history for contemporary readers will probably be that we are so accustomed to think of forest protection as a cause of the political left and yet, for most of history, it has been identified mostly with the right. The distinction between the political left and right is a modern one, possibly dating only from the French Revolution, where parties in parliament were seated according to their political views on the left or right side of a podium. It is not easy to say exactly what is the difference between the political left and right. Generally speaking, the left is, or at least aspires to be, more democratic and less elitist. Through most of history, it has been primarily the elites that identified most with the natural world, perhaps because they had the means to best protect themselves from its dangers, enjoy its beauties and plunder its resources. The right is also more oriented toward the past, the left toward the future, though I suspect that distinction between the two may be far more tribal than philosophical. At any rate, environmentalism is now a major part of every left-wing party's platform, while it is minimalized or disregarded completely by the right.

In rural societies where forests were a relatively communal property, such as those of the Woodland people of the American Northeast or the peasantry of the early Middle Ages, they were used for a wide range of purposes, such as gathering firewood, collecting herbs or hunting. The boundary between the worlds of nature and humankind was a very gradual continuum. As one ventured further into the forest, human control gradually decreased and natural, or supernatural, beings became more prominent, but even the distinction between human beings and nature spirits could be very porous.

It is hard to say just when and how a sharp distinction between the realms of nature and humankind first came about. In the relatively anthropocentric culture of Greece and Rome, all major deities had a human form, though they occasionally transformed into animals. Some, like Apollo and Athena, were associated strongly with the human domain, while others, such as Dionysius and Artemis, were identified with forests and other landscapes. The former were more detached and sober, while the latter, especially Dionysius, were given to frenzy and madness.

Contrary to what is often supposed, the rise of Christianity brought no immediate, dramatic change in relations between human beings and the natural world. For one thing, Christianity, for the most part, proved very good at absorbing or being absorbed by folk beliefs. As to whether Christianity was more anthropocentric than Greco-Roman paganism, that is not clear. Christ was in some respects more unequivocally human than the Greco-Roman deities, since he was, like human beings, subject to excruciating pain and death. He was nevertheless a deity of vegetation, much closer to Dionysus than to Apollo.

Christianity became notably less tolerant with Charlemagne's genocidal war against the pagan Saxons around the end of the eighth century, in which he made death the penalty for refusing baptism or blaspheming Jesus. This was immediately followed by his assertion of greater control over the forests, the home of the Saxons, which began to lose their status as a communal territory. Most especially, he began to set aside large areas of the forest as hunting preserves, a practice that would be imitated by other monarchs and nobles throughout Europe in the centuries to come.

Charlemagne did not do this, however, in the name of human dominance. On the contrary, he asserted his power over the forests by claiming the authority of nature. This was, as we have already seen, affirmed in the highly ritualized hunt of the stag. The laws against deforestation and the restrictions on the use of the forests by peasants were a means of protecting nature against human encroachment. It was also a way of asserting the authority of the monarch since nature was understood as a divine, hierarchal order that conferred his authority. In many respects, peasants could be considered subordinate to animals, such as deer, and even trees.

This order partially changed in at the end of the Middle Ages. Though royal and noble hunting preserves continued, forests were increasingly cut down to make way for human settlement. As they disappeared, they were glamorized in knightly epics and in fairy tales as places of romance and adventure where conventional rules did not apply. As capitalism

Lucas van Valckenborch, *Spring*, 1595, oil on canvas. Even with the arrival of spring with its wonderful profusion of flowers, the subjects continue to wear very formal dresses. In the background is a Renaissance garden, meticulously laid out in many symmetrically shaped little plots.

gradually emerged out of the feudal order, deforestation and control of forests was undertaken in the name of human dominion.

The difference can perhaps most clearly be seen in the design of gardens. The Renaissance style of gardening, which reached its culmination in Louis xiv's palace at Versailles, dramatized human domination of nature, particularly through the imposition of symmetrical, geometric forms on gardens through neatly rectangular flower beds and on trees through elaborate topiary. Louis xiv, who is still thought of as the ultimate model of an absolute ruler, chose the sun as his emblem and was known as the 'Sun King'. He identified not with Christ but with Apollo, god of the sun and the most highly anthropomorphic deity of the Greco-Roman pantheon, who represented the arts of civilization and the perfection of the human form. Forests, which block the sun, became identified with backwardness and superstition.

The early modern style, epitomized in the eighteenth-century English garden, was based not on domination of nature but on claiming her authority and power. Nature might indeed be supreme but was personified in the ruler or lord of the manor. This style featured asymmetrical designs and curving lines. Even more than the Renaissance gardens, it emphasized control of the landscape by diverting streams, creating artificial lakes, changing topography and choosing where trees were to stand. Such gardens may have appeared natural, but that was only because the artifice was concealed, and the owners manipulated the landscape on a prodigious scale.[1]

The Renaissance style was unabashedly anthropocentric, while the early modern style aspired to be, and perhaps really was, biocentric. Both, however, served essentially the same cause in practice, which was authoritarian governance. What Humphry Repton, an originator of the English garden, called 'objects of mere convenience' were not allowed near the manor house, which was to dominate the entire landscape. Such objects included barns, schools, kitchen gardens, churchyards and anything else that had a strictly practical purpose.[2] Entire villages were sometimes demolished on the grounds that they interfered with the impression of a harmonious landscape centred around a noble residence.[3] Occasionally, a working farm might be hidden by the counterfeit ruin of a castle or church, buildings of greater distinction.[4] The manor house was an expression of nature, the order of which allegedly placed the wealthy above the rest of humankind.

The Whig gardens of Lancelot 'Capability' Brown and others partially gave way to the Tory gardens, which in some respects carried the identification of the owner with nature even further. The manicured landscapes of the former gave way to a simulation of 'wild' nature. The ideology of the Whig gardens was a combination of *laissez-faire* capitalism with aristocratic privilege, while the Tory ones were inspired partly by a reaction against the emerging capitalist order. They often looked back to an idealized feudal order of Old England, in which neither man nor nature was subject to the vicissitudes of the market. The manor was portrayed not as the representation of a new order so much as the administrative centre of an idealized community.[5] This also entailed weakening the concept of private property and a partial revival of the commons, which included forests. It culminated in the idea of state property, the origin of national parks.[6]

A vivid symbol of this identification of royalty and nobility with nature may be seen in many depictions of Charles II of England hiding in an oak tree from Cromwell's soldiers. John Evelyn dedicated his book *Silva*, first published in 1664, to the king, called Charles II *Nemorensis Rex* or 'King of the Woods' and referred to the tree as 'that holy oak, which you have consecrated with your presence'.[7] One illustration of the scene

Samuel Wale, *Adam and Eve in the Garden of Eden*, *c.* 1773, engraving. Paradise is here imagined on the model of a botanical garden, where Adam and Eve are the proprietors. Their dominance is strong but unobtrusive, and they tend flora and fauna from locations throughout the globe.

Display dish with Charles II in a tree, *c.* 1680, slip-decorated earthenware by Thomas Toft.

is an earthenware plate by Thomas Toft, made in about 1680 and now in the Metropolitan Museum of Art, New York. Like many others, it shows the young king not merely sitting in the branches but merging with the oak. Two branches form his arms, while the tree trunk becomes his neck and leads to his head. All around his head are oak leaves. Rampant on one side of the oak is a lion, symbol of England and of wild nature. On the other is a unicorn, also rampant, with a long, golden chain around its neck.[8] The traditional chain may symbolize the authority of Scottish kings. Especially in this context, the chain could further symbolize natural law, which allegedly affirmed the authority of the monarch. He is one with the tree and with the forest, whose numinous power affirms his right to rule.

The Timber Shortage

Particularly in France, the forests became the centre of ongoing power struggles among royalty, the nobility, the bourgeoisie and the peasantry. The debates may have been conducted in mostly practical terms, but symbolism, which could become almost as complicated as the power struggles themselves, was never very far from the surface. These began in the seventeenth century, as people in the powerful nations of Europe began to worry about an impending shortage of wood. They needed the wood not only for building, lighting, heating, blacksmithing and glass blowing but for blast furnaces designed to smelt ores on an industrial scale. In addition, many of these needs, for firewood especially, were aggravated by a decline in global temperature known as the Little Ice Age, lasting from about 1450 to 1850. The most dramatic need for wood, as far as many European governments were concerned, was for building ships, which required timber in huge quantities. The resulting debates about conserving wood sometimes resemble contemporary ones, and it is even tempting to see them as the beginning of the environmental movement. But none of the parties was in the least concerned about the environment, at least as we would understand the term today.

As ever more forests were cut down, trees increasingly became a luxury and a status symbol. Monarchs and aristocrats planted trees for elaborately landscaped pleasure gardens, where they might stand alongside statues of Venus, artificial ruins of 'ancient' temples and the like. Rows of trees were planted at regular intervals along important roads to provide shade and to absorb rainwater. Huge ones would often lead up to the gateway of a royal or aristocratic palace to dramatize the importance of the place.

In 1662 John Evelyn presented a paper to the newly formed English Royal Society, in which he advocated the planting of trees to provide wood for the British Navy. Two years later he expanded the paper into a book entitled *Sylva; or, The Propagation of Forest Trees*. In addition to giving copious advice on matters such as what trees grow best on various types of soil, Evelyn encouraged landowners to plant and conserve forest trees by appeals to tradition, in which, from Homer onwards, trees were greatly valued for their beauty and as signs of the proprietor's greatness.

Evelyn was far more concerned about preserving forests as a patrimony than as a material for building ships. He wrote in a preface, 'I did not altogether compile this work for the sake of our ordinary rustics (mere foresters and woodmen) but for the more ingenious – the benefit and diversion of gentlemen, and persons of quality, who often refresh themselves in these agreeable toils of planting.'[9] It does not seem likely that English aristocrats would have cheerfully given up their prize trees, cultivated by their families for generations, for the purpose of strengthening the navy. In any case, England was starting to import most of its timber for shipbuilding from Russia, the Baltic states and the American colonies, and it did not need to be self-sufficient.[10]

In 1669 Jean-Baptiste Colbert, the powerful finance minister to Louis XIV of France, issued his *Ordonnance des Eaux et Forêts* (Ordinance Concerning Waters and Forests), in which he laid out a programme for the preservation of French forests, which was designed to assure his nation's military power. France, unlike England and the Netherlands, had indigenous reserves of timber that might potentially meets the needs of a growing navy, but this would only be possible with careful husbandry.[11] The system used primarily in management of French forests was summed up in the often-repeated formula *Le taillis sous futaie* or 'coppice under the high trees', which resonates like a political slogan. The large trees suggest the royalty and nobility, while the coppice beneath is for more humble people. The understorey might provide firewood and serve other everyday purposes. The high trees, which could take almost a century to grow, were to provide long boards for the sides of navy ships and poles for their masts. Rather than clearcutting, the system allowed people to take timber more or less as needed.

The approach of *taillis sous futaie*, however, had practical, environmental and aesthetic problems. For one thing, having two sharply distinguished heights of trees (that is, very tall and short) offered considerably less variety than you would find with natural regeneration, in which there would be a broad mix of many elevations and species. In addition, the canopy of the large trees might close, making it impossible for the trees below to get sufficient light. To have cutting dictated by the market and military needs also did not leave a forester much flexibility. Evelyn, who knew vastly more about forestry than Colbert, had objected to mixing coppices with high trees, on the grounds that the two would compete for space and resources. He recommended instead that timber trees be placed on the periphery of a field 'so that their branches may freely spread'.[12]

Colbert's ordinance reflected the king's desire to centralize authority and assert it over his nobles. It granted the navy vast control over the forests of France, even when owned by members of the nobility, including the privilege of marking and preserving promising trees. Those who wished to sell timber had to retain ten of the best trees, preferably oaks, in each lot that was sold for eventual use in shipbuilding. The ordinance, however, was not enforced consistently, especially since the king's wars and building projects created a financial strain, and even the king sold wood indiscriminately in violation of the provisions to finance his ambitions.[13]

If *taillis sous futaie* was the arrangement appropriate to a feudal society, the Prussian system of raising conifers of the same age in evenly spaced rows and clearcutting was that of an early industrial one. Unlike France and England, Prussia had no great aspiration to be a maritime power. It was concerned far more with the quantity than with the quality of wood, which was intended to supply fuel not only to heat homes and for small businesses but for major industries such as mining. Hans Carl von Carlowitz was director of the mines in Saxony, a part of Prussia, which required vast amounts of wood for supporting mineshafts and for furnaces to transform raw ore into metal. He published his *Sylvicultura oeconomica* (Economic Forestry) in 1706, and the book is widely considered the beginning of scientific forestry. Its foundation was the principle of sustainability (*Nachhältigkeit*), which stated that one should never take more wood than was currently being grown.[14] Ironically perhaps, this idea was the result of extreme commodification, something contemporary environmentalists often warn against. It was an extension of a familiar maxim of business – that one should balance the budget.

Rosgiebing Manor, *c.* 1700, woodblock print. This was published by the *Fruchtbringende Gesellschaft* (Fruit-Bringing Society), a benevolent organization of aristocrats intended, above all, to improve the German language. It shows how monocultures of conifers had been planted by nobles on their estates, especially in Germany, before that became an official policy in Prussia.

Understood in a far broader way than Carlowitz intended, the concept was to become a foundation of ecology.

Carlowitz advocated clearcutting followed by massive planting of seeds, essentially the sort of harvesting and replanting practised by farmers with their crops. He favoured conifers, especially spruce, on the grounds that they grow very quickly. Reforesting on a massive scale with lines of conifers had already been practised by aristocrats landscaping their estates, but the work of Carlowitz extended the practice to industry.

Though his basic orientation was commercial, Carlowitz devoted a good deal of attention to the religious and cultural significance that woods had throughout the ages. He was possibly the first to call attention to the '*silvae horridae*', the forests of terror, described by Tacitus.[15] This fitted in with an emerging aesthetic of industrialization, which evoked awe through grandeur of scale. Ecologically harmful though they were, the enormous areas of planted conifers had a sort of splendour. The vast monocultures of spruce trees were not indigenous, but they quickly came to be associated with Prussia. This would also provoke a reaction in the centuries to come and inspire Romantic nostalgia for the oaks and linden trees of former days.

Both the French and the Germans took pride in their forests. The Germans often liked to believe that their country was more densely forested than France. The French, meanwhile, considered the forests in their country more natural than those in Germany. In any case, the Prussian system proved more consistent with the emerging capitalist order. No other country, so far as I can tell, adopted the French *taillis sous futaie*. Other European nations, including France, increasingly adopted the Prussian practice of replacing indigenous trees with conifers,[16] even in the seemingly primeval woods of Fontainebleau.[17]

Britain led the world in industrialization, and in consequence had the greatest need for fuel. By 1805 old-growth forests were reduced to covering only 4.5 per cent of Britain.[18] Many landscapes, including some around historic buildings, were denuded of trees to the point where they appeared desolate. Nevertheless, the consequences of deforestation in Britain and Continental Europe were largely confined to aesthetic and long-term environmental factors. The lack of wood neither inhibited the building of naval ships nor the growth of industry.

The consensus of researchers is that concern about an imminent dearth of timber, at least considered as a commodity, in Britain and

After a painting by George Henry Boughton, *The Heir Presumptive*, after 1873, engraving.
The huge trees indicate the antiquity of the estate the little boy is set to inherit. The word
'presumptive' rather than 'apparent' is used ironically and suggests
that the legacy is unsure. The boy and his mother are attended by a Black servant or
slave, and the painting was done a few years after the American Civil War.
The aristocratic order of the American Southeast was doomed.

Continental Europe had been overly dramatized.[19] Everywhere, the need
for wood as fuel was being gradually eased by the growing availability of
coal. Evelyn used the need for timber in navy shipyards mostly as a pre-
text for writing about an expensive hobby. Colbert was attempting to
bring forests under the control of the state. Carlowitz's plan commodified
the forests for commercial purposes, while denying, or at least interfer-
ing with, many traditional uses of forests by both the peasantry and the
nobility. In general, Evelyn spoke for the nobility, Colbert for the king
and Carlowitz for the emerging bourgeoisie. The only way in which they
anticipated contemporary environmentalism was that they thought in
the long term, on a scale of many decades and even centuries. People had
been doing this almost from time immemorial with reference to family
names and ancestral homes.

But perhaps Evelyn, Colbert and Carlowitz shared an agenda here that
went beyond politics. There have been periodic scares about the death of
forests which turned out to be overstated, for example, in Continental
Europe in the 1980s. It is hard to untangle pragmatic concerns from
symbolic ones, but the idea that forests are a primeval heritage serves
to amplify any sense of crisis. The forests, as we have seen, have been

consistently identified with times gone by, particularly with the monarchy and nobility, and these institutions were increasingly coming under attack. To protect them meant to preserve a legendary past against the assaults of modernity.

As belief in the divine right of kings gradually declined, their identification with forests did as well.[20] In 1792, the year in which Louis XVI was arrested, the revolutionary government of France planted 60,000 trees, predominantly oaks, which were called 'Liberty Trees'. These were an expression of confidence in the future at a time when many saw the French Revolution as a new dawn for humankind. The same year the government approved a dating system that counted years not from the appearance of Jesus Christ but from the founding of the First Republic, though it was only used for a short time. Liberty Trees were generally placed in public spaces so that citizens might gather in their shade. The symbolism, like the Republican form of government, remained contested. In 1852 Napoleon III, who had just reestablished the monarchy in a coup at the end of the preceding year, ordered what remained of the Liberty Trees to be cut down. The tradition was replaced by that of 'President Pines', which symbolized excellence in an orderly, hierarchal state.[21]

Nazi Environmentalism

The political symbolism of trees and forests became more complicated as they reflected not simply conflicts between monarchy and republicanism but also several others, for example between *laissez-faire* capitalism and socialism, religion and secularism, nationalism and internationalism, or the Western and Soviet blocs. In general, however, conservation of forests was identified with the political right until roughly the last third of the twentieth century. This culminated in the Third Reich. The Nazi seizure of power was followed immediately by an unprecedented series of highly detailed laws concerning the protection of nature, including two on forests, several on animals and one on the hunt. These culminated in the Law on the Protection of Nature of June 1935.[22] These laws were pervaded by the ideology of 'blood and soil' and the idea that concern for animals and nature was a demonstration of German ethnic superiority, but they also contained many provisions that were humane or environmentally sound. Germany became the first European country to protect the wolf and other predators.[23] It banned all billboards in the countryside.[24]

Hermann Göring, arguably Hitler's second in command, assumed the titles of 'Master of German Forests' and 'Master of the German Hunt', together with the right to appropriate land for the purpose of conservation without compensating the owner.[25] In 1935, at a hunting festival, Göring said, 'We are accustomed to think of the German people as eternal. There is no better image for this than the forest.'[26]

The leading Nazis were, with notable exceptions such as Joseph Goebbels, vehemently anti-urban and believed the German people drew their strength from the forests.[27] Foresters had the second highest rate of membership in the Nazi party of any profession, exceeded only by veterinarians.[28] Ancestral Heritage, the branch of Heinrich Himmler's ss devoted to research, planned a massive study comprising over sixty volumes devoted to the relationship between Germans and their forests, though little of it came to fruition.[29] The project served imperialistic goals by claiming areas that had allegedly been part of a primeval forest as German heritage. The Nazis planned to 'Germanify' and reforest vast areas of their conquered territories, including almost all of Ukraine.[30]

The blockbuster documentary film *Ewiger Wald: Bedeutung der Natur im Dritten Reich* (Eternal Forest: The Meaning of Nature in the Third Reich), released in 1936 by the Militant League for German Culture, identified the German people with their forests by alternating scenes of nature and German history. It began by showing pagan rituals such as dances around the maypole in the forest. Subsequent scenes showed battles fought in the forest by German warriors, Teutonic knights and Prussian militias.[31] The forests were shown as commercially exploited in the Weimar Republic but revived under the Nazis, and the final scene was a triumphant May Day celebration beneath the forest canopy.[32] The message was that the German people would always triumph, like the forest from which they had emerged.[33] Ironically, when the film showed an area being reforested after a battle, it was with evenly spaced spruce, which had been favoured only since about the start of the eighteenth century, not with indigenous trees.

Despite having been written about by many outstanding scholars such as Raul Hilberg and Richard Overy, the Nazi period and the Holocaust remain half-repressed today, still surrounded by all sorts of traumas and sensitivities that can make it difficult or impossible to discuss constructively. All sides in political conflicts caricature the Nazi movement to make it seem the opposite of whatever cause they advocate. They then dismiss every indication to the contrary as propaganda. But such arguments lead us in endless circles, and I think environmentalists should freely acknowledge that the Nazis did share several of their ideas, especially to shield those ideas from further abuse. The Nazis were identifying state power with the natural world, a tradition that goes back at least to Charlemagne. Hitler stated in 1933 that 'Man should never fall into the misconception that he has really risen to be lord and master of nature.'[34] These words were not said in a spirit of humility but to claim a mandate from nature for his rule. The best lesson from that historical era may be that nature does not have a human face.

Meanwhile, most of the left, particularly the Bolsheviks, generally regarded concern with nature and forests as sentimental, indulgent and escapist.[35] In his poem 'To Posterity', Bertolt Brecht wrote that, 'to speak of trees is almost a crime, for it is a kind of silence about injustice!'[36] When the Green Party was first founded in West Germany around 1980, many worried that it would lead to a revival of fascism.[37] Conservation became not only entirely respectable on the left but a fundamental principle, a change that was accomplished so completely that most people have entirely forgotten the long association of forests with the political right.

One obvious reason for the reversal is the increased awareness on the left of climate change and the accompanying hazards. Another reason is that the right, particularly in its defence of forests, was driven by anti-modernism. For quite some time, the modern era, often dated by historians from 1800 through 1950, seemed to be almost an eternal condition. As long as there would be human beings, each generation was expected be more 'modern' and less traditional than the one before. Today, modernism is rapidly fading into the past and has become an object of nostalgia. But, for the left, the modern era is increasingly associated with slavery, colonialism, misogyny, genocide and environmental destruction.

Today, there are green parties like the German one in all European democracies and even a small one in the United States. By now, they are a familiar part of the political landscape and no longer appear particularly radical. They are all regarded as left or centre-left, and it is very clear that the initial fears about them were greatly overblown. A revival of ecofascism such as that in Nazi Germany – which could come either from the right, the left or, most likely, some combination of the two – is, however, a genuine possibility. That could be brought on as the problems associated with climate change increase in severity and democratic governments continue to show themselves incapable of dealing with them. One scenario is that those who have most vehemently denied the reality of human-induced climate change could suddenly become aware of it, insisting that the problem could be managed only through authoritarian controls. Should that happen, however, I am convinced that ecofascism would also fail.

Deforestation, resulting in climate change, is not the sort of problem that we can ever simply solve and forget. It is embedded in an extremely complex matrix of cultural, historical, economic, technological and legal conditions.[38] Addressing the problem constructively will involve a lot more than bold initiatives by charismatic leaders. That will require organic adjustments and coordination on many levels, in ways that are much too numerous and subtle to always be carried out on command. We must be less like an army and more like a forest.

Francis Quarles, *Hieroglyph XIV*, from the book *Emblems* (1696).
The flame and the falling leaves are two traditional symbols of transience.

15

The River in the Forest

The past is never dead. It's not even past.

WILLIAM FAULKNER

Time seems utterly real, and yet it is completely intangible. You cannot store it in a jar or point to it with your finger. Michael Marder is a philosopher who has extensively studied the ways in which plants challenge our notions of identity and thereby the basic ontologies with which we try to understand the world. He writes, 'the meaning of vegetal life is time.'[1] Plants express time through their seasonal cycles, their regular growth, as recorded in rings of a stump, and their patterns of germination and decay.

Plants, from cut flowers to autumn leaves, have always been symbols of transience. From Japanese haiku to Renaissance sonnets, they are invoked to remind people that human accomplishments do not last forever. Take the opening lines of Shakespeare's sonnet 73:

> That time of year thou mayst in me behold
> When yellow leaves, or none, or few, do hang
> Upon those boughs which shake against the cold,
> Bare ruined choirs where late the sweet birds sang.[2]

Before calendars and the countless devices people use for the measurement of time, it was mostly brought to human awareness by vegetation, and that is still largely the case in lyric poetry.

We may measure time with watches, but we construct it, like everything else, with images. There are no straight lines in a forest, and so it is hard to think of time, or anything else, as linear. That understanding gradually emerges in the cities, perhaps most especially in the Zoroastrian and Abrahamic tradition, which views time as leading up to a final battle between good and evil. Like a straight board, time is sawed in two. The city comes to represent the future, while the forest represents the past. The present is the space between them. Every traditional image of the forest is also a reconstruction of the past. Like the past, the forest is full of secrets, which it may hoard, release or destroy. In medieval forests, this is a past of wondrous adventures. In the Rococo forest, it is a time of ubiquitous eroticism. In Gothic forests, it is one of profound faith. In the jungle, it is primitive and violent.

My inventory of ways in which people understood the forest is very broad, yet they have a few things in common. In our traditions, from the royal hunting preserve to the Rococo forest, the forest is a sort of mythic past, which contrasts, for better or worse, with a demythologized present. In just about every case, the world of the forest is animistic, contrasting with the humanistic perspective that prevailed, and still mostly prevails, in Western culture. If people see the past as one of great fertility, the forest will be eroticized, as it is in Rococo art. If they see it as terrifying, the forest will be deep and dark, as it is in many European fairy tales. Indeed, just about every Western representation of the forest is a different conception of a primeval state.

The sharp division of time into future and past is closely bound to other dualities – civilization and savagery, humankind and nature, order and chaos, reason and madness. People have projected traits they wished to disown, such as 'savagery', outwards into the forest. They have tried to claim aspects of the forest such as 'antiquity' as their own. I speak of these ideas of the forest as being more poetically than socially constructed, because they are not primarily a reflection of relationships among different human beings. Rather, they are statements about humankind, understood in relation to a rather mystical other self. Every conception of the forest is a kind of cosmology.

Human management and cultivation are almost as old as the forests themselves. The expansion of what we know as civilization has required frequent deforestation, which has continually generated, and reaffirmed, a nostalgia for some vaguely imagined primeval world. As physical forests were increasingly objectified, those of literature were spiritualized. Caring for forests became increasingly technocratic, while images of them grew less realistic and more romantic.

People have traditionally thought of the forest as almost outside of history, a place where humankind began. It was a sort of fixed point against which humankind could measure how far it had come. One early indication that, for a few people at least, this was starting to change, is in Shakespeare's play *Macbeth*. The three weird sisters tell Macbeth:

> Macbeth shall never vanquished be until
> Great Birnam Wood to high Dunsinane Hill
> Shall come against him. (4.1.105–7)

Macbeth takes that to mean that he is invulnerable, for that can never happen. When Malcolm leads an invading army against Macbeth, he tells his men to each take a branch of a tree and march with it so as to conceal their numbers. A servant reports to Macbeth that the wood has begun to move, and the usurper is soon overthrown. Forests are no longer, as Macbeth had imagined, part of a changeless order but subject to alteration. Nevertheless, at least until very recently, they have continued to represent a potentially eternal condition, something to preserve, escape or return to.

Forests Yesterday and Today

Forestry today is a highly technical subject in which almost everything quantifiable is quantified. Forests are described statistically in terms of the density, diameter, species composition, age and other characteristics of trees. More emotional or aesthetic factors are likely to be mentioned by forestry professionals only in passing, but they are always in the background and unobtrusively drive discussions. Foresters also conscientiously record all possible uses of trees. In New York State, where I live, these include harvesting timber, keeping bees, maple sugaring and growing shiitake mushrooms, to name just a few. Now one more has been added, carbon sequestration, with an urgency that makes all of the others fade into insignificance.

From the point of view of those who love forests, carbon sequestration is also the benefit by far the least immediately apparent. This value is not directly perceived on a local level, nor is it to be seen on a small scale of time. If the massive task of stabilizing the climate enters our awareness as we walk through a forest at all, that will be on a level closer to that of myth rather than that of immediate practicality. We can conjecture that trees are in some sense sentient, yet we do not know what they see or hear. We know they are constantly exchanging messages, yet we cannot decipher or translate them. And we know they are helping to stabilize the global climate, yet we do not view this process in an immediate way. Nevertheless, carbon sequestration gives a reason, or sometimes an excuse, to protect forests, which may resonate beyond boundaries such as the neighbourhood, the region or the nation.

Today, deforestation is taking place at a rate far beyond any point in history, even the frantic cutting down of trees in North America memorialized in the stories of Paul Bunyan. Rates of deforestation and reforestation have now roughly stabilized in temperate zones of Europe and North America. Almost all the loss of forests is in the tropical regions of Latin America, Africa and Asia.[3] In 2021 the tropics lost 80 million acres of forest, an area approximately the size of Belgium.[4] But the responsibility lies at least as much with wealthy countries of the north as with tropical ones. The deforestation is driven mostly by the demand for timber and agricultural products in wealthy countries of the northern hemisphere.

The ideal of preserving or restoring wilderness dominated conservation until about the last quarter of the twentieth century, especially in the United States, and it remains influential today. In practice, this very often becomes a justification for ever more aggressive human intervention in natural processes. Most of the time, it has taken the form of eradication of invasive species or reintroduction of native ones. At times, these endeavours have been very successful, as when the reintroduction of wolves to Yellowstone National Park led to a renaissance of vegetable life. At other times, biologists may have inadvertently killed off native species along with introduced ones by spraying landscapes with herbicides or injecting poisons into streams.[5]

When the period that environmentalists are trying to restore is more remote, the intervention is likely to be more intense. George Monbiot, for example, has proposed restoring the ecosystem of remote times to large parts of Britain in his book *Feral*. Since many of the animals that lived then are now extinct, it would involve bringing in their relatives such as lions and elephants instead. The project would simultaneously entail extirpating 'invasive' ones such as sheep. Monbiot denies he is trying to recreate a specific landscape of the past and instead wishes to create one that is more vibrant and spontaneous, but the Paleolithic past is obviously his template.[6] I fear that trying to realize this vision would in practice lead to the opposite of what he wishes to accomplish. Upon reintroduction, even species that had only recently become extinct in the wild, such as whooping cranes and California condors, need to be extensively trained, constantly watched and regularly examined for poisons. The lions and elephants would need to be carefully monitored, and the restored jungle would be filled with hidden cameras. The plan could turn Britain into a safari park.

While the great majority of environmentalists support the eradication of many invasive species, there are a few dissenters. Fred Pearce in his book *The New Wild* argues that we should support, or at least accept, the globalization of wildlife, which will ultimately lead to greater diversity. He argues that, while invasive species may initially spread explosively, they eventually reach a natural limit, as their resources become scarce, their prey find defenses and their predators multiply. An example he gives is cane toads, which were initially imported to Queensland, Australia in 1935 to eat beetles that were damaging the sugar cane crop. They soon began to devastate a wide range of insects, lizards and other wildlife. Human attempts to eradicate the toads had little success, but eventually, according to Pierce, other animals learned how to keep them under some control. The toads are protected from predators by a poisonous gland inside their heads, but predators from crows to crocodiles figured out how to devour their flesh while avoiding the venomous parts.[7]

Similar controversies come up with reference to other modern problems that are confronting our forests, such as increasingly destructive wildfires, huge numbers of deer that prevent forest regeneration by eating young shoots and, of course, climate change. All these problems are largely caused by human beings. Does that mean that human beings should now withdraw from forests, interfere as little as possible and let nature take over? Or does it mean that human beings should intervene more aggressively to undo the damage we have created? There is no simple answer to this dilemma, but nearly all scientific environmentalists believe that human intervention is now required to prevent further destruction of our forests.

That is also my opinion. Without much doubt, life on earth will eventually recover from the current crises of species extinction and climate change. It has recovered from several mass extinctions and geological upheavals in the past, some of which were far worse than even the most pessimistic current projections about loss of biodiversity, but the process has taken millions of years. Furthermore, the idea of non-intervention seems to presuppose, and also re-enforce, a sharp separation between human beings and the natural world. This would, at the very least, be extremely difficult to maintain, and would condemn us to a perpetual sense of alienation. Instead, I believe people need to reclaim a place in the natural world. Human influence on the environment can be benign, as it was in the American Northeast before the arrival of Europeans.

This is also why, unlike some of my friends, I support careful, judicious logging in forests. It is often necessary to open up a closed canopy in the forest, so that new shoots will have sunlight. It may also be needed to reduce the spread of an arboreal pathogen or to prevent any species of tree from becoming overly dominant. Beyond that, I believe that this, and related activities, help to affirm our bonds with the natural world. If somebody has a coffee table or bowl with wood of an exquisite grain, it will serve as a perpetual reminder of the forest that produced it.

The Postmodern Forest

Jean François Lyotard announced in his book *The Postmodern Condition* (French edition, 1979) the end of 'grand narratives'. By these he meant essentially what we usually call 'ideologies', glorified histories of institutions such as science or democracy, intended to inspire public support.[8] For a while, this idea became itself a sort of 'grand narrative'. 'Postmodernism' became the trendiest academic buzzword since 'Futurism' in the early twentieth century, but it outlived the flurry of publicity. Freudian Psychoanalysis and Marxism, the leading ideologies of the early and mid-twentieth century, have faded, and nothing has taken their place.

For some, the renunciation of grand narratives has become a reason to focus only on narrow specializations, but these are trivial in isolation. I would like it to be instead a reason to use structures that are broadly encompassing yet flexible. A vast range of cultural phenomena may be brought together in an organic unity that is less like that of a system such as psychoanalysis or communism and more like that of a poem.

The grand narrative that ruled forestry had been that of a climax state, a balanced condition that any forest would allegedly move toward in time if left alone by human beings. Even more broadly, it was the idea of an eternal 'natural state' that one might preserve or return to.[9] That is essentially a version of a 'virgin' or 'primeval' forest, one that is purely a product of nature and owes nothing to humankind. This concept can inspire reverence, and reputed fragments of such a forest have been set aside as sacred groves, royal hunting grounds or national parks. The idea of a 'virgin' forest can inspire aggression, becoming the object of a frequently eroticized conquest.

That concept is now widely rejected, leaving us with what we might call 'postmodern forestry'. The notion of forests as representing some changeless order or balance has been discarded by foresters and scientific environmentalists in the twenty-first century. With or without human intervention, the composition of forests is in constant flux. Disturbances such as fires, violent storms and beaver-dam-created floods are no longer viewed simply as accidents to be avoided but as part of the way forests grow and adapt. Foresters try to mimic the effects of such disruptions, primarily by judicious cutting down of carefully selected trees.[10] Particularly in the United States, they are experimenting with controlled fires to clear the ground covering, release nutrients and preempt more violent conflagrations later on.[11]

But, even as I repudiate the idea of a primeval forest, I do not intend this as an exercise in debunking. It has contributed to important works of literature from Virgil's *Aeneid* and Dante's *Inferno* to medieval romances and the fairy tales of Grimm. It has inspired painters such as Caspar David Friedrich and Thomas Cole. Their works do not suddenly become invalid. The forest remains an image of primordial chaos, wonder, terror and hope. But simply by placing the primeval forest at a mythic beginning of the human ascent, we set up barriers between history and prehistory, humanity and nature, civilization and wilderness.

We perpetually construct an ideal of a primeval forest, but we then destroy such forests in the name of progress. This is a ritualistic cycle that became especially apparent in the modern era, as people constantly sought out seemingly untouched wilderness to cut it down, mourn it and attempt to recreate it. This sequence goes all the way back to the start of civilization with *The Epic of Gilgamesh,* and it seems to have become more pronounced in the modern era. The forest becomes a sort of sacrificial offering. Like religious rituals, this helps to affirm our values. But it involves destruction on a scale that is rendering it unsustainable. As long as we identify the forest with a past from which we often wish to escape, this pattern will probably continue.

A forest is characterized at least as much by its ambiance as by its biological composition. It is not easy to say what is the physical difference, if indeed there is one, between a forest and a 'woodland', a 'jungle', an 'arboreal park', a 'swamp', a 'wooded pasture' and so on. We should also remember that landscapes are highly individual and do not necessarily fit neatly into our preconceived categories, just as human personalities do not necessarily fit into a list of standard types.

While people have given a wide range of definitions, the concept of a 'forest' has usually been understood for at least the last few hundred years or so in relation to the primordial wilderness as an ideal type. If we reject that as a model, what can take its place? One possibility is the idea of a forest as an organic whole, resembling a single animal or plant yet composed of innumerable species, which are in constant communication with one another. We might even think of the forest as an enormous mind, while we human beings that stroll through it are thoughts.

If any ideal has taken the place of restoring the 'balance of nature' in forestry so far, it is complexity. When rich forests were spread across almost the entire American Northeast, transitions between one habitat and another could be very gradual. Now, when forests are more fragmented and less healthy, ranges of species need to be concentrated over a smaller area. The goal now is to have as much variety as possible in a forest. With respect to trees, this means a range of species, ages, heights, levels and so on.[12] After a harvest, some trunks and branches should be left on the ground, to provide a space for animals to seek cover and forage for insects. Leaves and remains of other decomposing vegetation should also be left to provide a habitat for worms, beetles and fungi. A variety of habitats is especially necessary because the environments where birds nest are not necessarily those in which they forage. The scarlet tanager, for example, breeds in a mature forest but otherwise prefers the understorey of a young forest.

I am happy to accept complexity on an interim basis as an organizing principle, but I am not convinced that it is either precise enough to offer much scientific guidance or inspiring enough to motivate people over generations. It does not have the mythic resonance of the 'primeval' or 'climax' forest. Besides, contemporary life is complicated enough already, and people are likely to crave simplicity. But, like the forests themselves, our mythopoeic images of them continue to evolve.

There does not necessarily need to be a single strategy for conservation, and it may help to have a range of competing approaches. Currently, in New York State where I live, 74 per cent of forested land is privately owned by individuals and families in lots averaging about 20 acres in size.[13] The owners generally keep their forest not for commercial reasons so much as for recreational, personal and environmental ones. In consequence, they take a wide variety of approaches to conservation from simply leaving forests alone to very aggressive intervention. We are able to learn from all approaches, especially by comparing the results achieved by them.

For now, the most locally specific goals of forest management are likely to be the most reliable, for example the preservation of a particular tree, lizard or bird. A few forests in New York State are managed to provide the highly specialized habitat required by the cerulean warbler. In the long run, my hope is that, in rejecting the concept of a primeval condition, we will cease to be dominated by an imagined past and more open to the present beauty of the forest.

Anthropocentrism

A strictly linear view of time has been closely tied to anthropocentrism, since it has historically regarded 'man' as the centre, the driving force and the culmination of progress. On several grounds, we should reject that now. For one thing, we place a vast burden on humanity if we make it the sole focus of our dreams, hopes and aspirations. We doom ourselves to perpetual disappointment, which can eventually lead to misanthropy. Furthermore, anthropocentrism places a great limit on our imaginations and, thereby, our capacity for joy. In addition, human identity is something that has been constructed gradually over thousands of years. It does not even exist apart from the many other species that have helped supply the concepts, symbols and models with which we describe it. That is why, for example, we always have birds and flowers on our cards for Valentine's Day. But the most compelling reason to reject anthropocentrism is also the simplest. It just does not make much sense.

I do not, however, believe that moving beyond anthropocentrism can be nearly as simple as some of my friends and colleagues seem to suppose. For one thing, having been raised in a society that has been permeated with anthropocentric perspectives for hundreds of years, we cannot simply discard them at will. They are even implicit in our language, in so many ways that we can hardly even be aware of all of them.

Furthermore, in an anthropocentric perspective, ethical decisions are at least simpler. The noblest reason for making a decision once seemed to be the expectation that it would benefit humankind. We know, or at least usually think we know, what will be good for human beings. We do not know this very well with respect to other forms of life. We can simplify the problem a bit by presuming these interests are the same as ours, but that assumption itself is profoundly anthropocentric. Furthermore, the various alternatives such as biocentrism, Gaiacentrism and ecocentrism are, in my opinion, still very incompletely and imperfectly articulated.

Finally, we should not think of moving beyond anthropocentrism as a panacea. A biocentric perspective does not guarantee that we will treat other forms of life well any more than an anthropocentric one guarantees that we will be good to our fellow human beings. For one thing, despotism is about giving some human beings a far more exalted status than others, but it has little to do with human status in the cosmos. The late medieval kings of Europe were not anthropocentric, as we have seen, in that they identified with the natural world, but they often found greater value in woodland trees and animals than in the peasantry. The Nazis were not anthropocentric, since they organized their world not around humankind as a whole but a biotic community, which embraced some animals and plants but excluded many human beings.[14] A German dog might be valued more than a Jewish man.

In summary, those of us who study the relations between human beings and the natural world have our work cut out for us. It seems possible that the emphasis on enabling many forms of life to flourish, which we now find in forestry, represents a fundamental change in human culture such as we seldom see over centuries or millennia. People have often announced vast paradigm shifts before, only to find that culture reverted to something like its former state. The advent of the Internet at first seemed to usher in a new era of human equality, and now many fear that it may have done the opposite.

But there are many profound changes that have been almost unheralded, which I can only appreciate now, having crossed the threshold of threescore years and ten, the traditional allotment of a human life. I can remember how utterly anthropocentric the teaching of natural history was. All of the early forms of life, from algae to trilobites, existed to set the stage for the triumphant appearance of man. We learned how he shed his scales, climbed on to shore, developed warm blood, learned to stand upright, mastered fire, planted fields and embarked on the great work of civilization. Although some biologists still believe that some approximation of the human form may have been inevitable, centring natural history around the emergence of man, especially European man, is no longer openly done.

As late as the 1960s, it was widely assumed that human society developed in a linear way, and most Indigenous cultures such as the pygmies or Australian Aborigines were 'backward' or 'primitive'. This paradigm was challenged by many anthropologists such as Franz Boas and Claude Levi-Strauss. Various peoples from Native Americans to the !Kung San have been proposed as representing the 'natural' man, unchanged since the start of history, but subsequent research showed they were products of complex cultural developments.[15] The trajectory of human civilization was still thought of in a linear way and on a Western model, with fixed stages from the development of agriculture and the advent of cities to the industrial revolution and beyond. According to a largely implicit technological determinism, human society was allegedly restructured when agriculture replaced hunting and gathering, compelling societies to formulate human relations in more hierarchic ways. This view has recently been questioned in *The Dawn of Everything* by David Graeber and David Wengrow.[16] The forest, like human society, is never 'virgin' or 'primeval' but the product of continual environmental evolution.

Physicists today regard time as an illusion,[17] though, if this is the case, it is one that is not easy to lay aside. In a sense, forests may still represent the remote past, before the start of civilization, but it is folded into an eternal present. Time no longer has any forward or backward, hence there can be no political left (oriented towards the future) or right (oriented towards the past). There is only a greatly enhanced, and often bewildering, range of possibilities. Other dualities break down as well, for example, that between civilization and savagery.

Basically, time is a sort of rhythmic pattern based on repetition, with which we organize our experience. It is very different depending on whether we mark time by the hands of a watch, the decay of a radioactive element, the sun, the moon, the changing colours of leaves or the rings of growth on a tree. It is certainly perceived very differently by various animals and plants. What I propose is simply that we recognize time as only one way to classify events among many, recognizing that it is subject to considerable variation. The forest may show us how.

A disadvantage of a less linear view of time is that it complicates an individual's attempts to construct a personal identity and find a place in the cosmos. We do this primarily through stories, and these generally have a beginning, middle and end. It is harder where transitions are fluid. An advantage of a less linear view of time is that death loses much of its terror. In the vegetation of a natural, mixed forest, even dead wood is alive in that it can host insects, woodpeckers, moss, lichens, fungi, vines and other organisms. The roots of a fallen tree can continue to pass nutrients to other vegetation. Death is everywhere, but it is not the opposite of life. The two blend inextricably, as organic matter takes on an endless parade of forms.

Perhaps the best image to describe time may be that of the pre-Socratic philosopher Heraclitus, who compared it to a river. But let us remember that a river, especially in a forest, never runs entirely straight. It also does not flow at a constant pace. The water must move around rocks and accelerate over falls. It may swirl on the surface or flow backwards underneath. It may collect in stagnant pools beside the bank. It is decreased by evaporation and increased by rain. The banks narrow and expand. Near where I live, the Hudson River regularly reverses its direction with the tides.

The metaphor suggests a vision of time that is not unequivocally cyclic, progressive or entropic. It is the organic time of experience, not the time of a wristwatch. We do not actually encounter time as a steady progression from the past, by means of the present, to the future. We do not live only in the present; we cannot live only for the future. We cannot even conceive of one temporal stage in isolation from the other two. They are irrevocably woven together through memory, sensual intensity and anticipation. Time is a meandering stream with many islands and subsidiaries, not a straight canal with walls of reinforced concrete. And even upon reaching the sea, its currents will not cease to flow.

Epilogue

Going to the woods is going home.

John Muir

The late medieval kings were not truly masters of their hunting preserves. English gentlemen from the seventeenth until the nineteenth centuries were not masters of their country estates. These were carefully cultivated illusions, stage settings for elaborate public masquerades. In fact, the result of human intervention in a forest environment is only roughly predictable at best. But, in acknowledging this, we open the possibility of becoming participants in the landscape. The forest is a community that even human beings may join. It does not demand great knowledge or vast wisdom of us. It asks only that we be willing to take our place alongside the other citizens of that realm.

Not very long ago, I took a course from the New York State Department of Environmental Conservation to become what they call a Master Forest Owner (MFO). The title may impress the reader as a little too grand, and that is certainly how it impressed me. I have a lot of trouble thinking of myself as an owner, still more thinking of myself as a master. But I admire the programme and am proud to be part of it. The DEC refers people who own forested land to me. At their request, I walk the land and offer suggestions on environmentally sound ways to manage it.

On the first such occasion, I at first felt utterly intimidated, but I soon discovered that I am actually not so bad at offering guidance. I have learned something about forestry, but my knowledge does not at all compare with that of a professional forester. What I do have is the experience that enables me to empathize with the dilemmas of other owners. I now realize, as I once did not, that people who own forest land are not necessarily wealthy, but forests encourage grand dreams that can easily outrun their means. I know the difficult choices that must be made, both intellectually and emotionally.

There is something highly personal, and therefore unpredictable, about the dilemmas that I have faced. One for me was presented by a large beech tree in my forest, of which I was fond. It formed a large part of a closed canopy that blocked light in a very strategic area for wildlife, the confluence of two streams. I had walked the land countless times and could hear very few birds. Apart from deer, few animals were to be seen. I might have attributed the lack to my own deficiency of perception, but I remembered the land in my childhood. In the stream, you would see a turtle basking in the sun on just about every large rock. I remember vividly coming up the streams to see two great blue herons, which stood majestically for a few moments and then flew away. The turtles had not been seen for decades, and the herons were long absent as well. A major problem was that the canopy of the forest had closed and admitted hardly any sun. There was very little ground cover and little understorey. Since much of the land was on a slight slope, this meant that the good soil, with nothing to hold it in place, was constantly being washed away in storms.

Beech trees produce nuts that feed wildlife but not nearly as often as some other trees such as oaks. The leaves of beeches take a very long time to decompose. The leaf litter is good for worms, toads and other small creatures, but it had kept other plants from growing. I could have learned more, as one always can, but, after a certain point, the information becomes more technical but not more useful. A decision had to be made. I ordered the beech tree and several others in the vicinity cut down.

Afterwards, the woods looked terrible, as they usually do after a timber harvest, with stumps and bare logs lying forlornly on the ground. I felt sad yet did not lose faith. It was autumn, and I sowed seeds of native wildflowers in the newly cleared ground. In winter, I scattered birdseed in the snow and erected bird houses. Next spring, the first sign of vindication was that grass appeared in great plenty where there had formerly been only mud. What delighted me and made me think that perhaps my decision was right after all was when I visited the property shortly after a rain. There was a large puddle in the small meadow that the timber harvest had created and in it were hundreds of tadpoles. Then I saw several other puddles and they were teeming with life as well. Eventually, I also began to hear more birdsong.

After a long absence, both red-eared turtles and alligator turtles have been sighted on the property. This spring I came upon a wood frog. These amphibians burrow in the leaf cover as winter approaches. Their breathing and their hearts stop. Then, the next spring, as the land revives, they

Wood frog by a stream on the author's property. This animal freezes during winter so completely that its heart ceases to beat, but it revives in spring.

thaw out, are resurrected and soon ready to breed. Perhaps that might be a metaphor for the land, which had been resurrected as well. I might call this a happy ending, but for the forest it is no ending at all. It is just an episode in a history which may last hundreds, even thousands, of years.

And I still feel sad whenever I pass the forlorn stem of the beech tree. I am waiting for the time when it will be covered with lichens and insects, in other words, when it will once again come to life. The ability of beeches to root sprout often enables them to take over a landscape, especially when one has been cut down. As expected, a few shoots have emerged from the ground. On the side where there is a small meadow and more sun, they will not be able to compete with maples and oaks. A few shoots probably will survive near the river where there is more shade, but they will not become dominant, at least not for a long time to come.

Such agonizing about a tree can at times seem odd to rural people, some of whom chuckle at the emotion those who live in cities invest in decisions like cutting one down. Farmers, at least traditional ones, are more used to both birth and death since they observe both constantly among domestic and uncultivated plants and animals. They think of nature with, I believe, much the same sort of spirituality as city people but focus a bit less on individual creatures and more on natural rhythms.

At the beginning of this book, I wrote of how walking through a forest is like going back in time, in terms of language, to an era when meaning was not confined to words but pervaded everything. Another way to say this is that language was not confined to humans. Plants and animals are constantly signalling to one another, through sounds, motions, chemicals and so on. I am part of this process, for the sound of leaves crushed beneath my shoe, the scent of my perspiration, a slight stumble against a rock and a wave of my arms as I regain balance all send out messages, of which I am barely or not at all aware. I am a sentence with which the forest is talking to itself.

There is also a language in a stump as it becomes ever more overgrown with moss, as its roots end out new shoots, as it invites ants, slugs and woodpeckers. It tells a story of death and resurrection. A poet might translate this into words. A painter might render it in lines and colours. But I cannot check the words in any dictionary or the lines against any diagram. I can just look for a while and move on.

On this property at least, the influence of climate change has not been entirely negative. The most remarkable part is without doubt the island, an area of 16 acres completely surrounded by water opposite the confluence of the two streams. The relative isolation makes it a sort of ecosystem unto itself and ideal for wildlife. Now, however, I can see from year to year a sort of geological change that one might have expected to take centuries. The increase in rain over the past two years is making the entire area where the two streams meet into a miniature lake with several islands, where trees are starting to sprout. The water remains completely clear and shallow enough that you can see every stone, large or small, in the riverbed. Perhaps we are seeing the emergence of a different sort of landscape appropriate to what we sometimes call, rather deceptively, the Anthropocene or Age of Man.

There are things that I have learned about forests that cannot be expressed in strictly empirical terms. I know how a bit of forest that is very small in terms of acreage can seem very big to an owner, while a big one can seem very small. It is similar with the writing of this book. I have a formal background in intellectual history and literature. I have also done extensive work in folklore, but here I have strayed beyond my major areas of expertise. My justification is that, in this era of specialization, the larger picture is often lost in a mass of detail. Epic problems require us to think on an epic scale. To use a familiar expression, we must not be unable to see the forest for the trees.

Most forests are today subject to constant threats such as invasive species, botanical pandemics, large herds of deer and uncontrolled fires. Furthermore, the temperate forests of the northern hemisphere may soon, because of climate change, need to survive in semi-tropical conditions. An increase in severe storms, droughts, and temperature is expected. Eventually, nature will be able to adjust, but the changes will probably come too suddenly for this to be accomplished without serious damage. Should we simply wait and see what happens? Should we start to replant parts of the forest with trees from warmer climates? Should we compromise by taking modest steps such as reducing the density of trees to make them more resilient? At any rate, we are coming to see that trees share with us what may have once seemed a uniquely human vulnerability.

I worry that the continual stress may cause us to lose sight of their beauty. The woods, which were a refuge from the city in Victorian times, can start to seem like the proverbial urban jungle. The hazards are easier to write about than the pleasures of a walk in the woods. Perils can be inventoried and monitored, but beauty must be continually rediscovered. For this reason, especially, the work of poets and artists has become anything but a luxury. We need it to remind us of why the work to preserve our forests is profoundly important, despite all the effort, isolation and uncertainty that it may at times entail.

TIMELINE OF FORESTS IN CULTURE

c. 10000 BCE   The end of the Pleistocene, as glaciers retreat leaving North America and Europe covered mostly with spruces, firs and pines

c. 8000 BCE   Birches become common in North America and Northern Eurasia. They are followed by other trees such as beeches, oaks and maples

c. 2100 BCE   The earliest known version of the *Epic of Gilgamesh* in Sumerian tells of cutting down the cedars of Lebanon and the consequences that follow

c. 1000 BCE   The chestnut arrives in what is now the American Northeast and gradually becomes the most dominant tree

98 CE   Tacitus publishes *Germania*, where he describes the Germans as a people of the forest, a document that will later have a great influence on German identity

c. 800   Carolingian kings and nobles assert their dominion over forests, place them under regulations and set many of them aside as hunting preserves, a practice that is gradually adopted by rulers in Britain and other European kingdoms

c. 800   Maya civilization reaches its peak of about 3 million people and begins to rapidly collapse, probably because of environmental factors, leaving large settlements in Central America to be reclaimed by the surrounding forest

c. 1000   Clearing of land in forests and the cultivation of maize and beans becomes common among the Woodland Indians of what is now Canada and America

c. 1079   William I of England creates the New Forest of about 71,500 acres as a royal hunting preserve

c. 1150–1500   There is a proliferation of Arthurian epics in Britain, France, Germany and other parts of Europe, in which magical forests become a setting for fantastic adventures

c. 1320   Dante completes *The Divine Comedy*, in which his journey to hell begins in 'a dark wood'

c. 1400   The beginning of the Age of Exploration, in which Europeans will sail to distant lands throughout the world, a process that will frequently lead

	to exploitation, colonization, deforestation, importation of invasive species and extensive spread of diseases
c. 1500	Conrad Celtis of Nuremberg rediscovers Tacitus's *Germania* and uses it to create a romanticized image of the primeval German forests
c. 1600–1900	The pace at which forests are cut down to open land for agriculture increases in China until the land is almost entirely deforested except for remote, mountainous areas
c. 1650–*c.* 1950	Large areas of indigenous forests in the northern hemisphere are cut down and replaced by monocultures of fast-growing conifers, especially Norway spruce. This begins in Prussia, but the practice eventually spreads throughout much of Northern Europe, including France and England. This is also done in Canada and the United States.
1664	In England, John Evelyn publishes *Sylva*, a guide to the cultivation, use and conservation of trees
1669	Jean-Baptiste Colbert, the minister of finance under Louis xiv of France, proclaims a new body of laws for the national forests entitled 'L'ordonnance des eaux et forêts' (Ordinance of Water and Forests). It places forests under greatly increased regulation in order to preserve wood for military purposes
1697	Charles Perrault publishes his *Histoires ou contes du temps passé* (Stories or Tales of Times Past), in which he sets most of his fairy tales in a Rococo sort of forest
c. 1700	Japan institutes extensive policies for the conservation, management and replanting of forests
c. 1700–present	Massive forest fires become common in North America
1713	Publication of *Sylvicultura Oeconomica* (Economic Forestry) by Hans Carl von Carlowitz in Saxony, considered the first work of scientific forestry and the first to articulate the concept of sustainability
c. 1710–70	Painters at the French court such as Jean-Antoine Watteau, François Boucher and Jean-Honoré Fragonard depict heavily landscaped forests in the Rococo style as places of play and courtship.
1725	Giambattista Vico publishes his *La Scienza Nuova* (The New Science) in Naples, in which he theorizes that human civilization began in forests
1792	In France, 60,000 trees, primarily oaks, are planted and called 'freedom trees' in honour of the French Revolution
1812–58	Seven editions of *Kinder- und Hausmärchen* (Tales for the Hearth and Home) by Jacob and Wilhelm Grimm in Germany popularize the motif of the enchanted forest

c. 1825–48	Thomas Cole becomes the unofficial founder and leader of the Hudson River School of painters. They endeavour to depict what remained of the original American landscapes before European settlement as well as to document their gradual destruction
c. 1850–present	The diversity of forests is increasingly reduced worldwide by the unintended importation of insects and arboreal pathogens to areas where they are not indigenous. In the United States, these include the gypsy moth (1869), chestnut blight (*c.* 1900), beech scale (1920), Dutch elm disease (1928), the butternut canker (1967) and the Emerald Ash Borer (2002). The chestnut in North America is entirely destroyed
1864	The founding of Yosemite National Park in the Sierra Nevada Mountains of California
1884–5	The West Africa Conference takes place in Berlin, where European powers divide up Africa, with the largest shares going to Britain and France, leading to colonization of Africa and consequent deforestation
c. 1900	Deer, especially white-tailed deer, are nearly extirpated in most of the United States through overhunting
1914–32	W. B. Laughead, a former logger and advertising manager for the Red River Lumber Company in California, publishes a series of pamphlets to publicize stories of lumberjack Paul Bunyan, which celebrate the destruction of American forests
1936	The Revolutionary League for German Culture releases the film *Eternal Forest: The Meaning of Nature in the Third Reich*, which identifies the German people with the forests
c. 1960–present	The area of forests in North America and Western Europe stabilizes or increases. This, however, is more than offset globally by the accelerating destruction of forests in the tropics, for example in Nigeria and Brazil, where they are deliberately burned or cut down, primarily for the sake of agriculture
c. 1980	The first Green Party is formed in West Germany, providing a model that will be followed throughout Europe and much of the world. The party emphasizes the protection of nature, especially forests
1995	The Second Assessment Report on the Intergovernmental Panel on Climate Change (IPCC) confirms that human activity is having a global impact on weather and temperature. The importance of forests for carbon sequestration becomes universally recognized by the scientific community
1997	The industrialized nations meeting in Kyoto, Japan, agree to reduce carbon emissions. The United States Senate, however, declines to ratify the Kyoto Protocols

c. 2000   Restrictions on hunting not only lead to a comeback of deer in the United States, but deer become probably more common than in any previous time

2022   There is a major wave of wildfires in Europe and North America, particularly severe in the Mediterranean region, which is in part due to a climate that has become warmer and drier

REFERENCES

Introduction: Forests and Memory

1 Charles Watkins, *Trees in Art* (London, 2018), pp. 81–3.
2 Thomas Hardy, 'During Wind and Rain', www.poetryfoundation.org, accessed 20 May 2022.
3 Attorney A. S. Embler, *David E. Brundage and Wife to Bluma Sax* (Newburgh, NY, 1933).
4 Hugh Canham, 'History of the New York Forest Owners Association, Part 1', *New York Forest Owner* (September/October 2021), p. 4.
5 James H. Wandersee and Elisabeth E. Schussler, 'Preventing Plant Blindness', *American Biology Teacher*, LXI/2 (1999), p. 82.
6 Frederic Edward Clements, *Plant Succession: An Analysis of the Development of Vegetation* (Washington, DC, 1916), pp. 102–7.
7 Jack Santino, *All Around the Year: Holidays and Celebrations in American Life* (Chicago, IL, 1995), p. 173.
8 Michael Williams, *Americans and Their Forests: A Historical Geography* (Cambridge, 1992), pp. 35, 38.
9 Charles D. Canham, *Forests Adrift: Currents Shaping the Future of Northeastern Trees* (New Haven, CT, 2020), pp. 77–8.
10 Ibid., p. 76.
11 Ibid., p. 69.
12 Ibid., p. 68.
13 Herman Hesse, *Trees: An Anthology of Writings and Paintings by Hermann Hesse*, ed. Volker Michels, trans. Damion Searls (San Diego, CA, 2022), p. 1.
14 Maurice Maeterlinck, *The Intelligence of Flowers*, trans. Alexander Teixeira de Mattos (New York, 1913), pp. 26–30.

1 Wood and Leaves

1 Richard Elton Walton, 'Deer Are Consuming the World's Largest Organism, Killing Off Its Opportunity for Growth', www.cnn.com, 29 November 2021.
2 Stefano Mancuso, *The Revolutionary Genius of Plants: A New Understanding of Plant Intelligence and Behavior*, no trans. given (New York, 2018), p. 91.
3 C. J. Turlings, John H. Loughrin et al., 'How Caterpillar-Damaged Plants Protect Themselves by Attracting Parasitic Wasps', *Proceedings of the National Academy of Science*, XCII (May 1995), pp. 4169–74.
4 Mancuso, *Plants*, pp. 216–17.
5 Ibid., p. 96.
6 United States Department of Health and Human Services, 'NIH Human Microbiome Project Defines Normal Bacterial Makeup of the Body', www.NIH.gov, 13 June 2012.

7 René Descartes, 'Meditations on First Philosophy', in *Descartes: Selected Philosophical Writings* (Cambridge, 2006), Meditation Six, pp. 119–20.

8 Michael Marder, *Plant Thinking: A Philosophy of Vegetal Life* (New York, 2013), p. 39.

9 Sara Black, Amber Ginsburg et al., 'The Legal Life of Plants', in *Botanical Speculations: Plants in Contemporary Art*, ed. Giovanni Aloi (Cambridge, 2021), pp. 29–47.

10 Virgil, *Aeneid*, trans. Frederick Ahl (Oxford, 2007), VIII, 314–25, pp. 194–5.

11 John Leighton, and James K. Colling, *Suggestions in Design* (New York, 1881), p. 55.

12 Nathaniel Altman, *Sacred Trees* (San Francisco, CA, 1994), pp. 73–80.

13 Alexander Porteous, *The Lore of the Forest: Myths and Legends* (London, 1994), p. 157.

14 Dennis Tedlock, trans., *Popol Vuh: The Mayan Book of the Dawn of Life*, revd edn, ebook (New York, 1996), pp. 158–69.

15 Vladimir Bibikhin, *The Woods*, trans. Arch Tait (Cambridge, 2021), p. 8; Marder, *Plant Thinking*, p. 66.

16 Corinne J. Saunders, *The Forest of Medieval Romance: Avernus, Broceliande, Arden* (Woodbridge, England, 1993), pp. 19–24.

17 Corinna Jenal, *'Das ist kein Wald, Ihr Pappnasen!' Zur sozialen Konstruktion von Wald. Perspektiven von Landschaftstheorie und Landschaftspraxis* (Berlin, 2019), p. 38.

18 Peter Marshall, *The Philosopher's Stone: A Quest for the Secrets of Alchemy* (New York, 2001), p. 29.

19 Eduardo Kohn, *How Forests Think: Toward an Anthropology Beyond the Human*, ebook (Berkeley, CA, 2013), location 3890.

20 Pedro Pitarch, *The Jaguar and the Priest: An Ethnology of Tzeltal Souls* (Austin, TX, 1996), pp. 1–59.

21 Kohn, *How Forests Think*, locations 166–9, 1849–70.

22 Ibid., location 66.

23 Michel Foucault, *The Order of Things: An Archeology of the Human Sciences*, trans. not given (New York, 1994), pp. 70–73.

24 Ibid., pp. 417–22.

25 Brent Berlin, 'The First Congress of Ethnozoological Nomenclature', *Journal of the Royal Anthropological Institute*, 12 (2006), pp. 23–37.

26 Ibid., pp. 37–40.

27 Dante Alighieri, *La Divina Commedia di Dante Alighieri* (Milan, 1911), Inferno, Canto I, lines 1–6, p. 1. The translation is my own.

28 Charles Watkins, *Trees in Art* (London, 2018), pp. 150–51.

2 The Spirituality of Trees

1 Aristotle, 'De Anima (On the Soul)', in *The Basic Works of Aristotle*, ed. Richard McKeon (New York, 2001), section 413 a–b, pp. 556–8.

2 Mary Douglas, *Purity and Danger: An Analysis of the Concepts of Pollution and Taboo* (New York, 1994), pp. 40–41.

3 Ibid., p. 54.

4 Ibid., p. 56.

5 Ibid., p. 11.

6 James George Frazer, *The Golden Bough: A Study in Religion and Magic*, abridged edn (Mineola, NY, 2019), pp. 324–84.

7 Joseph Bruchac, *Native Plant Stories* (Golden, CO, 1995), p. xi.

8 David Attenborough, *The First Eden: The Mediterranean World and Man* (Boston, MA, 1987), pp. 140–41.

9 Carol Kaesuk Yoon, *Naming Nature: The Clash between Instinct and Science* (New York, 2009), pp. 50–51.

10 Francis James Child, ed., *The English and Scottish Popular Ballads in Five Volumes*, vol. II (Mineola, NY, 2003), verses 5 and 6, p. 4.

11 Ibid., verses 19 and 20, p. 285.

12 T. H. Philpot, *The Sacred Tree; or, The Tree in Religion and Myth* (New York, 1897), p. 84.

13 Boria Sax, *Imaginary Animals: The Monstrous, the Wondrous and the Human* (London, 2013), pp. 216–17.

14 Anonymous, 'The Seeress's Prophesy', in *The Poetic Edda* (Oxford, 1996), trans. Carolyne Larrington, verses 19–20, p. 6.

15 Anonymous, 'Grimnir's Sayings', in *The Poetic Edda*, verses 31–4, p. 56.

16 Anonymous, 'The Seeress's Prophesy', ibid., verse 47, p. 10.

17 Anonymous, 'Grimnir's Sayings', ibid., verse 35, p. 57.

18 Anonymous, 'Vafthrudnir's Sayings', ibid., verse 45, p. 47.

19 Mircea Eliade, *Shamanism: Archaic Techniques of Ecstasy* (Princeton, NJ, 1974), pp. 272–3.

20 Nathaniel Altman, *Sacred Trees* (San Francisco, CA, 1994), pp. 78–9.

21 Vladmir Bibikhin, *The Woods*, ed. Artemy Magun, trans. Arch Tait (Cambridge, MA, 2021), p. 59.

22 Anonymous, 'The Dream of the Rood', trans. Michael Alexander, *The First Poems in English*, ed. Michael Alexander, ebook (London, 2008), Kindle locations 758–926.

23 Jacobus de Voragine, *The Golden Legend: Readings on the Saints*, trans. William Granger Ryan, 2 vols (Princeton, NJ, 1993), vol. II, chap. 37, pp. 168–73.

24 Maurice Maeterlinck, *The Intelligence of Flowers*, trans. Alexander Teixeira de Mattos (New York, 1913), pp. 10–11.

3 Mythic Beings of the Forest

1 John Burroughs, *Wake-Robin* (Cambridge, MA, 1900), p. xiii.

2 Philippe Descola, *Beyond Nature and Culture*, trans. Janet Lloyd (Chicago, IL, 2013), p. 26.

3 Ibid., p. 29; Daniel Cohen, *The Encyclopedia of Monsters* (New York, 1982), pp. 74–5.

4 Nathaniel Altman, *Sacred Trees* (San Francisco, CA, 1994), pp. 71–85.

5 Michael Williams, *Deforesting the Earth: From Prehistory to the Global Crisis, an Abridgement* (Chicago, IL, 2006), pp. 224–5.

6 David D. Gilmore, *Monsters: Evil Beings, Mythical Beasts and All Manner of Imaginary Terrors* (Philadelphia, PA, 2003), pp. 75–81.

7 Ibid., p. 2.

8 Nigel J. Smith, *The Enchanted Amazon Rain Forest: Stories from a Vanishing World* (Gainesville, FL, 1976), pp. 42–52, 178–9.

9 Williams, *Deforesting the Earth*, pp. 224–5.

10 N. K. Sanders, trans., *The Epic of Gilgamesh* (New York, 1970), p. 63.

11 Andrew George, trans., *The Epic of Gilgamesh* (New York, 2016), pp. 1–21.

12 Lise Gotfredsen, *The Unicorn* (New York, 1999), p. 15.

13 Jeanne-Marie Leprince de Beaumont, 'Beauty and the Beast', in *Folk and Fairy Tales*, ed. Martin Hallett and Barbara Karasek, 5th edn (Peterborough, Canada, 2018), pp. 128–37.

14 Sara Graça da Silva and Jamshid J. Tehrani, 'Comparative Phylogenetic Analyses Uncover the Ancient Roots of European Fairy Folktales', *Royal Society Open Science*, iii/1 (January 2016), p. 8, https:// royalsocietypublishing.org.

15 Cohen, *Monsters*, pp. 3–17.

16 John Ayto, *Dictionary of Word Origins: The Histories of More than 8,000 English-Language Words* (New York, 1990), p. 374.

17 Wu Cheng'en, *Journey to the West*, trans. Anthony Yu, 4 vols (Chicago, il, 1980), vol. iii, pp. 220–37.

18 Mark Elvin, *The Retreat of the Elephants: An Environmental History of China* (New Haven, ct, 2004), pp. xvii, 44–7, 78, 321–68.

19 Sophia Suk-mun Law, *Reading Chinese Painting: Beyond Forms and Colors: A Comparative Approach to Art Appreciation*, trans. Tony Blishen (New York, 2016), pp. 74–93.

20 Peter Wohlleben, *The Hidden Life of Trees: What They Feel, How They Communicate – Discoveries of a Secret World*, trans. Mike Grady (New York, 2006), ebook, locations 110–27.

21 Ibid., p. 26.

22 Brian Morris, *Animals and Ancestors: An Ethnography* (New York, 2000), p. 226.

23 Chinua Achebe, *Things Fall Apart* (New York, 1958), p. 148.

24 Ben Okri, *The Famished Road*, ebook (New York, 2016), p. 19.

4 Conquest of the Woods

1 Bertrand Hell, 'Enraged Hunters: The Domain of the Wild in North-Western Europe', in *Nature and Society: Anthropological Perspectives*, ed. Philippe Descola and Gisli Palsson (London, 2004), p. 555.

2 J. Hansman, 'Gilgamesh, Humbaba and the Land of the Erin-Trees', *Iraq*, xxxviii (Spring 1976), p. 24.

3 Andrew George, trans., *The Epic of Gilgamesh* (New York, 2016), pp. 104–22.

4 Hansman, 'Gilgamesh', p. 35.

5 Sara Graça da Silva and Jamshid J. Tehrani, 'Comparative Phylogenetic Analyses Uncover the Ancient Roots of European Fairy Folktales', *Royal Society Open Science*, iii/1 (January 2016), p. 7, https:// royalsocietypublishing.org.

6 Jeremy Black and Anthony Green, *Gods, Demons and Symbols of Ancient Mesopotamia: An Illustrated Dictionary* (Austin, tx, 1992), p. 106.

7 Michel Pastoureau, *The Bear: History of a Fallen King*, trans. George Holoch (Cambridge, ma, 2011), pp. 34–59.

8 Ibid., pp. 11–26.

9 E. Douglas Van Buren, 'Mesopotamian Fauna in the Light of the Monuments. Archaeological Remarks Upon Landsberger's "Fauna Des Alten Mesopotamien"', *Archiv für Orientforschung*, VI/II (1936–7), pp. 20–21.

10 Pastoureau, *The Bear*, pp. 11–33.

11 George, trans., *Gilgamesh*, pp. 36–46.

12 F.N.H. Al-Rawi, and A. R. George, 'Back to the Cedar Forest: The Beginning and End of Tablet V of the Standard Babylonian Epic of Gilgameš', *Journal of Cuneiform Studies*, 66 (1914), p. 74.

13 George, trans., *Gilgamesh*, pp. 37–96.

14 William Faulkner, 'The Bear', in *The Faulkner Reader* (New York, 1971), pp. 219–314.

15 Anonymous, 'Davy Crockett Theme Lyrics', www.lyricsondemand.com, accessed 28 August 2022.

16 Pastoureau, *The Bear*, p. 92.

5 The Royal Hunt

1 Georges-Louis Leclerc, Comte de Buffon, *Buffon's Natural History*, trans. not given, 10 vols (London, 1792), vol. VI, p. 50.

2 Ibid., pp. 27–8.

3 John Ayto, *The Dictionary of Word Origins: The Histories of More than 8,000 English-Language Words* (New York, 1990), p. 161.

4 Bertrand Hell, 'Enraged Hunters: The Domain of the Wild in North-Western Europe', in *Nature and Society: Anthropological Perspectives*, ed. Philippe Descola and Gisli Palsson (London, 2004), p. 540.

5 Jean-Dennis Vigne, 'Domestication ou appropriation pour la chasse: histoire d'un choix socio-culturel depuis le néolithique. l'exemple des Cerfs (Cervus)', in *Exploitation des animaux sauvages à travers le temps: xiiie rencontres internationales d'archéologie et d'histoire d'antibes – ive colloque international de l'homme et l'animal*, ed. J. Desse and F. Andoin-Rouzeau (Juan les Pins, France, 1993), p. 203.

6 Ibid., p. 204.

7 Maya Wei-haas, 'Prehistoric Female Hunter Discovery Upends Gender Role Assumptions', *National Geographic* (4 November 2020): www.nationalgeographic.com, accessed 15 March 2021.

8 Hell, 'Enraged Hunters', pp. 533–9.

9 Jacobus de Voragine, *The Golden Legend: Readings on the Saints*, trans. William Granger Ryan, 2 vols (Princeton, NJ, 1993), vol. II, pp. 266–71.

10 Sean Kelly and Rosemary Rogers, *Saints Preserve Us! Everything You Need to Know About Every Saint You'll Ever Need* (New York, 1993), pp. 139–40.

11 Gilbert White, *The Natural History of Selborne, and the Naturalist's Calendar* (London, *c.* 1890), letter vii, p. 21.

12 Jacob and Wilhelm Grimm, *The German Legends of the Brothers Grimm*, trans. Donald Ward, 2 vols (Philadelphia, PA, 1981), vol. I, legend 309, p. 245.

13 Hell, 'Enraged Hunters', pp. 550–54.

14 Martine Chalvet, *Une histoire de la forêt*, ebook (Paris, 2011), pp. 460–67.

15 Charles Watkins, *Trees, Woods and Forests: A Social and Cultural History* (London, 2016), p. 38.

16 Ovid, *Metamorphoses*, trans. Rolfe Humphries (Bloomington, IN, 1955), III, 138–248, pp. 61–4.

17 J. Donald Hughes, *Pan's Travail: Environmental Problems of the Ancient Greeks and Romans* (Baltimore, MD, 1994), pp. 94, 216.

18 Chalvet, *Histoire*, location 1464.

19 Roland Bechmann, *Trees and Man: The Forest in the Middle Ages*, trans. Katharyn Dunham (New York, 1990), p. 14.

20 Theodore Roosevelt, 'Conservation and Democracy', *Roosevelt Wildlife Bulletin*, III/3 (September 1926), p. 498.

21 Corinne J. Saunders, *The Forest of Medieval Romance: Avernus, Broceliande, Arden* (Woodbridge, 1993), pp. 10–19.

22 Bechmann, *Trees and Man*, p. 13.

23 Saunders, *Medieval*, p. 5.

24 John Manwood and William Delson, *Treatise on Forest Law*, 5th edn (London, 1761), p. 158.

25 Saunders, *Medieval*, p. 3.

26 Chalvet, *Histoire*, pp. 1467–90.

27 Gabriel Bise, and Gaston Poebus, *Medieval Hunting Scenes ('the Hunting Book' by Gaston Poebus)*, trans. J. Peter Tallon (Huntsville, OH, 1978), pp. 58–67.

28 Francis Klingender, *Animals in Art and Thought to the End of the Middle Ages*, trans. Evelyn Antal and John Harthan (Cambridge, MA, 1971), pp. 468–9.

29 Keith Thomas, *Man and the Natural World: A History of the Modern Sensibility* (New York, 1983), p. 29.

30 Matt Cartmill, *A View to a Death in the Morning: Hunting and Nature through History* (Cambridge, MA, 1993), pp. 64–5.

31 Hell, 'Enraged Hunters', p. 540.

32 Watkins, *Trees, Woods and Forests*, pp. 52–5.

33 Kenneth Clark, *Animals and Men: Their Relationship as Reflected in Western Art from Prehistory to the Present Day* (New York, 1977), pp. 142–3.

34 Thomas Malory, *Le Morte D'arthur*, ebook (Boston, MA, 2017), Kindle locations 124, 572–3.

35 Louis Charbenneau-Lassay, *The Bestiary of Christ*, trans. D. M. Dooling (New York, 1991), pp. 117–26.

36 Bechmann, *Trees and Man*, pp. 30–31.

37 Manwood and Delson, *Treatise on Forest Law*.

38 Rose-Marie Hagen and Rainer Hagen, *Masterpieces in Detail: What Great Paintings Say* (Cologne, 2000), pp. 146–51.

39 Mauro Agnoletti, *Storia del bosco: il paesaggio forestale italiano*, ebook (Bari, Italy, 2020), pp. 38, 43–4.

40 Hughes, *Pan's Travail*, pp. 169–76.

41 Bechmann, *Trees and Man*, p. 33.

42 Ibid., p. 31.

43 Cartmill, *A View to a Death in the Morning*, pp. 60–61.

44 Naomi Sykes, *Beastly Questions: Animal Answers to Archeological Issues* (London, 2015), p. 72.

45 Virginia DeJohn Anderson, *Creatures of Empire: How Domestic Animals Transformed Early America* (New York, 2004), p. 59.

46 John Cummins, *The Art of Medieval Hunting: The Hound and the Hawk* (Edison, NJ, 2003), p. 74.

47 Stephen Knight, 'Robin Hood and the Forest Laws', *Bulletin of the International Association for Robin Hood Studies*, 1 (2017), p. 1.

48 White, *Selborne*, letter viii, p. 21.

49 Wilhelm Heinrich Riehl, 'Feld and Wald', in *Gesammelte Werke Wilhelm Heinrich Riehls*, ebook (Cleveland, OH, 2020), locations 38529–619.

50 Clark, *Animals*, p. 102.

51 Anderson, *Empire*, p. 60.

52 Ibid., p. 62.

53 James Fenimore Cooper, *The Deerslayer* [1841] (New York, 1991).

54 Felix Salten, *Bambi: A Life in the Woods*, trans. Whittaker Chambers (New York, 1928), p. 286.

55 Ibid., frontmatter.

56 Jim Sterba, *Nature Wars: The Incredible Story of How Wildlife Comebacks Turned Backyards into Battlegrounds* (New York, 2012), pp. 113–14.

57 Ibid., p. 106.

58 Ibid., p. 107.

59 Peter Smallidge, Director of Cornell University's Arnot Forest, personal communication.

6 The Forest and Death

1 Hansjörg Küster, *Der Wald: Natur und Geschichte* (Munich, 2019), p. 192.

2 Pliny the Elder, *Natural History: A Selection*, trans. John F. Healy (New York, 1991).

3 Tacitus, *Germania*, in *The Agricola and the Germania*, trans. S. A. Handford (Harmondsworth, 1986), chap. 5, p. 104.

4 Ibid., chap. 19, p. 117.

5 Ibid., chap. 9, p. 109.

6 Tacitus, *The Annals of Imperial Rome*, trans. Alfred John Church and William Jackson Brodribb (New York, 2007), Book 1, Nook ebook section 53.

7 Johannes Zechner, *Der Deutsche Wald: Eine Ideengeschichte Zwischen Poesie und Ideologie* (Darmstadt, 2016), p. 20.

8 Tacitus, *Annals*, Book 1, location 51.

9 Ibid., Books 1 and 2, locations 49–108.

10 Ibid., Book 2, location 108.

11 J. Donald Hughes, *Pan's Travail: Environmental Problems of the Ancient Greeks and Romans* (Baltimore, MD, 1994), p. 80.

12 Ibid.

13 Zechner, *Der Deutsche Wald*, p. 20.

14 Küster, *Der Wald*, pp. 185–6.

15 Edward Hyams, *The English Garden* (London, 1966), p. 15.

16 Martine Chalvet, *Une histoire de la forêt*, Kindle edn (Paris, 2011), ebook location 794–808.

17 T. Hudson-Williams, 'Dante and the Classics', *Greece and Rome*, XX/58 (January 1951), p. 38.

18 Dante Alighieri, *La Divina Commedia di Dante Alighieri* (Milan, 1911), *Inferno*, Canto XIII, pp. 247–52.

19 Ibid., Canto V, pp. 15–24.

20 Zechner, *Der Deutsche Wald*, pp. 18–19.

21 Leonard Forster, 'Introduction and Commentary', in *Selections from Conrad Celtis, 1459–1508*, ed. Leonard Forster (Cambridge, 1948), pp. 100–111.
22 Christopher S. Wood, *Albrecht Altdorfer and the Origins of Landscape*, 2nd edn (London, 2014), p. 134.
23 Ibid.
24 Celtis, *Selections from Conrad Celtis*, pp. 24–5.
25 Wood, *Altdorfer*, p. 154.
26 Ibid., p. 190.
27 Ibid., pp. 156–7.
28 Ibid., p. 189.
29 Anonymous and Ralph Caldicott, *Babes in the Wood* (London, 1879), pp. 30–31.
30 John Keats, 'Ode to a Nightingale', in *On Wings of Song: Poems About Birds*, ed. J. D. McClatchy (New York, 2000), lines 6–8, 50–58, pp. 218–20.
31 Johann Wolfgang von Goethe, 'Wanderers Nachtlied II (Ein Gleichnes)', in *Deutsche Gedichte: Von Den Anfängen bis zur Gegenwart*, ed. Echtermeyer and Benno von Wiese (Düsseldorf, 1979), p. 194. The translation is my own.
32 'Kickelhahn', www.wikipedia.com, accessed 5 July 2021.
33 Joseph Leo Koerner, *Caspar David Friedrich and the Subject of Landscape* (London, 2009), p. 194.

7 Lord of the Forest

1 Edward Topsell, *The History of Four-Footed Beasts, Serpents and Insects* (facsimile of the 1658 edition), 3 vols (London, 1967), vol. I, pp. 551–2.
2 Neil Evernden, *The Social Creation of Nature* (Baltimore, MD, 1992), p. 41.
3 Bruno Bettelheim, *The Uses of Enchantment: The Meaning and Importance of Fairy Tales* (New York, 1977), p. 94.
4 Matilde Battistini, *Symbols and Allegories in Art*, trans. Stephen Sartarelli (Los Angeles, CA, 2005), p. 244.
5 Wolfram von Eschenbach, *Parzival*, trans. A. T. Hatto (New York, 1980), p. 132.
6 Anonymous, 'Sir Gawain and the Green Knight', in *Sir Gawain and the Green Knight, an Authoritative Translation, Contexts, Criticism*, ed. Marie Borroff and Laura L. Howes (New York, 2010), pp. 3–64.
7 Alice E. Lasater, *Spain to England: A Comparative Study of Arabic, European, and English Literature of the Middle Ages* (Jackson, MS, 1974), pp. 189–96.
8 Max Lüthi, *The European Folktale: Form and Nature*, trans. John D. Niles (Bloomington, IN, 1986), pp. 32–3.
9 Sara Graça da Silva and Jamshid J. Tehrani, 'Comparative Phylogenetic Analyses Uncover the Ancient Roots of European Fairy Folktales', *Royal Society Open Science*, III/1 (January 2016), https://royalsocietypublishing.org.
10 Max Lüthi, *The Fairy Tale as an Art Form and Portrait of Man*, trans. John Erickson (Bloomington, IN, 1987), pp. 135–44.
11 Bernard Roger, *The Initiatory Path in Fairy Tales*, Nook ebook (Rutledge, VT, 2015).
12 Boria Sax, *The Frog King: On Legends, Fables, Fairy Tales and Anecdotes of Animals* (New York, 1990), p. 49.

13 Albert B. Friedman, 'Morgan Le Fay in Sir Gawain and the Green Knight',
Speculum, XXXV/2 (April 1960), pp. 269–72.

14 Joseph L. Henderson, 'Ancient Myths and Modern Man', in *Man and His
Symbols*, ed. Carl G. Jung (New York, 1968), p. 123.

15 Anonymous, 'Bricriu's Feast', in *Early Irish Myths and Sagas*, ed. and trans.
Jeffrey Gantz (New York, 1985), pp. 219–55.

16 Thomas Malory, *Le Morte D'arthur* (Boston, MA, 2017), chap. XXI–II,
pp. 671–4.

17 Jonathan Hughes, *The Rise of Alchemy in Fourteenth-Century England:
Plantagenet Kings and the Search for the Philosopher's Stone* (New York, 2012),
pp. 81–3.

18 Dennis William Hauck, *Sorcerer's Stone: A Beginner's Guide to Alchemy*
(New York, 2004), p. 189.

19 Hughes, *The Rise of Alchemy*, p. 84.

8 Lady of the Forest

1 Laurence Half-Lancer, 'Fairy Godmothers and Fairy Lovers', in *Arthurian
Women: A Casebook*, ed. Thelma S. Fenster (New York, 1996), pp. 142–3, 48.

2 Matilde Battistini, *Symbols and Allegories in Art*, trans. Stephen Sartarelli
(Los Angeles, CA, 2005), p. 244.

3 Alexandr Afans'ev, *Russian Fairy Tales*, trans. Norbert Guterman (New York,
1973), pp. 441–3.

4 Andreas Johns, *Baba Yaga: The Ambiguous Mother and Witch of the Russian
Folktale* (New York, 2010), p. 272.

5 Ibid., p. 273.

6 Afans'ev, *Russian Fairy Tales*, pp. 439–47.

7 Vladimir Propp, *Theory and History of Folklore*, trans. Ariadna Y. Martin and
Richard P. Martin, vol. V: *Theory and History of Literature* (Minneapolis, MN,
1984), p. 117.

8 Ibid., pp. 116–18.

9 Ibid., p. 117.

10 Vladimir Propp, *The Morphology of the Folk Tale*, trans. Laurence Scott
(Austin, TX, 1968).

11 Joanna Hubbs, *Mother Russia: The Feminine Myth in Russian Culture*
(Bloomington, IN, 1988), pp. 48–51.

12 Ibid., p. 35.

13 Jacob Grimm and Wilhelm Grimm, *The Annotated Brothers Grimm*,
ed. and trans. Maria Tatar (New York, 2004), pp. 73–85.

14 Ibid., p. 72.

15 Afans'ev, *Russian Fairy Tales*, pp. 76–9.

16 Johns, *Baba Yaga*, p. 97.

17 Jacob and Wilhelm Grimm, *The German Legends of the Brothers Grimm*,
trans. Donald Ward, 2 vols (Philadelphia, PA, 1981), vol. I, legend 171, p. 57.

18 Sabine Baring Gould, *Curious Myths of the Middle Ages*, ed. Edward Hardy
(New York, 1987), pp. 79–82.

19 Josef Freiherr von Eichendorff, 'Waldgespräch', in *Deutsche Gedichte: Von
den Anfängen bis zur Gegenwart*, ed. Echtermeyer and Benno von Wiese
(Düsseldorf, 1979), p. 372. The translation is my own.

20 Suzanne Simard, *Finding the Mother Tree: Discovering the Wisdom of the Forest* (New York, 2021), p. 513.

21 Richard Powers, *The Overstory*, ebook (New York, 2019).

9 Classical, Rococo and Gothic Woods

1 Michael Williams, *Deforesting the Earth: From Prehistory to the Global Crisis, an Abridgement* (Chicago, IL, 2006), p. 91.

2 Ibid., p. 117.

3 Oliver Rackham, *History of the Countryside* (London, 2020), p. 133.

4 Ibid., p. 134; Charles Watkins, *Trees, Woods and Forests: A Social and Cultural History* (London, 2016), pp. 219–23.

5 Giambattista Vico, *The New Science of Giambattista Vico* (Ithaca, NY, 1984).

6 Martine Chalvet, *Une histoire de la forêt*, ebook (Paris, 2011), Kindle location 3773.

7 Barbara Novak, *Nature and Culture: American Landscape and Painting, 1825–1875* (New York, 1980), pp. 204–5.

8 Ibid., p. 35.

9 Jennifer Milam, *Fragonard's Playful Paintings: Visual Games in Rococo Art* (Manchester, 2006), plate V.

10 Chalvet, *Une histoire de la forêt*, Kindle locations 2384–98.

11 Charles Perrault, *Perrault, Contes* (Paris, 1981), pp. 169–78.

12 Ann Radcliffe, *The Romance of the Forest* [1791] (Oxford, 2009), pp. 266–9.

13 William Wordsworth, 'Lines Composed a Few Miles above Tintern Abbey, on Revisiting the Banks of the Wye During a Tour. July 13, 1798', in *Favorite Poems, William Wordsworth*, ebook (Mineola, NY, 1992), Kindle locations 333–85.

14 John Ruskin, *Ruskin's Writings on Art*, ed. Joan Evans (Garden City, NY, 1959), pp. 228–34.

15 Ibid., p. 167.

10 The Primeval Forest

1 Boria Sax, 'Mermaids', in *Storytelling: An Encyclopedia of Mythology and Folklore*, ed. Josepha Sherman, 2 vols, vol. II (Armonk, NY, 2008), p. 304.

2 Boria Sax, 'The Basilisk and Rattlesnake, or a European Monster Comes to America', *Society and Animals*, II/1 (1994), pp. 3–15.

3 Henry Wadsworth Longfellow, 'Evangeline: A Tale of Acadie' [1847], https://poets.org.

4 William Cullen Bryant, 'A Forest Hymn' [1824], www.poemhunter.com.

5 Michael Williams, *Deforesting the Earth: From Prehistory to the Global Crisis, an Abridgement* (Chicago, IL, 2006), p. 25.

6 William Cronon, *Changes in the Land: Indians, Colonists, and the Ecology of New England*, Nook edn (New York, 2011), p. 27.

7 Williams, *Deforesting*, p. 60.

8 Meehan Christ, 'The Age of Acceleration', *Orion*, XLI/2 (Summer 2002), p. 31.

9 Ibid., p. 147.

10 Edmund Burke, *A Philosophical Enquiry into the Origin of Our Ideas of the Sublime and Beautiful* (Oxford, 2015), pp. 47–9.

11 Barbara Novak, *Nature and Culture: American Landscape and Painting, 1825–1875* (New York, 1980), p. 38.

12 John Muir, *Our National Parks* (San Francisco, CA, 1991), p. 248.

13 Anne Whinston Spirn, 'Constructing Nature: The Legacy of Frederich Law Olmstead', in *Uncommon Ground: Rethinking the Human Place in Nature*, ed. William Cronon (New York, 1996), pp. 91–6.

14 Kenneth R. Olwig, 'Reinventing Common Nature: Yosemite and Mount Rushmore: A Meandering Tale of Double Nature', in *Uncommon Ground*, ed. Cronon, pp. 363, 68.

15 Richard Grant, 'The Lost History of Yellowstone: Debunking the Myth That the Great National Park Was a Wilderness Untouched by Humans', *The Smithsonian* (January/February 2021), pp. 54–5, 116–17.

16 Thomas Cole, *Essay on American Scenery* (Catskill, NY, 2018), pp. 20–21.

17 Henry David Thoreau, 'Walking', in *The Portable Thoreau*, ed. Jeffrey S. Cramer (New York, 2012), pp. 562–71.

18 Linda S. Ferber, *The Hudson River School: Nature and the American Vision* (New York, 2009), p. 191.

19 Ibid., pp. 193–8.

20 Barbara Babcock Millhouse, *American Wilderness: The Story of the Hudson River School of Painting* (Hensonville, NY, 2007), p. 86.

11 The Forest of Dreams

1 P. L. Travers, *What the Bee Knows: Reflections on Myth, Symbol and Story* (Wellingborough, UK, 1989), pp. 265–6.

2 Anonymous, *A Perceforest Reader: Selected Episodes from Perceforest: The Prehistory of King Arthur's Britain*, trans. Nigel Bryant (Woodbridge, 2012), pp. 85–102.

3 Noémie Chardonnens, 'D'un Imaginaire à l'autre : la belle endormie du roman de perceforest et son fils', *Études de lettres*, III/4 (2011), p. 198.

4 Giambattista Basile, 'Sun, Moon, and Talia', in *Folk and Fairy Tales*, ed. Martin Hallett and Barbara Karasek (Peterborough, Canada, 2018), pp. 79–82.

5 Charles Perrault, 'The Sleeping Beauty in the Wood', in *Folk and Fairy Tales*, ed. Hallett and Karasek, pp. 83–8.

6 Jacob and Wilhelm Grimm, *The Annotated Brothers Grimm*, ed. and trans. Maria Tatar (New York, 2004), pp. 232–9.

7 Roland Beechmann, *Trees and Man: The Forest in the Middle Ages*, trans. Katharyn Dunham (New York, 1990), pp. 261–2.

8 Michael Imort, 'A Sylvan People: Wilhelmine Forestry and the Forest as a Symbol of Germandom', in *Germany's Nature: Cultural Landscapes and Environmental History*, ed. Thomas Lenkan and Thomas Zeller (New Brunswick, NJ, 2005), pp. 61–2.

9 Wolf Burchard, *Inspiring Walt Disney: The Animation of French Decorative Arts* (New York, 2021), pp. 185–7.

10 Ibid., pp. 107–17.

12 Law of the Jungle

1 Saskia Huma, 'The Real-Life Captain Kurtz', *Daily Mail*, 15 May 2021.
2 Frederick Jackson Turner, 'The Significance of the Frontier in American History (1893)', www.historians.org, accessed 14 February 2022.
3 Christopher Mcintosh, *The Swan King: Ludwig II of Bavaria*, ebook (London, 2012), pp. 193–8.
4 Elyse Nelson, 'Sculpting about Slavery in the Second Empire', in *Fictions of Emancipation: Carpeaux's Why Born Enslaved! Reconsidered*, ed. Elyse Nelson and Wendy B. Walters (New York, 2022), p. 56.
5 John Thompson, 'Africa Geographicus', 1813, www.geogrphaphicus.com, accessed 17 February 2022.
6 John Rankin, *Africa* (London, c. 1860).
7 Peter Parley, *The Second Book of History: The Modern History of Europe, Africa, and Asia* (Boston, MA, 1845), p. 162.
8 John Ayto, *Dictionary of Word Origins* (New York, 1990), p. 310.
9 Roland Beechman, *Trees and Man: The Forest in the Middle Ages*, trans. Katharyn Dunham (New York, 1990), p. 283.
10 Candace Slater, 'Amazonia as Edenic Narrative', in *Uncommon Ground: Rethinking the Human Place in Nature*, ed. William Cronon (New York, 1996), pp. 110–17.
11 Joseph Conrad, *Heart of Darkness* (New York, 2012), p. 38.
12 Ibid., pp. 6–7.
13 Ibid., pp. 56–7.
14 Ibid., p. 80.
15 Matthew White, *The Great Big Book of Horrible Things: The Definitive Chronicle of History's 100 Worst Atrocities* (New York, 2012), p. 542.
16 Hannah Arendt, *Eichmann in Jerusalem: A Report on the Banality of Evil* (New York, 2006).
17 Conrad, *Heart*, p. 33.
18 Adam Hochschild, *King Leopold's Ghost*, ebook (New York, 2020), pp. 533–53.
19 Marshall Everett, *Roosevelt's Thrilling Experiences in the Wilds of Africa: Hunting Big Game* (Houston, TX, 1909), unpaginated back matter.
20 Ibid., p. 165.
21 Ibid., unpaginated back matter.
22 Ibid., caption to unpaginated illustration entitled 'The Happy Anticipation of a Fine Feast'.
23 Edgar Rice Burroughs, *Tarzan of the Apes*, ebook (Overland Park, KS, 2012), Kindle location 1906–63.
24 Ibid., Kindle location 2617.
25 Rudyard Kipling, *The Jungle Book*, ebook (Seattle, WA, 2017), Kindle location 184.
26 Ibid., Kindle location 293–308.
27 Ibid., Kindle location 910–25.
28 Allen F. Roberts, *Animals in African Art: From the Familiar to the Marvelous* (New York, 1995), pp. 16–18.

13 The Man with the Big Axe

1 W. B. Laughead, *The Marvelous Exploits of Paul Bunyan* (Middletown, DE, 2021), pp. 1–9.
2 Carl Sandburg, *The Complete Poems of Carl Sandburg* (New York, 1970), p. 496.
3 B. A. Botkin, *A Treasury of American Folklore: Stories, Ballads, and Traditions of the People* (New York, 1944), pp. 491–2.
4 *Legends of Paul Bunyan*, ed. Harold W. Felton (New York, 1947), pp. 221–48.
5 Michael Edmonds, *Out of the Northwoods: The Many Lives of Paul Bunyan*, Kobo edn (2009), pp. 302–4.
6 Ibid., p. 298.
7 Ibid., p. 314.
8 Ibid., p. 309.
9 Michael Williams, *Americans and Their Forests: A Historical Geography* (Cambridge, 1992), pp. 222–3.
10 Edmonds, *Northwoods*, p. 16.
11 Ibid., pp. 87–93.
12 Ibid., pp. 240–42.
13 Laughead, *Exploits*.
14 Ibid., pp. 243–5.
15 Richard M. Dorson, *Folklore and Fakelore: Essays toward a Discipline of Folk Studies* (Cambridge, MA, 1976), pp. 335–6.
16 Ibid., p. 27.
17 Gifford Pinchot, *Breaking New Ground* (Washington, DC, 1998), pp. 27–8.
18 Edmonds, *Northwoods*, pp. 401–2.
19 Keith Thomas, *Man and the Natural World: A History of the Modern Sensibility* (New York, 1983), pp. 194–6.

14 The Politics of Trees

1 Edward Hyams, *The English Garden* (London, 1966), p. 22.
2 Nigel Everett, *The Tory View of Landscape* (New Haven, CT, 1994), p. 39.
3 Ibid., pp. 41, 44.
4 Ibid., p. 40.
5 Ibid., pp. 183–203.
6 Ibid., pp. 204–8.
7 John Evelyn, *Sylva; or, A Discourse of Forest Trees and the Propagation of Timber*, 3rd edn [1706] (Chapel Hill, NC, 2012), p. lxxvi, at www. projectgutenberg.org, accessed 16 June 2022.
8 Thomas Toft, *Display Dish with Charles II in a Tree*, c. 1680, www. metropolitanmuseum.org, accessed 16 June 2022.
9 Evelyn, *Sylva*, p. xcix.
10 Kieko Matteson, *Forests in Revolutionary France: Conservation, Community and Conflict, 1669–1848* (Cambridge, 2015), p. 37.
11 Ibid., pp. 35–6.
12 John Evelyn, *Sylva; or, A Discourse on Forest Trees* (Cambridge, 2013), vol. II, p. 5.
13 Ibid., p. 37.

14 Hanns Carl von Carlowitz, *Sylvicultura Oekenomica* (Leipzig, 1713), p. 106.

15 Hansjörg Küster, *Geschichte des Waldes: Von der Urzeit bis zur Gegenwart* (Munich, 2013), p. 176.

16 Matteson, *Forests*, p. 167.

17 Charles Watkins, *Trees in Art* (London, 2018), p. 158.

18 Oliver Rackham, *History of the Countryside* (London, 2020), pp. 135–6.

19 Martine Chalvet, *Une Histoire De La Forêt*, ebook (Paris, 2011), Kindle locations 2319–47.

20 Küster, *Geschichte*, p. 182.

21 Matteson, *Forests*, pp. 244, 47–54.

22 Robert Delort and François Walter, *Histoire de l'environnement européen* (Paris, 2001), p. 309.

23 Boria Sax, *Animals in the Third Reich*, 2nd edn (Pittsburgh, PA, 2013), pp. 64–5, 100–113, 164–73.

24 Raymond H. Dominick III, *The Environmental Movement in Germany: Prophets and Pioneers, 1871–1971* (Bloomington, IN, 1992), p. 106.

25 Ibid., pp. 105–6.

26 Bernd A. Rusinek, 'Wald und Baum in der arische-germanische Geistes- und Kulturgeschichte' in *Der Wald. Ein deutscher Mythos*, ed. Albrecht Lehmann and Klaus Schriewer (Hamburg, 2000), www.archivportal-d.de, accessed 22 July 2022, p.4. The translation is my own.

27 Dominick, *Environmental*, pp. 111–15.

28 Ibid., p. 113.

29 Rusinek, 'Wald und Baum', p. 6.

30 Jost Hermand, *Old Dreams of a New Reich: Völkish Utopias and National Socialism* (Bloomington, IN, 1992), p. 281.

31 *Ewiger Wald* (Kampfbund für deutsche Kultur, 1936), www.youtube.com, accessed 28 June 2022. This only contains the first half or so of the film. Much was probably omitted to minimize its association with Nazism.

32 Anonymous, 'Ewiger Wald', Alchetron, last modified 14 April 2022, https://alchetron.com, accessed 28 June 2022.

33 Victoria Urmersbach, 'Von Wilden Wäldern und der Liebe Zur Linde: Waldgeschichten Zwischen Realität und Mythos', in *Der Wald in Der Vielwalt Möglicher Perspektiven*, ed. Corinna Jenal and Karsten Berr (Berlin, 2022), pp. 29–30.

34 Dominick, *Environmental*, p.90.

35 Michael Williams, *Deforesting the Earth: From Prehistory to the Global Crisis, an Abridgement* (Chicago, IL, 2006), p. 390.

36 Bertolt Brecht, 'An Die Nachgeborenen', in *Deutsche Gedichte: Von den Anfängen biz zur Gegenwart*, ed. Echtermeyer and Benno von Wiese (Düsseldorf, 1979), p. 632. The translation is my own.

37 Dominick, *Environmental*, pp. 111–12.

38 Williams, *Deforesting*, pp. 402–4.

15 The River in the Forest

1 Michael Marder, *Plant-Thinking: A Philosophy of Vegetable Life* (New York, 2013), p. 179.

2 William Shakespeare, *Shakespeare's Sonnets* (New York, 2011), p. 175.

3 Michael Williams, *Deforesting the Earth: From Prehistory to the Global Crisis*, abridged edn (Chicago, IL, 2007), pp. 172, 395–6.

4 Ashley Junger, 'Saving Our Forests for the Trees: Deforestation Is Threatening Critical Ecosystems Throughout the World', www.earthwatch. org, accessed 8 July 2022.

5 Jordan Fisher Smith, 'The Wilderness Paradox', *Orion* (September–October 2014), p. 37.

6 George Monbiot, *Feral: Rewilding the Land, the Sea, and Human Life* (Chicago, IL, 2017).

7 Fred Pearce, *The New Wild: Why Invasive Species Will Be Nature's Salvation* (Boston, MA, 2015), pp. 96–8.

8 Jean François Lyotard, *The Postmodern Condition: A Report on Knowledge*, trans. Geoff Bennington and Brian Massumi (Minneapolis, MI, 1984), pp. 31–8, 60.

9 William Cronon, 'Introduction: In Search of Nature', in *Uncommon Ground: Rethinking the Human Place in Nature*, ed. William Cronon (New York, 1996), pp. 25–6.

10 Brian J. Palik, Anthony W. D'Amato et al., *Ecological Silviculture: Foundations and Applications* (Long Grove, IL, 2021), pp. 37–50, 293–5.

11 Elizabeth Weil, 'Forever Fire', *New York Times Magazine*, 16 January 2022, pp. 33–43.

12 Palik, *Silviculture*, pp. 115–42.

13 Stacey Kazacos, 'From the President', *New York Forest Owner*, LX/5 (September–October 2022), p. 3.

14 Boria Sax, *Animals in the Third Reich* (Pittsburgh, PA, 2013), pp. 167–76.

15 Jonathan Marks, *What It Means to Be 98% Chimpanzee: Apes, People and Their Genes* (Berkeley, CA, 2002), pp. 165–72.

16 David Graeber and David Wengrow, *The Dawn of Everything: A New History of Humanity* (New York, 2021).

17 Jim Holt, 'The Grand Illusion', *Lapham's Quarterly*, VII/4 (2014), pp. 187–91.

FURTHER READING

These are books that I have found especially helpful, either for background information or in addressing more specific questions. I have not included primary sources since those are discussed explicitly in my book and are not difficult to find. The one exception is the *Epic of Gilgamesh*. Because the original sources are fragmentary and very remote in time, any translation involves a great deal of interpretation, and so I have included three English versions. I have not included works that are either highly specialized or tangential to the topic of forests in human history and culture. Contrary to my usual practice, I have included a few books in languages other than English, though only when I thought they had information or perspective that was not easily available in English.

Agnoletti, Mauro, *Storia del bosco: il paesaggio forestale italiano* (Bari, Italy, 2020).
    In Italian, a history of the forests of Italy.
Altman, Nathaniel, *Sacred Trees* (San Francisco, CA, 1994). A broad survey of
    trees in myth and legend.
Anderson, Virginia DeJohn, *Creatures of Empire: How Domestic Animals
    Transformed Early America* (New York, 2004). A study of the contrasting
    relationships to flora and fauna among early European colonists and
    Native Americans.
Barr, Karsten, and Corinna Jenal, eds, *Der Wald in der Vielfalt Möglicher
    Perspektiven* (Berlin, 2022). In German, a collection of essays on the social
    and historical significance of forests.
Beechmann, Roland, *Trees and Man: The Forest in the Middle Ages*, trans.
    Katharyn Dunham (New York, 1990). A detailed discussion of medieval
    forests, especially in France.
Bibikhin, Vladimir, *The Woods (Hyle)*, trans. Arch Tait (Cambridge, 2021).
    A philosophical and etymological discussion of our concept of the woods
    by a leading Russian philosopher.
Bruchac, Joseph, *Native Plant Stories* (Golden, CO, 1995). A collection of traditional
    Canadian and American Indian tales by a Native American author.
Canham, Charles D., *Forests Adrift: Currents Shaping the Future of Northeastern
    Trees* (New Haven, CT, 2020). A forester's account of how woodlands of the
    American Northeast have developed and how they are likely to evolve in the
    decades and centuries to come.
Cartmill, Matt, *A View to a Death in the Morning: Hunting and Nature through
    History* (Cambridge, MA, 1993). A cultural history of hunting.
Chalvet, Martine, *Une histoire de la forêt* (Paris, 2011). In French, an account of
    forests, especially in France, from Neolithic times to the present and broader
    cultural and historical trends.

Corvol, Andrée, *L'Homme aux Bois: Histoire des relations de l'homme et la forêt XVIIe–XXe siècle* (Paris, 1987). In French, a study of relations between people and forests in France during the modern era.

Cronon, William, *Changes in the Land: Indians, Colonists, and the Ecology of New England* (New York, 2011). A highly influential modern classic, which was among the first books to look critically at the ideal of a primordial landscape.

Cronon, William, ed., *Uncommon Ground: Rethinking the Human Place in Nature* (New York, 1996). A collection of essays on the history of American forests, emphasizing how they were extensively managed to create an impression of primeval purity.

Dalley, Stephanie, trans., *Myths from Mesopotamia: Creation, the Flood, Gilgamesh, and Others*, trans. Stephanie Dalley (Oxford, 1992). Contains translations of two versions of *The Epic of Gilgamesh*, which are notable for their strict adherence to the original tablets.

Delort, Robert, and François Walter, *Histoire de l'environnement européen* (Paris, 2001). In French, a history of the natural environment in Europe.

Descola, Philippe, *Beyond Nature and Culture*, trans. Janet Lloyd (Chicago, IL, 2013). A comprehensive study of ways in which human societies relate to their natural environments.

Ferber, Linda S., *The Hudson River School: Nature and the American Vision* (New York, 2009). A scholarly introduction to the painters of the American Hudson River School with extensive illustrations.

George, Andrew, trans. *The Epic of Gilgamesh: The Babylonian Epic Poem and Other Texts in Akkadian and Sumerian*, 2nd edn (New York, 2019). Combines several versions of *The Epic of Gilgamesh* together in one narrative with extensive notes.

Harrison, Robert Pogue, *Forests: The Shadow of Civilization* (Chicago, IL, 1993). A study in the cultural significance of forests, with special emphasis on those of Italy.

Jenal, Corinna, *'Das ist kein Wald, Ihr Pappnasen!' Zur sozialen Konstruktion von Wald. Perspektiven von Landschaftstheorie und Landschaftspraxis* (Berlin, 2019). In German, a historical and philosophical study of how the concept of a wood has been socially constructed.

Kohn, Eduardo, *How Forests Think: Toward an Anthropology Beyond the Human* (Berkeley, CA, 2013). A philosophical/anthropological discussion of the significance of forests, with special emphasis on those of Latin America.

Küster, Hansjörg, *Der Wald: Natur Und Geschichte* (Munich, 2019). In German, a discussion of how forests and their terrain have changed over the centuries, written from a perspective of environmental geography.

Maeterlinck, Maurice, *The Intelligence of Flowers*, trans. Alexander Teixeira Mattos (Cambridge, MA, 1906). By a winner of the Nobel Prize in literature, this book makes a case for the sentience of plants and is arguably the first in the discipline now known as 'plant studies'.

Marder, Michael, *Plant Thinking: A Philosophy of Vegetal Life* (New York, 2013). A philosophical investigation of the fundamental ontologies of plant life and their implications.

Matteson, Kieko, *Forests in Revolutionary France: Conservation, Community and Conflict, 1669–1848* (Cambridge, 2015). A detailed discussion of how forests

were impacted by the wide range of governments in France, from Louis XIV
to Napoleon III.
Monbiot, George, *Feral: Rewilding the Land, the Sea, and Human Life* (Chicago,
IL, 2017). Argues for a radical rewilding, which the author believes would
restore something close to the Paleolithic landscapes in Britain.
Novak, Barbara, *Nature and Culture: American Landscape and Painting, 1825–
1875* (New York, 1980). A discussion of the philosophical and aesthetic
foundations of painters in the Hudson River School, especially the works
depicting the vanishing American forests.
Palik, Brian J., et al., *Ecological Silviculture: Foundations and Applications* (Long
Grove, IL, 2021). A practical guide to the foundations of contemporary
forestry.
Pearce, Fred, *The New Wild: Why Invasive Species Will be Nature's Salvation*
(Boston, MA, 2015). Argues the unconventional thesis that we should
accept the globalization of wildlife and that it will ultimately contribute to
biodiversity.
Perlin, John, *A Forest Journey: The Story of Wood and Civilization* (Woodstock, VT,
2005). A study of how a nearly insatiable demand for wood has influenced
Western culture from ancient times to the advent of fossil fuels.
Rackham, Oliver, *History of the Countryside* (London, 2020). A detailed history
of British landscapes.
Sandars, N. K., trans. *The Epic of Gilgamesh* (New York, 1977). A relatively free
but artistically very effective translation.
Saunders, Corinne J., *The Forest of Medieval Romance: Avernus, Broceliande, Arden*
(Woodbridge, 1993). A detailed study of the role of the forest in Medieval
European romances.
Simard, Suzanne, *Finding the Mother Tree: Discovering the Wisdom of the Forest*
(New York, 2021). An autobiographical account by an important figure
in contemporary forestry, in which she discusses how the discipline has
developed.
Smith, Nigel J., *The Enchanted Amazon Rain Forest: Stories from a Vanishing World*
(Gainesville, FL, 1976). A study of the folklore of the Brazilian Amazon.
Sterba, Jim, *Nature Wars: The Incredible Story of How Wildlife Comebacks Turned
Backyards into Battlegrounds* (New York, 2012). An account of how human
protection has created a dramatic comeback for deer, turkeys and other
American animals but also revived old resentments of them.
Thomas, Keith, *Man and the Natural World: A History of the Modern Sensibility*
(New York, 1983). A modern classic that explores many facets of the
relationship between human beings and the natural world.
Watkins, Charles, *Trees in Art* (London, 2018). A extensive and beautifully
illustrated discussion of the conventions and ideals reflected in graphic art
depicting trees.
––, *Trees, Woods and Forests: A Social and Cultural History* (London, 2016).
A discussion of the changing attitudes towards forests, especially in Britain,
as reflected in the literary and graphic arts.
Wessels, Tom, *Reading the Forested Landscape: A Natural History of New England*
(New York, 1999). A book on forest forensics, which reconstructs the
history of a landscape from clues in the terrain and vegetation, centred
around the American Northeast.

Williams, Michael, *Americans and Their Forests: A Historical Geography* (Cambridge, 1992). An extensive history of American forests.
——, *Deforesting the Earth: From Prehistory to the Global Crisis, an Abridgement* (Chicago, IL, 2006). A detailed history of deforestation throughout the world.
Wohlleben, Peter, *The Hidden Life of Trees: What They Feel, How They Communicate – Discoveries from a Secret World*, trans. Tim Flannery (New York, 2017). A bestselling book on forest management, particularly of old-growth forests.
Zechner, Johannes, *Der Deutsche Wald: Eine Ideengeschichte zwischen Poesie und Ideologie* (Darmstadt, 2016). In German, a discussion of how the changing concepts of the forest are reflected in poetry and the other arts.

ACKNOWLEDGEMENTS

I wish to thank the National Convention of Independent Scholars (NCIS) and Mercy College for grants for research materials that helped me write this book. Thanks especially to my wife, Linda Sax, for her generous support and many helpful suggestions. Tom Christensen has taken many beautiful photos on my property, and he has graciously allowed me to reproduce them in this book. Thanks also to the people at Reaktion Books for their confidence in the project.

PHOTO ACKNOWLEDGEMENTS

The author and publishers wish to express their thanks to the below sources of illustrative material and/or permission to reproduce it. Some locations of artworks are also given below, in the interest of brevity:

Alte Nationalgalerie, Staatliche Museen zu Berlin: p. 164 (*top*); Amon Carter Museum of American Art, Fort Worth, TX: p. 174; from *Anne Anderson's Old, Old Fairy Tales* (Racine, WI, 1935): p. 186; Art Institute of Chicago: p. 156; Artokoloro/ Alamy Stock Photo: p. 59; Ashmolean Museum, University of Oxford: p. 29; Autry Museum of the American West, Los Angeles: p. 171 (photo Library of Congress, Prints and Photographs Division, Washington, DC); Basilica di San Francesco, Arezzo: p. 45; Bayerische Staatsbibliothek, Munich: pp. 38 (MS Cod.icon. 26, fol. 59r), 44 (MS Clm 15710, fol. 60v – photo World Digital Library); Beinecke Rare Book and Manuscript Library, Yale University, New Haven, CT: p. 133 (Mellon MS 110, fol. 131v); Bibliothèque nationale de France, Paris: pp. 74 (MS Latin 9474, fol. 191v), 84 (MS Français 616, fol. 87r), 127 (MS Réserve OD-60 PET FOL, fol. 19r); British Library, London: p. 125 (Cotton MS Nero A x/2, fol. 94v); photos Tom Christensen: pp. 6, 68, 99, 253; collection of the author: pp. 10 (*left*), 11, 34, 51, 57, 93, 100, 101, 138, 139, 150, 160, 161, 164 (*bottom*), 169, 172, 173, 196, 199, 206, 207, 208, 214, 227, 231, 233, 238; from Taxile Delord, *Les fleurs animées*, vol. II (Paris, 1847): p. 36; Dover Pictorial Archive: pp. 28, 42, 96, 112; from Brothers Grimm, *Hansel and Grethel and Other Tales* (London, 1920), photo University of North Carolina at Chapel Hill Library: p. 134; from Richard Huber, *A Treasury of Fantastic and Mythological Creatures: 1,087 Renderings from Historic Sources* (New York, 1981), photo Dover Pictorial Archive: p. 63; Kunsthistorisches Museum, Vienna: p. 88; from John Leighton, *1,100 Designs and Motifs from Historic Sources* (New York, 1995), photos Dover Pictorial Archive: p. 22; Library of Congress, Prints and Photographs Division, Washington, DC: pp. 216 (photo Carol M. Highsmith), 219; The Metropolitan Museum of Art, New York: pp. 55, 56, 85, 110, 115 (*bottom*), 130, 157 (*bottom*), 197, 228; The Morgan Library and Museum, New York: p. 32 (MS G.5, fol. 18v); Museum für Islamische Kunst, Staatliche Museen zu Berlin: p. 41; Muzeum Narodowe, Warsaw: p. 33; National Galleries of Scotland, Edinburgh: p. 92; New-York Historical Society: pp. 177, 178, 179, 180; The New York Public Library: pp. 54, 115 (*top*), 222; private collection: pp. 104, 157 (*top*), 198, 225; Royal Collection Trust/© His Majesty King Charles III 2023: p. 151; photos Boria Sax: pp. 10 (*right*), 218; Schloss Charlottenburg, Berlin: p. 162; Toledo Museum of Art, OH: p. 155; Unsplash: p. 189 (photo Dylan Bman); U.S. Capitol Building: p. 194; The Wallace Collection, London: pp. 9, 159; Wikimedia Commons: pp. 48 (photo Osama Shukir Muhammed Amin FRCP (Glasg), CC BY-SA 4.0), 67 (photo Rama, CC BY-SA 3.0 FR – Musée du Louvre, Paris), 188 (photo © Thomas Wolf/www.foto-tw.de, CC BY-SA 3.0 DE).

INDEX

Page numbers in *italics* refer to illustrations